THE GRENADA REVOLUTION

CARIBBEAN
STUDIES
SERIES

Anton L. Allahar and Shona N. Jackson
Series Editors

THE GRENADA REVOLUTION

Reflections and Lessons

Edited by Wendy C. Grenade

University Press of Mississippi / Jackson

www.upress.state.ms.us

The University Press of Mississippi is a member
of the Association of American University Presses.

First printing 2015
∞
Library of Congress Cataloging-in-Publication Data

Grenade, Wendy C.
  The Grenada Revolution : reflections and lessons / edited by Wendy C.
Grenade.
     pages cm. — (Caribbean studies series)
  Includes bibliographical references and index.
  ISBN 978-1-62846-151-0 (cloth : alk. paper) — ISBN 978-1-62846-152-7
(ebook) 1. Grenada—History—1974–1983. 2. Grenada—Politics and
government—1974–1983. 3. New Jewel Movement (Grenada) 4. Coard,
Bernard, 1944-—Interviews. 5. Grenada—History—American Invasion,
1983—Causes. I. Title.
  F2056.8.G79 2015
  972.9845—dc23   2014029777

British Library Cataloging-in-Publication Data available

CONTENTS

vii   Foreword

xi   Acknowledgments

3   1. Introduction
Wendy C. Grenade

PART I
Historicizing Grenada

13   2. Grenada, 1949–1979: Precursor to Revolution
Curtis Jacobs

37   3. Grenada: Socioeconomic Overview, 1960–2012
Kari H. I. Grenade

PART II
Insiders' Perspectives on the Grenada Revolution

59   4. A Retrospective View from Richmond Hill: An Interview with
Bernard Coard
Wendy C. Grenade

87   5. Grenada Once Again: Revisiting the 1983 Crisis and Collapse of
the Grenada Revolution
Brian Meeks

114   6. Remembering October 19: Reconstructing a Conversation with
a Young Female NJM Candidate Member about Her Recollections
of October 19, 1983
Patsy Lewis

PART III
Theoretical Critiques of the Grenada Revolution
and Lessons for the Future

121   7. Grenada: Noncapitalist Path and the Derailment of a Social
          Democratic Revolution
       Hilbourne A. Watson

152   8. C. L. R. James and the Grenada Revolution: Lessons Learned and
          Future Possibilities
       Tennyson S. D. Joseph

179   9. The Challenges for Revolutionary Change in the Caribbean
       Horace G. Campbell

PART IV
The Caribbean Left, Party Politics, and Political
Transitions in Grenada

213   10. The Grenada Revolution and the Caribbean Left: The Case of the
           Guyana Working People's Alliance
       David Hinds

241   11. Exploring Transitions in Party Politics in Grenada, 1984–2013
       Wendy C. Grenade

264   12. The Spirit and Ideas of Maurice Bishop Are Alive in Our
           Caribbean Civilization
       Ralph E. Gonsalves

275   Contributors

279   Credits

281   Index

FOREWORD

On March 13, 1979, Grenada's New Jewel Movement stunned its Anglophone Caribbean neighbors by summarily removing from office the country's prime minister, Eric Matthew Gairy, in the subregion's first overthrow of an elected government. Grenada had become legally independent from Britain in February 1974, and March 1979 came just after the end of the country's fifth year as an independent nation. Gairy had been accused of abusing the electoral system, and the New Jewel Movement was generally considered, even by detractors, to have the support of a majority of Grenada's voting-age population.

Four years after the overthrow of the Gairy government, what had come to be known as the Grenada Revolution collapsed after bloody infighting and the murders of prime minister Maurice Bishop, other ministers of government, and members of the public. From the United States, the Reagan administration used the opportunity to invade and ensure the demise of a regime of which it had become increasingly more suspicious. The Grenada Revolution was over. The year was 1983.

Now, after thirty years during which many key participants in the Grenada events have said little, Wendy Grenade brings together in this collection a broad variety of contributors—key participants as well as scholars and commentators on the events—to help us analyze not only what took place but also, more importantly, what lessons might be learned from the triumphant beginning and painful end of the Grenada Revolution. The perspectives are varied. One major detail that all contributors appear to agree on is that brutal executions occurred on October 19, 1983.

Contributors to this collection take differing approaches to analyzing the nature of Grenada's New Jewel Movement and the political process that it led for four and a half years. One describes the end of the process as Stalinist; another comments that there was nothing Stalinist about it. There are differences, too, when contributors interrogate the role of the vanguard party and consider whether the collapse of the revolution indicated the failure in Grenada of notions of the Leninist vanguard, or the failure of the NJM leadership to fully understand the nature and meaning of vanguardism.

The varied approaches in this collection recall the responses to the 1983 collapse itself. They evoke the confusion and recrimination of the Caribbean

Left and the profound sadness and self-examination that the October 1983 choices of the Grenada revolutionaries brought to Caribbean political organization and to supportive political movements internationally. Each contribution to the collection, not the least of these the editor's interview with Bernard Coard, the surviving half of the Coard-Bishop duo most obviously at the center of the 1983 tensions, arouses complex emotions and doubtless, for many, disturbing memories.

The variety of perspectives is both informative and necessary, urging the reader to consider themes of memory and history. In his book *States of Memory: Continuities, Conflicts, and Transformations in National Retrospection*, Jeffrey Olick reminds his readers:

> Stable images of the past are not always demonstrably true images. Sometimes false ideas are transferred across generations and accepted as if they were true. And sometimes we do not know whether an account of the past is true or not. Truth value and its resistance to revision is plainly not the only source of the past's stability.[1]

Different versions of a painful story are to be expected, and the phenomenon of recording several different truths, which is obvious in this collection, is not unique to the Grenada story. By engaging with memory and interrogating history, the collection challenges critics of Caribbean political processes to be informed in their praxis by the lessons drawn from the errors and triumphs of the Grenada Revolution. Throughout the collection, readers are both informed by the recounting of memories and encouraged to analyze by the outlining of historical and political circumstances. The juxtaposition of the two makes fascinating and informative reading. Thirty years after the end of the political process that came to be known as the Grenada Revolution, the reader might find it useful, when confronted with a recounting of the emotions surrounding both the beginning and the end of those four and a half years of Grenada's story, to consider what Pierre Nora has to say about memory and history:

> Memory and history, far from being synonymous, are . . . in many respects opposed. Memory is life, always embodied in living societies, and as such in permanent evolution, subject to the dialectic of remembering and forgetting, unconscious of the distortions to which it is subject, vulnerable in various ways to appropriation and manipulation, and capable of lying dormant for long periods, only to be suddenly awakened. History, on the other hand, is the reconstruction, always problematic and incomplete, of what is no longer. Memory is always

a phenomenon of the present, a bond tying us to the eternal present; history is a representation of the past. Memory, being a phenomenon of emotion and magic, accommodates only those facts that suit it. It thrives on vague, telescoping reminiscences, on hazy general impressions or specific symbolic details. It is vulnerable to transferences, screen memories, censorings, and projections of all kinds. History, being an intellectual, nonreligious activity, calls for analysis and critical discourse. Memory situates remembrance in a sacred context. History ferrets it out; it turns whatever it touches into prose. Memory wells up from groups that it welds together, which is to say, as Maurice Halbwachs observed, that there are as many memories as there are groups, that memory is by nature multiple yet specific; collective and plural yet individual. By contrast, history belongs to everyone and to no one and therefore has a universal vocation.[2]

Some of the contributions to this collection suggest reminiscences and still anguished analysis by key participants in the events. Some present perspectives by those who had close alliances with key participants or with the New Jewel Movement. Others suggest a complex engagement with memory and history or an attempt to focus more on what historical and political processes suggest. Participants and commentators appear more willing, in this thirtieth year, to discuss the triumph and the tragedy of the Grenadian and wider Caribbean story and to suggest lessons for new generations. For those interested in examining the lessons of sociohistorical and political processes, this is an excellent anthology.

—Merle Collins
Department of English
University of Maryland
2013

Notes

1. Jeffrey K. Olick, *States of Memory: Continuities, Conflicts, and Transformations in National Retrospection* (Durham: Duke University Press, 2003), 102.

2. Pierre Nora, *Realms of Memory: The Construction of the French Past* (New York: Columbia University Press, 1996), 3.

ACKNOWLEDGMENTS

The genesis of this volume of essays can be traced to many conversations held over several years with numerous persons who generated ideas, raised questions, and inspired action. I wish to especially thank my colleague and friend David Hinds for our frequent and intense discussions about Caribbean politics. I also wish to record my appreciation to my friends Faye Thompson and Rita Joseph for sharing with me their experiences as women in the Grenada Revolution. Through my interactions with Faye and Rita, I encountered several former revolutionaries, from both sides of the 1983 conflict, who shared their memories of the period from 1979 to 1983. This enabled me to find a balanced perspective on the Grenada Revolution.

This book would not have been possible without the valuable reflections, ideas, and critical insights of the contributors. I thank them for their commitment and cooperation throughout the completion of the project. A special thanks to Professor Merle Collins for writing the foreword to the book. I also wish to thank all the interviewees for their contributions. I especially thank Bernard Coard for allowing me to interview him behind prison walls. I thank him for sharing his perspective on the Grenada experience. I also express my appreciation to Dr. Francis Alexis, the late George Brizan, Prime Minister Keith Mitchell, Joan Purcell, and other key political actors in Grenada who took time over the years to share their experiences with me.

Thanks to the University Press of Mississippi for agreeing to publish the book. Special thanks to the editors for their guidance and oversight of the process. Several colleagues, friends, and mentors at the University of the West Indies, Cave Hill Campus, were also invaluable to the process: Cynthia Barrow-Giles, Tennyson Joseph, Sherma Roberts, Halimah DeShong, Kristina Hinds Harrison, and Don Marshall. I thank them for their deep intellectual insights, mentorship, and camaraderie. I am also privileged to benefit from lifelong friends who have constantly provided genuine friendship and emotional nourishment over time and distance. Thanks to Suronna Bruno, Charmaine Blackette, Dawn Walker, Thelma Blair, Evadne Brewster-Wiltshire, and several others. I am most grateful for their encouragement and support.

My close-knit family has nurtured and sustained me: my dad, Cletus Grenade; my late mum, Olga; siblings Claudia, Nedd, Tedd, and Kari; nephews and nieces Taskah, Kion, Ty, Tia, Kyanna, Sage; and countless relatives in Grenada and abroad. They are my rock. I draw on their wisdom, take refuge in their kindness, and anchor in their unwavering love.

Above all, I give God thanks for yesterday's breakthroughs, today's opportunities, and tomorrow's possibilities.

THE GRENADA REVOLUTION

1. Introduction

Wendy C. Grenade

Thirty years after the collapse of the Grenada Revolution and the U.S. invasion of Grenada, a confluence of forces has ushered in a complex world. *The Grenada Revolution: Reflections and Lessons* uses the benefit of thirty years' hindsight to reflect on and critique the Grenada Revolution. The principal aim of the book is to use the Grenada Revolution as the point of departure to revisit a critical period in the postcolonial Caribbean experience to glean lessons for contemporary Caribbean politics and society. A central question is: Why did the Grenada Revolution lose its way, and what is its legacy? Perhaps more important, what are the lessons from the Grenada experience for democratic transformation in the twenty-first century?

Why the Grenada Revolution?

On March 13, 1979, during the Cold War, the New Jewel Movement (NJM) led by Maurice Bishop seized power from Eric Gairy's dictatorship in what was the making of the Grenada Revolution (1979–83). This period marked a "crucial turning point in the history and character of the Caribbean" (Lewis 1987, 1). Grenada was the first in the Anglophone Caribbean to experience a successful "Golpe" (coup), breaking for the first time the tradition of West Indian constitutionalism; the first where its prime minister was assassinated; and the first to be invaded by the United States (Lewis 1987, 2). Those events placed Grenada at the center of Cold War machinations. Fundamentally, the Grenada Revolution was an attempt to break with the past and create new pathways for economic and social transformation. The revolutionary experiment in Grenada was not an isolated event but part of a larger struggle throughout the Third World for self-determination and social justice.

    An extensive body of work on the Grenada Revolution, its demise, and the subsequent U.S. invasion has been written by academics, journalists, government officials, political activists, think tank experts, and others (Lewis 1987, ix); and with this, a wide range of views has emerged on the revolution's significance. One strand in the literature locates the revolution within the Cold War conjuncture. A dominant view on the right argues that the revolution "was designed to create a Communist society and to bring Grenada into the Soviet orbit" (Ledeen and Romerstein 1984, 3). It is argued that U.S. "president Reagan felt 'that America was being kicked around as it had been when Carter was in charge,' and that if he could not react in Beirut, in Grenada 'he bloody well could react—and would'" (Payne, Sutton, and Thorndike 1984, 150–51; cited in Morales 1994, 80). A second view, from the left, locates the Grenada affair with the anti-imperialist struggle and the Caribbean radical tradition. Rupert Lewis observes:

> Grenada is the beginning of the end of the Caribbean radicalism that really begins with the late 1960s, rises to a high point in 1970 in Trinidad, and then with the Manley period in Jamaica, and develops in most of the islands as critical groupings and organizational activities and which, from a regional point of view, has a sense of itself as having a common agenda for change, with different groups having different ideological positions, but being all part of a movement for change in the sixties and seventies. That ends quite definitively in Grenada in 1983. (Lewis, quoted in Scott 2001, 158)

In the aftermath of the crisis, several scholars and other observers turned their gaze on Grenada, seeking to understand the events of October 1983, given its geopolitical significance (Boodhoo 1984; Payne, Sutton, and Thorndike 1984; Thorndike 1985; Pastor 1986; Lewis 1987). However, these earlier works focused on the immediate aftermath of the collapse of the Grenada Revolution and the U.S. invasion. With the end of the Cold War, interest in Grenada subsided.

With the passage of time, there is need for fresh analyses. Recently there has been a rekindling of scholarly interest in the "Grenada affair" (Meeks 2001; Scott 2007; Collins 2003; Puri 2010).[1] The contributions in this book seek to add to the discourse. The book builds on a conversation that began at the 33rd Annual Caribbean Studies Association Conference in San Andres, Colombia, in May 2008 on the panel "Transcending Silence: Revisiting Grenada Twenty-five Years Later." It further elaborates on a previous publication, "Grenada Revolution (30) Years After," a special issue of the *Journal of Eastern Caribbean Studies* (September–December 2010), in which several of the chapters in this book were presented as preliminary reflections that have since been significantly advanced for the current work.

Purpose and Structure of the Book

The implosion of the Grenada Revolution and the subsequent U.S. invasion of Grenada in 1983 occurred at a critical juncture in world affairs. The Cold War was coming to an end, and a new world economic order was dawning. The convergence of those events and forces exacerbated old problems and brought to the fore new, complex issues for the small developing states of the Commonwealth Caribbean. This book combines various perspectives to tell a Caribbean story that weaves together historical and contemporary analyses to draw lessons for the present and future. By examining the possibilities and contradictions of the Grenada Revolution, the contributors use thirty years' hindsight to illuminate a crucial period of the Cold War in a new dispensation. The book seeks to unsettle old debates while providing fresh understandings about a critical period in the Caribbean's postcolonial experience. It throws into sharp focus the centrality of the Grenada Revolution and offers a timely collection of articles as a contribution to Caribbean scholarship and praxis.

Part I: Historicizing Grenada

Following this introduction, part 1 lays the historical foundation for the book. In chapter 2, Curtis Jacobs constructs a broad framework that weaves together global events, regional developments, and Grenada's particularities. Jacobs discusses the rise and eventual fall of Eric Gairy, the rise of Maurice Bishop, and the historical currents that led to the making of the Grenada Revolution on March 13, 1979. Jacobs contends that as Gairy's political challenges mounted, and as his authoritarian tendencies became more apparent, he reintroduced violence as a necessary prerequisite for the conduct of politics. For Jacobs, Gairy opened the door to his being toppled from office by the very methods that he used to maintain his rule.

In chapter 3, Kari Grenade provides a socioeconomic overview of Grenada from 1960 to 2012, with specific focus on economic performance in the era of the People's Revolutionary Government (PRG) of 1979 to 1983. Grenade reviews the economic environment during the Gairy era, specifically 1960 to 1978, and discusses the different approaches to economic development pursued by Gairy and by the PRG. Grenade then delves into several aspects of development planning and policy, as well as the performance of the four key economic sectors (real, fiscal, monetary, and external) from 1979 to 1983. The chapter then provides a brief socioeconomic overview of Grenada (focusing primarily on economic growth performance) since the collapse of the Grenada Revolution through the end of 2012.

Part II: Insiders' Perspectives on the Grenada Revolution

In part 2 the contributors provide a retrospective gaze on the Grenada Revolution. Chapter 4 reproduces an interview I conducted with Bernard Coard at the Richmond Hill Prison, Grenada, on October 17, 2008, before his release in September 2009. Bernard Coard was the deputy prime minister in the PRG and was imprisoned for twenty-six years, charged, along with others, for the murder of Maurice Bishop, Fitzroy Bain, Norris Bain, Evelyn Bullen, Jacqueline Creft, Keith Hayling, Evelyn Maitland, Unison Whiteman, and others on October 19, 1983. Coard's interview has deliberately been placed at the beginning of this part of the book, given the critical role he played in the making and collapse of the Grenada Revolution. Coard locates the Grenada Revolution within the context of "the many revolutionary upsurges of the Grenadian people over centuries." Coard centers the anti-Gairy struggle in Grenada within the larger anti-imperialist and antidictatorial struggles of the Caribbean Left. Coard reflects on the highs and lows of the Grenada Revolution and admits that the revolutionaries made many grave errors.

After the release on September 5, 2009, of Coard and the six remaining prisoners convicted of the murder of Maurice Bishop and others, there has been cause for a flurry of new conferences, papers, letters, and communiqués on the Grenada Revolution and its tragic demise. In chapter 5 Brian Meeks revisits the 1983 crisis and collapse of the Grenada Revolution. As one of the many regional workers in the revolution, Meeks sets out to rethink and restate his knowledge of events "for a new generation and a completely different world." Meeks tackles some of what he considers to be flaws in the new round of debates on the crisis and collapse of the Grenada Revolution and offers alternative explanations. He concludes that the story is yet to be fully told.

In fact, the story of the Grenada Revolution and its demise is a tapestry of narratives, where the truth is still elusive. In chapter 6, Patsy Lewis, a Grenadian who was an active supporter of the Grenada Revolution, presents a narrative account of the tragic events of October 19, 1983. Lewis seeks to recount the events of the day through the eyes of a junior member of the NJM who had been summoned to Fort Rupert (now Fort George) along with other members of the NJM. The narrative is based on an actual interview with a young woman in her mid-twenties a year after the tragedy. The piece is written from the perspective of the interviewee but shifts in the last paragraph to the perspective of the interviewer, who provides the reader with some insight into her responses to the interview. This chapter takes the reader back to the moment when both sides squared off in the final hours before the implosion of the Grenada Revolution.

Part III: Theoretical Critiques of the Grenada Revolution and Lessons for the Future

Part 3 provides theoretical critiques of the Grenada Revolution and lessons for the future. In chapter 7, Hilbourne Watson argues that the Grenada Revolution did not meet the requirements for a social revolution with a working-class character. He contends that Grenada, like most other Caribbean societies, simply lacked the foundation—material and otherwise—to build socialism, as there did not exist the deep inner structures of capital in science, technology, industry, finance, production, and labor to achieve and sustain a social revolution. For Watson, the crisis and collapse of the Grenada Revolution and the roles played by the Grenada revolutionaries had a great deal to do with an inherited authoritarian political culture.

Tennyson Joseph discusses C. L. R. James and the Grenada Revolution in chapter 8. He argues that many of the theoretical assumptions and tactical approaches of the Grenada Revolution were rooted in the experiences of early twentieth-century Russia. Joseph contends that the internal tensions within the Grenada Revolution largely ignored the pre- and post-Stalin theoretical debates within Communism and reflected little awareness of original Caribbean Marxist thought. Joseph argues that this was manifested in the limited impact of the Caribbean's foremost Marxist theoretician, C. L. R. James, on the revolutionary process in Grenada, although James's theoretical contributions addressed concerns that bore direct relevance to the later implosion of the Grenada Revolution and to a post-Stalinist global Marxism. Joseph seizes the opportunity provided by James's critique of the Grenada Revolution to widen the critique of James's thought by engaging in a wider analysis of the utility and relevance of James's key theoretical and methodological assumptions and approaches to the politics of the early twenty-first century, to identify what remains useful and what requires further formulation.

In chapter 9, Horace Campbell discusses the challenges for revolutionary change in the Caribbean. Similar to Joseph, Campbell examines the new revolutionary place in the twenty-first century as popular forms of expressions are breaking out as peoples develop new techniques at self-organization and mobilization. Campbell focuses on the lessons from the Haitian, Cuban,

Rastafarian, and Grenadian revolutions and counterrevolutions to conceptualize revolutionary change for the next thirty years. He zeros in on the
Zapatistas and the Bolivarian revolution, the women's movement, the antiracist movement, and the environmental justice movement to enrich struggles
for change beyond the single-issue struggles that have in the past influenced
political mobilization.

Part IV: The Caribbean Left, Party Politics, and Political Party Transitions in Grenada

Part 4 focuses on the implications of the demise of the Grenada Revolution
for the Caribbean Left and for party politics in Grenada. In chapter 10, David
Hinds offers an analysis of the Grenada Revolution and the Caribbean Left,
using the case of Guyana's Working People's Alliance (WPA). Hinds contends that the politics of most Caribbean Left parties were influenced by the
experience of the Grenada Revolution and its ultimate demise. The chapter
looks at the relationship between the NJM and WPA before and during the
revolution, including the impact of the revolution on the WPA's fight against
the Forbes Burnham–led People's National Congress (PNC) dictatorship in
Guyana. Finally it draws a connection between the demise of the revolution
in October 1983 and the shift in the WPA's tactics and strategy in the period
after the demise.

In chapter 11, I trace the twists and turns of party politics in Grenada from
1984 to 2013. I discuss the construction of the new political architecture and
its subsequent splintering, the emergence of an unstable multiparty system, the thirteen-year dominance of the Keith Mitchell–led New National
Party (NNP) (1995–2008), and intraparty splintering and the breakdown of
the National Democratic Congress (NDC) (2008–13). I argue that although
Grenada has transitioned to formal electoral democracy, there exists today
an unsettled "settling" to the two-party system. I argue, however, that Grenada has a collective resilient impulse that promotes stability in the midst of
volatility.

Chapter 12 reproduces a speech by Prime Minister Ralph Gonsalves of
Saint Vincent and the Grenadines, on the occasion of the naming of the Maurice Bishop International Airport (MBIA) in Grenada in May 2009. Gonsalves
argues that the spirit and ideas of Maurice Bishop were alive and flourishing
among the people of Grenada and the Caribbean. He applauded the naming
of the airport as an act of the Grenadian people coming home to themselves
out of their agony and compromises, their pain and joys, and their triumphs
and defeats of the past.

It is my hope that this book generates fresh insights for those who lived through the period of the Grenada Revolution and can benefit from thirty years' hindsight. I trust that the chapters here also ignite scholarly interest in the Grenada Revolution for the generation of Grenadian and Caribbean youth who are unaware of its significance. Importantly, as developing countries and ordinary peoples continue to search for social justice, equality, freedom, and hope in an increasingly uncertain world, this work is intended to provoke debate and inspire conscious action.

Notes

1. At the annual Caribbean Studies Association Conference in San Andres (2008), Jamaica (2009), Barbados (2010), and Grenada (2013), panels on the Grenada Revolution attracted large audiences and generated intense debates.

References

Boodhoo, K. 1984. *Grenada: The Birth and Death of a Revolution.* Latin American and Caribbean Center, Florida International University.

Collins, M. 2003. *Lady in a Boat.* Leeds, UK: Peepal Tree Press.

Grenade, W. C., ed. 2010. "Grenada Revolution: (30) Years After." *Journal of Eastern Caribbean Studies* 4 (3).

Lewis, G. K. 1987. *Grenada: The Jewel Despoiled.* Baltimore: John Hopkins University Press.

Ledeen, M., and H. Romerstein. 1984. *Grenada Documents: An Overview and Selection.* Washington, DC: U.S. Department of State and U.S. Department of Defense.

Meeks, B. 2001. *Caribbean Revolutions and Revolutionary Theory: An Assessment of Cuba, Nicaragua, and Grenada.* Mona, Jamaica: University of the West Indies Press.

Morales, W. Q. 1994. "U.S. Intervention and the New World Order: Lessons from Cold War and Post–Cold War Cases." *Third World Quarterly* 15 (1): 77–101.

Pastor, R. 1986. "Does the United States Push Revolutions to Cuba? The Case of Grenada." *Journal of Interamerican Studies and World Affairs* 28 (1): 1–34.

Payne, A., P. Sutton, and T. Thorndike. 1984. *Grenada: Revolution and Invasion.* London and Sydney: Croom Helm.

Puri, S. 2010. "Legacies Left: Radical Politics in the Caribbean." Special issue, *Interventions: International Journal of Postcolonial Studies* 12 (March).

Scott, D. 2001. "The Dialectic of Defeat: An Interview with Rupert Lewis." *Small Axe* 10:85–177.

———. 2007. "Preface: The Silence People Keeping." *Small Axe* 11 (22): v–x.

Thorndike, T. 1985. *Grenada: Politics, Economics, and Society.* London: Frances Pinter.

PART I
Historicizing Grenada

2. Grenada, 1949–1979: Precursor to Revolution

Curtis Jacobs

This chapter discusses the rise and eventual fall of Eric Gairy and the rise of Maurice Bishop as a public figure, leading to the consolidation of the Grenada Revolution in 1979. A British colony, Grenada had endured World War II, including the sinking of the *Island Queen* (Steele 2011). Many Grenadians had served in Europe, North Africa, and Asia (see Brizan 2002). The Moyne Commission Report of 1945 had commented that constitutional development was necessary if social reform was to be wisely conceived and efficiently conducted.[1]

The activism of T. A. Marryshow, C. L. R. James, and others had borne fruit.[2] The 1947 meeting in Jamaica worked out the general arrangements for "closer union" and set the stage for the establishment of the British West Indies Federation. By 1950 the gradual transfer of executive power from the governor to elected officials had begun. Britain had by then granted independence to India and Pakistan in 1947, Ceylon (Sri Lanka) in 1948, and was poised to grant independent status to Gold Coast (Ghana) in 1957.

The global post-1945 period was dominated by the Cold War, the rivalry between the United States and the Soviet Union. Mahan's ideas were more crucial to American interests.[3] With petroleum the basis of the world's military-industrial complex, the United States was reluctant to exploit its domestic reserves of petroleum in the event of war with the Soviet Union. The safety of supplies from the commercial deposits in the Middle East became a matter of national security.

Grenada's geographical position at the southeastern corner of the Caribbean archipelago placed her at the gateway of the most important sea lanes of the American oil tankers on their way to the refineries of the southeastern United States, the Panama Canal, and the Pacific Northwest. The United States and Britain became extremely concerned with developments in the island nations of this area, which includes Trinidad and Tobago. As Britain faded into a world power of lesser rank, she tacitly acquiesced to the U.S. domination of Caribbean affairs.

The events in Grenada beginning in 1950 and 1951 brought to a head developments that had been set in train since emancipation in 1834. The main theme of this period was the political enfranchisement of the peasantry and the working class, which after the collapse of the plantations had evolved from the formerly enslaved and their descendants who purchased land up to ten acres in extent (Brizan 1998, 248). Closely related to this group were the protopeasantry, tenant farmers and estate laborers who supplemented their wages with the produce of small lots that were either owned, rented, or given without charge by large proprietors (248). These workers were "a significant proportion of Grenada's working population, its main source of labor, and the predominant agents of domestic food supply" (Brizan 1998, 248). Despite their significance, they existed on the fringes of Grenadian society (248–49). The 1939 Moyne Commission found that the daily wage for an estate laborer had remained unchanged for a hundred years (259).

Nevertheless the peasantry had begun the conversion of the traditional plantation economy into the premodern contemporary phase by establishing villages and markets, as well as institutions such as schools and hospitals, and initiating the cooperative movement. Politically impotent, they were nevertheless a social force to be reckoned with (Brizan 1998, 251).

The focus of social life was the village, where life was lived on a small scale. This resulted in the deep sense of community engendered from shared experience (Douglas 2003, 22). The common shared experience produced a remarkable group cohesiveness and social solidarity, which institutionalized the *su-su*, a system of cooperative savings based on mutual trust among participants. The peasantry, protopeasantry, tenant farmers and estate laborers also formed friendly societies, which provided members with mutual aid and support for acute financial need of all types (Brizan 1998, 257–59). The *maroon* was an important institution for large projects such as land clearing and home construction (Douglas 2003, 31). Everyone contributed to the enterprise, with the expectation that they would be reciprocated when their turn came (31).

At the top of Grenada's social order was "a tiny clique of planter-merchants and professionals, who controlled the Legislative and Executive Councils of government, as well as the civil service and who owned most of the fertile land and wealth in the country" (Brizan 1998, 249). The period immediately before 1950 saw the relative decline of T. A. Marryshow. Weighed down with increasing debt and encroaching ill health, the "Old Bulldog" was past his prime even as self-government and federation loomed on the horizon. Despite his public identification with the poor and dispossessed, Marryshow, as a member of the legislature, was officially on the same footing as the planter-merchant and professional classes that dominated the highest levels of Grenada's political life. His absence from Grenada for most of the last decade and a half of his life may have left a leadership vacuum (see Sheppard 1987).

The old fire was still there. In September 1944, Marryshow's minority report rejected the Select Committee's main recommendations on constitutional reform. He advocated, among other things, unqualified universal adult suffrage and a fully elected lower house (Singham 1966, 115–16). This bore fruit in late 1949 when the British granted full universal adult suffrage at age twenty-one and a majority of elected members in the lower house, to be enshrined in the constitution of 1951 (116–17).

The vacuum left by Marryshow was filled by two events, occurring within two years of each other. The first was in 1949, when Eric Matthew Gairy returned to Grenada from Aruba. At Moyah, St. Andrew, on February 18, 1922, Gairy was born into a poor, working-class family. At primary school, Gairy gained the favor of his teachers and the local Roman Catholic clergy, where he became an acolyte (Steele 2003, 349). After leaving school, he became a pupil teacher at the La Filette Roman Catholic Primary School.

During the 1940s, Gairy first migrated to Trinidad, then to Aruba, and worked in the oil industry while learning the fundamentals of organized labor. Believed to have been expelled from Aruba for his militant labor activism, Gairy returned to Grenada, where the underlying dire condition of the working class was exacerbated by the sharp decline in the colony's wartime prosperity and an increasingly high cost of living.

The Grenada oligarchy's concessions to the working class had postponed the Caribbean-wide development of politically militant organized labor. In 1950 two unions with small memberships made up the Trades Union Council. Their leaders had accommodated themselves within the established order (Brizan 1998, 266).

The twenty-seven-year-old Gairy's entry into Grenada's mainstream political life happened with almost perfect timing. In 1949, Grenada's population was relatively young (Brizan 1998, 249). Two generations younger than Marryshow, Gairy's age alone appealed to the masses yearning for a leader to emerge from the accumulated effects of the postemancipation period. More importantly, Gairy was unafraid of the colonial authorities and poised to inherit the fruits of the labors of Marryshow and his predecessors (Singham 1966, 152). Ironically, it was at Aruba that Gairy first met Marryshow, who aroused his interest in Grenadian affairs (153).

Gairy began as a parochial champion for the poor and downtrodden of his native St. Andrew. The case that brought him to wider attention was the occasion that Gairy successfully took the new owner of an estate to court under the Tenants Compensation Ordinance on behalf of its evicted tenants (Singham 1966, 155).

Drawing on his experience in labor organization and activism, Gairy and George Otway established the militant and politically conscious Grenada Workers' Union in 1950. Gairy later claimed that by June 1951 he had a registered following of about 27,000 (Singham 1966, 153). Unlike in Aruba, Gairy's activities encountered less opposition from the British authorities in Grenada (153–55).

A series of strikes and general social unrest between 1950 and 1951 propelled Gairy from a local social activist to a Caribbean public figure, eclipsing T. A. Marryshow as the champion of the masses. He was able to obtain significant wage concessions from the employer class and raised the working class's standard of living. Gairy's arrest and detention in February 1951 were widely condemned by the rest of the British Caribbean (Singham 1966, 162).

In 1951, the second development occurred with the return of a family of five from Aruba, comprising a husband, wife, and three children, of which the eldest were daughters. The youngest, a seven-year-old son, was in fact born at Aruba on May 29, 1944, where his parents had migrated in 1939. His name was Maurice Rupert Bishop (Franklyn 1999, 63–65).

Bishop was the scion of one of Grenada's oldest and most distinguished families. His mother, born Alimenta La Grenade, great-granddaughter of Louis La Grenade, a free colored who took a pro-British, antirevolutionary stand during Fédon's Rebellion in 1795–96. The elder Bishop established himself as a businessman in the town of St. George, and the family assumed residence at Fairmount at Parade, a suburb of St. George's.

With elections based on universal adult suffrage due in 1951, Gairy used his newfound social prominence as a stepping-stone for his now openly political ambitions. This presented the opportunity to be elected to the legislature, which until then was the preserve of the ruling elite.

The legislative power that Gairy actually wielded was more apparent than real, as constitutional controls over the legislature were strict. After his election on October 10, 1951, Gairy "began to make quite reckless demands and to act as though he was above the law, such as refusing to register his union's accounts as required by law, driving without a valid driver's license, and calling work stoppages on individual estates. During this period, the government began to take legal action against him in a number of cases" (Singham 1966, 172). After the ruling of the arbitration board went against him in a dispute in 1953, Gairy threatened and called strike action. The island-wide strike called for November 1953 collapsed around December. In January 1954, Gairy induced about 50 percent of the workers to strike, but by the end of February, most had returned to work (172–73).

In the meantime, Gairy developed his cult of personality. He seemed uninterested in developing the organizational infrastructure of the Grenada Manual and Mental Workers' Union (GMMWU) and the Grenada United Labor Party (GULP) and let slip opportunities to organize the urban working class, relying instead on his rural supporters (Singham 1966, 173).

On December 20, 1954, the government introduced the committee system, which was meant to prepare elected legislators in the proposed British West Indies Federation by acquainting them with the knowledge and functions of government bureaucracy and procedures (Brizan 1998, 357). It lasted from 1955 to 1960, when it was superseded by the ministerial system of government (357).

In 1954, Dr. John Watts, an American-trained dentist, formed the Grenada National Party (GNP). The party had a systematic, comprehensive vision for Grenada. The GNP advocated a better Grenada for all its citizens, with a strong emphasis on education as the basis for sustainable development (Brizan 1998, 359).

In the meantime, the GULP lost ground, despite being elected to six of the eight seats contested in 1954. Gairy retained his seat with a significantly reduced majority (Singham 1966, 175). Then members of his party who had developed personal followings earned Gairy's displeasure. He appeared never to appreciate the importance of the organizational development of cadres, preferring to maintain links with groups and members only through himself. This practice came to a head in a conflict between Gairy and the member for St. John and St. Mark, L. C. J. Thomas. Thomas had won the seat on the GULP ticket, but differences with Gairy led to his expulsion (175). This was a significant loss. With the GULP seats now numbering five, and the other members unlikely to support the GULP, Gairy could easily be thwarted on any issue before the Legislative Council (175).

Other developments undermined Gairy's popularity. The exodus to Trinidad and the United Kingdom and new economic activities such as banana cultivation and export in the post–Hurricane Janet period reduced his following in cocoa, sugar, and nutmeg. The development of rival labor unions challenged his domination of organized labor (Singham 1966, 175–6).

In the 1957 elections, the GULP won only two seats to the Legislative Council. Two former GULP members held their seats. The GNP and the People's Democratic Movement won two seats each. About a month later, Gairy was convicted and disenfranchised for disrupting a rival party's meeting. He unsuccessfully appealed the conviction, thereby losing the right to take his seat in the legislature from 1957 to 1961, which disqualified him from the federal and general elections of the period (Singham 1966, 176–77).

H. A. Blaize presided over the entry of the first woman member of the legislature, with his nomination of Gertrude Protain to serve on the Education and Social Services Committee (Nyack Compton 2004, 16–23).

With Gairy in the political wilderness, Britain granted cabinet and ministerial government in 1959, where most executive power was vested in the office of the chief minister, which was first held by Blaize. The government commanded the support of the majority of the members of the elected legislature, itself comprising ten elected members, two nominated members, and one ex officio member. The administration was presided over by the administrator, whose office was granted reduced powers. There were also changes to the structure of the civil service (Steele 2003, 359–60; Brizan 1998, 358).

In early 1959, the Caribbean learned that the Cuban dictator Batista was overthrown by the 26th of July Movement, led by Fidel Castro Ruz. Cuba has a special place in the history of Grenada. It was in late 1814 that the British governor informed the council that Julien Fédon had escaped to Cuba. After Fédon's last official sighting on July 27, 1796, he was believed drowned attempting to escape to Trinidad, until the governor received information that he was in Cuba. After two years, the attempt to extradite Fédon was abandoned (Jacobs 2002). The Cuban Revolution presented the changed concept of revolution from the fundamental transformation of an existing social order to the seizure of the state apparatus to effect the social transformation.

In 1960, within the federation, Grenada received the full ministerial system of government, but no date was given for the dissolution of the old Legislative Council (Singham 1966, 177). Gairy demanded elections under this new constitution. In the Legislative Council, his erstwhile colleague L. C. J. Thomas and Preudhomme of the GULP resigned their seats in protest over the delay in calling elections. The administrator refused to lift the court-imposed ban on Gairy's political activities. The *West Indian* newspaper commented that the decision was judicial and not political (178). At length, the British government announced that elections would be held in March 1961.

Gairy made his disenfranchisement the major election issue. He announced that if he was not allowed to stand, Joshua Thorne, a supporter, would stand in his place (Singham 1966, 178). In the end, Thorne stood in the constituency for which Gairy normally stood.

The GULP won eight of the ten elected seats in the legislature. The GNP won the Town of St. George's and Carriacou. Cynthia Gairy, the wife of Eric Gairy, became the first woman to be elected to the Legislative Council in her own right (Steele 2003, 361).

The attorney George Clyne, a GULP member, was invited to be the chief minister. From April to June, Gairy's behavior bordered on the surreal:

> From April to June Gairy continued to behave as though he was Chief Minister. His private home came to be considered the real headquarters of the Legislative Council and the Executive Council by his party and by the people of Grenada.... He kept up a steady campaign for his re-enfranchisement ... arguing that there could be no government in Grenada until he was Chief Minister. The Administrator kept publicly silent on the controversial issue. (Singham 1966, 182)

Several diverse public figures supported his reinstatement. On June 6, the British government announced that a decision on Gairy's disenfranchisement may be decided by the Legislative Council. At the time, Gairy was in Britain at the federal conference on independence. On June 28, the bill ending Gairy's disenfranchisement was passed through the legislature in all its stages. Gairy returned to Grenada a hero (Singham 1966, 182).

Watts, chairman of the GNP, commented that if the due process of law was allowed to break down, you can never tell where it will end (cited in the *West Indian* by Singham 1966, 182).

Both in government and in opposition, Gairy displayed a distinct disregard for the rule of law and established procedure. His clashes with the administrators and other public officials had convinced him that the law was not neutral, and the people were being made to suffer under an unjust social order. He also believed that he was never accepted as a social equal by the "upper brackets" (Singham 1966, 184).

Gairy's movement faltered after 1961. The accumulated effects of developments since 1950 continued to undermine his popular support. What began as a genuine movement to alleviate the workers' dire socioeconomic situation became in the end a means to undercut the popular appeal of the person who stood up for the cause of the very working class (Singham 1966, 186–88).

Meanwhile Maurice Bishop completed primary school in 1957 and was awarded a scholarship to the Presentation Brothers' College (PBC), the premier secondary school for Roman Catholic boys (Franklyn 1999, 67). His favorite subjects were English, history, and literature, and a lifelong friendship with Kenrick Radix began.

At PBC Maurice read C. L. R. James and Kwame Nkrumah. His wide reading was the basis of his strength as a debater and a riveting, formidable public speaker. In 1962, Bishop was awarded the Principal's Gold Medal for Public Speaking (Franklyn 1999, 67). In 1963, at age nineteen, Bishop traveled to the

United Kingdom to study law at the Holborn College of Law, University of London.

Meanwhile Gairy was reelected to the Legislative Council following the resignation of Thorne and the ensuing by-election. Clyne then resigned as chief minister, making way for Gairy's appointment as chief minister and minister of finance in August 1961.

On January 22, 1962, the administrator appointed a commission "to enquire into the spending of public funds in Grenada during the financial year commencing 1 January 1961 and subsequently, and to report and make recommendations" (Brizan 1998, 358). The commission sat from February 5 to May 2. It heard evidence from thirty-seven persons, including twenty-three public servants and representatives of interest groups (358). Its report cited serious breaches of financial procedure, particularly by the minister of finance (358–59).

It was a scandal involving graft, misappropriation of public funds, and intimidation of the public service (Brizan 1998, 360). The commissioners found that the minister of finance "had disregarded and contravened the laws and regulations governing the control of expenditure." The government, particularly the minister of finance, was found to have engaged in "financial mismanagement and wasteful expenditure" (360). The arch offender of this "squandermania" was the minister of finance, E. M. Gairy (360).

Standing behind this scandal were serious issues of fiscal control in the British West Indies Federation. In his budget presentation, Gairy complained bitterly about his experience with the federal minister of finance to obtain funds for Grenada's development (Singham 1966, 223). The alternative was to raise revenue in Grenada itself, and Gairy introduced a series of taxes, called "Tax Like Fire" (223). His budget alienated all the major interest groups and sparked a "wave of dissatisfaction and unrest in the country" (*West Indian*, cited in Singham 1966, 225). It was against this background that the administrator appointed the commission into public expenditure on January 22. On June 18, 1962, the administrator officially suspended the 1959 constitution and assumed his reserve powers, including that of appointment of a minister of finance.

At the general elections of September 18, 1962, the GULP won four seats to the GNP's six, and the GNP was invited to form the government. Under Blaize the GNP used the proposed unitary statehood with Trinidad and Tobago as its major election issue. The GNP assumed the government, but its proposal for unitary statehood was abandoned owing to strong opposition in Trinidad and Tobago, despite much groundwork by both governments (Brizan 1998, 361–63).

Under the GNP, much work was done in agriculture, education, health, communications, and infrastructure (Brizan 1998, 363). Grenada had been a "grant-in-aid" colony since 1958, and under the GNP administration the colony received funds for development expenditure. Between 1963 and 1966, nearly $750,000 was received. Between 1965 and 1968, Grenada received some nearly $2.5 million (363). Several important standing committees of the legislature were established. The 1959 constitution was restored in 1966, which offered the possibility of constitutional advances.

On March 3, 1967, Grenada became an "associated state" of Great Britain. The constitution provided for a governor who represented the British monarch; a bicameral legislature comprising a nominated Senate and an elected House of Representatives; and cabinet government, which was presided over by a premier. Grenada was granted full internal-affairs self-government, while defense and external affairs remained under British control (Brizan 1998, 365). H. A. Blaize became the first premier, but in the 1967 elections, the GULP was returned to office by a margin of seven to three over the GNP.

Out of office, Gairy lived in "virtual penury" but in 1967 still commanded considerable popular support (Brizan 1998, 367). These were the final twelve years of Gairy's domination of Grenada's politics, years during which he enriched himself, becoming increasingly authoritarian and anti-working-class (367).

Gairy's final years actually began with making history. In the search for a new governor, his first choice was president of the Senate, Thomas Joseph Gibbs, former member of the Federal Parliament and staunch Gairyite (Brizan 1998, 474–7). Joseph Gibbs is believed to have declined and suggested his daughter, Hilda.[4] Hilda Gibbs Bynoe, born at Crochu, St. Andrew, on November 18, 1921, a medical doctor, became the first native governor of Grenada, the first and only female governor of Grenada, and the first female governor in the history of the British Commonwealth.

On Sunday, October 19, 1969, eleven years to the day after the death of T. A. Marryshow, the *West Indian* reported that Maurice Bishop had completed his studies in law and qualified as a barrister (cited in Franklyn 1999, 71). Bishop returned a changed man. Recently married to Angela Redhead, he had had a unique experience in London when the anticolonial movement had begun to accelerate. The world seemed to be hurtling along a radical political path, which included the rise of Black Power consciousness. Bishop must have imbibed these influences. This period also witnessed the assassinations of Malcolm X, Martin Luther King Jr., John F. Kennedy, and Ernesto "Che" Guevara; worldwide opposition to the Vietnam War; and the radical international student movements and their alliances with the working class.

If he did not encounter it before, Bishop must also have discovered the Marxist conception of history. As Henry Kissinger wrote, during the so-called Cold War, great-power rivalry was intimately associated with rival social philosophies (Kissinger 1979, 62). It was as if Kissinger foresaw the unfolding scenario in Grenada after 1979:

> The elusive problem of peace would have been difficult enough in any circumstances: in our time it is compounded by ideological conflict. In periods heavily influenced by ideology, political loyalties no longer coincide with national boundaries. Communist parties everywhere adhere to a philosophy that asserts historical inevitability and pay allegiance to a foreign nation often in conflict with their own; many new nations are swept by an ideology whose central tenet, if not Communism, is powerfully anti-Western in the name of anti-imperialism; a crucial new conflict is the struggle between moderates and radicals in the developing world. (Kissinger 1979, 68)

In Britain, Bishop also discovered details of his family's history, particularly Louis La Grenade and his role in Fédon's Rebellion from 1795 to 1796. Even as an aspiring revolutionary, inspired by Julien Fédon as Grenada's first anticolonial, antislavery, protonationalist hero, Bishop must have understood that this ideology implied a rejection of his famous ancestor's antirevolutionary past. The evidence suggests that Bishop never publicly discussed his famous ancestor (see Franklyn 1999, 66).

At the Miss World pageant in London in 1970, Grenada's entrant, Jennifer Hosten, became the first-ever nonwhite Miss World, under controversial circumstances.

In Grenada itself, Gairy attempted to perpetuate himself in power, even against popular wishes, using three main categories:

1. By making as many people as possible economically dependent on the Government and upon himself in order to control them politically.
2. By crushing dissent and making it difficult if not impossible for Parliamentary Opposition to operate and perform. By 1979 Parliament had become his personal property.
3. By creating a highly centralized bureaucracy where decision-making depended on the Cabinet, which, in effect, was Gairy himself. (Brizan 1998, 367)

The Firearms Act of 1968, for example, was in fact a ruse to seize the firearms of his political opponents and to have their licenses disapproved (Steele 2003,

363). Gairy seemed determined that the state maintain the monopoly on violence (Brizan 1998, 367–68).

Gairy then neutralized anyone who differed with him on any matter and cultivated an air of mystery about his person. He promoted his belief in the occult and participated in Afro-Caribbean religious ceremonies. He later publicly identified with the belief in alien visitations and unidentified flying objects (Steele 2003, 361). Gairy's membership in the Rosicrucian Order may also have enhanced this mysterious image, all this while the issues of governance were relegated to the proverbial back burner and the state apparatus became a weapon to settle his personal vendettas (363).

By then there were those already contemplating revolution. They were drawn from the social group opposed to Gairy throughout his public life: the "upper brackets." These were mostly young, overseas-educated professionals who had returned full of ideas about social transformation.

Maurice Bishop may have personified this new middle class. Twenty-two years younger than Gairy, a veteran of radical student politics and public service in London, Bishop was ready to resume where he had left off in Grenada in 1963, where he tried to establish the Assembly of Youth after Truth (Franklyn 1999, 68–70). Back home, this idea was reborn in the Movement for Assemblies of the People (MAP), an organization that he cofounded with Kenrick Radix (68).

Bishop often visited Trinidad and Tobago during the so-called Black Power Revolution of 1970 and used to be "around Geddes Granger," as he was known before becoming Makandal Daaga.[5] Most Grenadians would not be surprised to know that Makandal Daaga's father was the Grenada-born Urias Phillip Grainger, who migrated to and was recruited from Trinidad and Tobago to serve in the British armed forces during World War I (Besson and Brereton 1991, 415).

On May 10, 1970, about three hundred Grenadian youths, under the leadership of an as yet unidentified progressive professional element that later emerged as the New Jewel Movement, staged a mass demonstration in sympathy with the Trinidad Black Power advocates but focused their attention on the Grenada situation by demanding "more jobs now" (Jacobs and Jacobs 1980, 95).

Gairy's reaction was swift. On May 21, 1970, the Grenada legislature passed the Emergency Powers Act, giving the public authorities sweeping powers to search private premises for "subversive literature" and arms and ammunition without a warrant, to restrict the physical movement of persons, to limit the right to freely associate, and to ration essential services and commodities (Jacobs and Jacobs 1980, 95).

On May 23, 1970, Gairy announced his intention to "wet our house . . . in order to prevent the [Black Power] fire from spreading to Grenada." He announced, among other measures, the establishment of the body known today as the "Mongoose Gang," comprising the "roughest and toughest rough-necks," to deal with those whom he derided as "hot and sweaty youth," determined to emulate their counterparts in Trinidad and Tobago.

Gairy had legitimized in Grenada's political culture state-sponsored collective political violence as a necessary means of dealing with political discontent. In so doing, he made his own overthrow by collective political violence possible, feasible, and socially acceptable.

The folk expression "hot and sweaty" means "without much forethought; hurriedly; to undertake anything without giving it full consideration" (Mendes 2003, 88). For Gairy, Bishop was perhaps the "hot and sweaty boy" par excellence. After his return to Grenada, Bishop plunged directly into Grenada's radical political movement. During the nurses' strike of November 1970, twenty-two nurses were arrested and charged. Their attorney was Maurice Bishop.

Gairy's "land for the landless" program legislated the government's seizure of some thirty estates by 1978 (Steele 2003, 365). As laudable as its declared intentions were, many estates belonged to his political opponents. Others were not subdivided at all, as he sought to break his opponents' economic power (Brizan 1998, 368). This program may also have inadvertently compromised Grenada's potential to earn foreign exchange from its export plantation agriculture.

The elected boards of the producer cooperatives in nutmeg, bananas, and cocoa industries were abolished by acts of the legislature, and in their place interim government-appointed boards were installed. A government-appointed commission was appointed to inquire into the financial affairs of the Nutmeg Board, which was guided through the litigation by Maurice Bishop. The High Court ruled for the Nutmeg Board (Brizan 1998, 368–69).

In the 1972 elections, the first in which fifteen seats were contested, the GULP won thirteen seats, with the GNP holding on to Carriacou and St. Patrick West. For the first time, the GULP won the town of St. George, and Cynthia Gairy was reelected. The question of independence was an election issue, and after the elections, negotiations began with the British government on the question of independence for Grenada.

Meanwhile Bishop and MAP forged a relationship with the Joint Endeavours for Welfare, Education, and Liberation (JEWEL), led by Teddy Victor and Unison Whiteman. The urban intellectual middle class, along with those disillusioned with the corruption and failures of Gairy's rule, supported the movement. It also challenged Gairy's rural base (Franklyn 1999, 73).

On January 21, 1973, MAP and JEWEL publicly tried Lord Brownlow, the English owner of La Sagesse estate, who had denied public access to the beach. Brownlow was a cousin of Queen Elizabeth II.[6] Forty people were later charged with disorderly conduct and destruction of property. These charges were later dismissed (Steele 2003, 368).

On March 11, the New Jewel Movement (NJM) was officially formed out of MAP and JEWEL, and a People's Convention on Independence was arranged for May 6, 1973. Assemblies of the people were proposed as the new governmental structure for society. Bishop and Whiteman became "joint co-ordinating secretaries." The JEWEL's periodical, *Jewel*, became the *New Jewel*, and its motto changed from "Let's join hands to build a better land" to "Not just another society but a just Society" and "Let those who labour hold the reins" (Brizan 1998, 372).

At the People's Convention on Independence at Seamoon Pavilion on May 6, 1973, the NJM called for people's involvement in the independence constitution, as well as the initiation of positive and concrete steps to redress national issues. The NJM decried "flag and anthem" independence as having no substance for the people and their ills; instead the NJM advocated a meaningful, real, and genuine independence. It called for independence under a new progressive, imaginative, honest, and hardworking leadership. It demanded independence projects, not celebrations, and called for negotiations with the British for partial reparation of wealth exported from Grenada during the three centuries or so of British rule (Brizan 1998, 373–74).

Meanwhile, in Chile, the Nixon Doctrine bore fruit. On September 11, 1973, the world's first democratically elected socialist government of Salvador Allende, a personal friend of Fidel Castro of Cuba (Allende was in fact born on July 26) was toppled in a coup led by General Augusto Pinochet, who then led the so-called Dirty War against Chile's socialists and communists.

Gairy held a meeting at Grenville Market Square on May 6 at which he identified several NJM members present, whereupon his supporters set upon, beat, and brutalized them (Brizan 1998, 378). At Seamoon on November 4, 1973, twenty-seven charges were read out against the government (374–75). The government, found guilty of all charges, was called on to resign with effect from November 18, 1973 (375–76). Should the government refuse, the country would be subject to a general strike.

On Sunday, November 18, 1973, Gairy used the occasion of governor Dame Hilda Bynoe's birthday to attack the NJM's leadership meeting in Grenville. Maurice Bishop, Unison Whiteman, Kenrick Radix, Selwyn Strachan, Simon Daniel, and Hudson Austin were mercilessly beaten by the secret police under the supervision of Inspector Belmar, thrown into jail, and refused medical attention (Brizan 1998, 378). Bishop and Radix required extensive reconstructive surgery. The others fared only slightly better (Steele 2003, 371).

Bloody Sunday made martyrs of the six NJM leaders and precipitated the very strike they had intended to prevent (Brizan 1998, 378–79). The arrests and beatings were later justified by court testimony that the meeting was held for subversive purposes, and they were in possession of weapons with which to capture the Grenville police station, all of which were successfully refuted in court (Steele 2003, 371).

On November 19, 1973, the Committee of 22 was formed. It called for a general strike, which, the committee declared, would cease only when Gairy ordered the discipline of those directly responsible for Bloody Sunday and instituted a public inquiry into the incident, as well as those responsible for law enforcement (Steele 2003, 371). Recent evidence suggests that the NJM contemplated bearing arms against the state in the face of this sustained state-sponsored political violence, but the decision to create a military arm must also have been informed by security considerations and the possible seizure of political power once Gairy proved too difficult to dislodge via the ballot box.

In 1973 the ultrasecret National Liberation Army (NLA) was established. Ewart Layne, an early recruit and later a lieutenant in the People's Revolutionary Army (the successor to the NLA) wrote a history of the NLA from prison. Owing to ignorance of this body, many writers have not considered its activities and Gairy's response, particularly during the revolutionary upsurge from 1973 to 1974 (Franklyn 1999, 73). Maurice Paterson cites recruitment from the Grenada Boys' Secondary School Cadet Corps, amusing attempts to obtain arms and military training in Guyana (Paterson 1992, 5–24). During the revolutionary upsurge from October 1973 to February 1974, the NJM used every conceivable legal means to topple Gairy, including a propaganda campaign in the *New Jewel* (Franklyn 1999, 74).

The repercussions from the Bloody Sunday incident forced Gairy on December 1973 to establish the Commission of Enquiry into the Breakdown of Law and Order and Police Brutality in Grenada. It was nicknamed the Duffus Commission after its chairman, Sir Herbert Duffus, a retired chief justice of Jamaica. Its original scope was enlarged after the events of 1974, and it finally completed its hearings on May 16, 1974 (Brizan 1998, 381–84).

Before the Duffus Commission was finished, Grenada became the first associated state to become independent on February 7, 1974. Its Independence Constitution of 1973 made Grenada a sovereign realm of Great Britain. It inherited the Westminster model of constitutional government, a bicameral legislature, and a ceremonial head of state, the British monarch.

The buildup to Independence Day was turbulent. For most Grenadians, Gairy had been irreparably discredited by the events of Bloody Sunday. The general strike began in January 1974 and lasted a full month, with thousands at a time filling the streets and air with chants of "Gairy must go!" Dame Hilda Bynoe, traumatized by these and other events, resigned and migrated to Trinidad (Brizan 1998, 379).

January 21, 1974, was the first anniversary of the public trial of Lord Brownlow. With the Duffus Commission in session, Rupert Bishop was shot dead in St. George's, after which businesses were looted (Brizan 1998, 379). January 21, 1974, acquired a new name: Bloody Monday.

For Gairy, independence was imminent. Sir Leo De Gale was hastily installed as governor, and two weeks later, Grenada became independent. At the University of the West Indies, St. Augustine Campus, Trinidad and Tobago, from January 11 to 13, 1974, academics held a conference called "Independence for Grenada: Myth or Reality?" (Ryan 1974, 1).

The Independence Secretariat had completed its preparations for Grenada's inaugural independence celebrations. The major religious denominations refused to read Gairy's inaugural independence message. There was a power outage, and special arrangements were made to have power available at midnight on February 6. Maurice Bishop was temporarily held incommunicado until celebrations were complete. Many Grenadians were aghast that Britain had allowed the country to become independent at that moment (Steele 2003, 373). But Gairy was determined to be the "Father of Independence." He became Grenada's first prime minister, and the new nation officially joined the ranks of the Anglophone Caribbean.

Grenada inherited the Westminster model of government, a system that allows for regular electoral contests to decide which political organization holds the reins of power to make authoritative decisions for the whole society. It also provides for the separation of powers of the legislature, the judiciary, and the executive. The head of government—the prime minister and chairman of cabinet—is usually appointed by the head of state and is the person who, in the opinion of the head of state, commands the support of the majority of the members of the House of Representatives. The prime minister is *primus inter pares*, first among equals, and wields enormous executive power. He has the authority to hire and fire government ministers and the authority to call elections and appoint diplomats. A prime minister is a virtual dictator. Independence did not bring an end to the general strike, however. It lasted two weeks after the independence.

With the American oil lifeline passing between Trinidad, Tobago, and Grenada on its way to the United States, Grenada stood at a remarkable geopolitical and economic confluence in international affairs. This was particularly so after 1973, with the nationalization of the oil companies by the Arab states and the onset of the first oil shock, which sent oil prices soaring. The security of America's petroleum supplies became a matter of national concern.

Meanwhile, in Grenada, the NJM and NLA were both reorganized and strengthened between 1974 and 1977, after which they were "ready and able to overthrow the government" (Franklyn 1999, 75). The first major issue in Grenada's postindependence politics was the report of the Duffus Commission of May 1975 (Steele 2003, 373). The report "took away from the Gairy regime any shred of credibility it had left" (Brizan 1998, 381). The commission recommended sweeping changes to the organization of the police force; the removal of certain magistrates for failing to discharge their duties with impartiality and confidence; an inquiry into the conduct of the solicitor general with a view to removing him from office; and no further delay in addressing all criminal charges before the court involving violent incidents in the periods under the mandate of the commission (Steele 2003, 374).

Gairy's contempt for the commission's report was best illustrated when he placed Belmar on the GULP slate of candidates for the 1976 general elections.

By Act No. 17 of 1976, the Saint George's University (School of Medicine) Limited was established. The establishment of this institution, with no history and credibility whatsoever, occurred amid a series of bizarre scandals that had occurred during Gairy's final twelve years, including the Knights of Toledo fiasco and the Clancy brothers. As with the others, the St. George's University School of Medicine became the object of opposition politics.

Gairy visited and established diplomatic relations with the government of Chile under Pinochet, who apparently welcomed the opportunity to help subdue Grenada's socialist revolutionaries (Brizan 1998, 381). With the Newspaper Amendment Act of 1975, Gairy attempted to muzzle the press. The act increased the deposit required of anyone publishing a newspaper from EC$900 to EC$20,000. The real intention was the closure of the *New Jewel*, which then had a circulation of some 10,000 (Brizan 1998, 384). When this measure failed to stem the paper's rising popularity, the government made it a criminal offence to print, own, read, and circulate the newspaper.

For the general elections of 1976, Gairy's increasingly authoritarian rule brought the opposition groups together into the People's Alliance. Bernard Coard, after resigning his job at the University of the West Indies, returned to Grenada with his Jamaican-born wife Phyllis, ostensibly to conduct research in Grenada. He soon became prominent in the NJM and became its deputy leader. From her teaching position at the Anglican High School, Phyllis Coard was soon recruiting followers from students there and the Grenada Boys' Secondary School.

The general elections were called on November 7, 1976, the birthday of T. A. Marryshow. They were a straight contest between the GULP and the People's Alliance. Nevertheless the GULP won the elections by a margin of nine seats to six.

In the 1976 elections, Maurice Bishop was elected to the Grenada Parliament and was elected Leader of the Opposition. The other elected People's Alliance members were Herbert Blaize, Unison Whiteman, and N. Bain. In St. Andrew North East, Innocent Belmar was elected, and K. Radix ran a close but ultimately unsuccessful race against Mrs. C. B. Gairy (Brizan 1998, 481). The success of the People's Alliance was achieved against the odds, since the government banned their unlimited use of public address systems (384).

The 1976 election was the final occasion on which the NJM identified with Westminster-style parliamentary democracy. It had exhausted all socially acceptable means by which Gairy could be dislodged from office. Much of the movement's energies before 1976 had been devoted to acquiring arms and training as a security force. Paterson observes that security had been a priority, protecting the leadership at political meetings, particularly in the rural areas (1992, 13).

Perhaps the most sensational event of the immediate postelection period was the murder of Innocent Belmar. At the time, the government and the public-sector labor unions were in a dispute over wages for public servants as recommended by the Salaries Revision Commission. Gairy had banned the use of public address systems, which prohibited the unions from broadcasting the issues. The public workers had not received increases since 1974, and the commission recommended an 83 percent increase. Gairy not only refused to pay the recommended increases but threatened the labor leaders involved, the names of whom were later displayed on placards at a meeting before a hostile crowd (Brizan 1998, 385–86).

Gairy saw Belmar's election as a moral victory and the strikes as politically motivated. He admitted that in 1974 he had been caught napping; this was the last strike that the union leaders would call, and he boasted that he was well prepared. This was emphatically declared three times before religious leaders trying to mediate in the dispute. The options were money or the labor leaders' lives (Brizan 1998, 386). The unions were forced to accept whatever the government was prepared to concede. It was, as Brizan wrote, a sad day for organized labor. Gun and terror tactics had become the order of the day, the final arbiter in any major dispute (386).

Paterson comments that Belmar's assassination was a clear signal to Gairy that the opposition had entered a military phase. The security around him and government ministers was tripled instantly. More Chilean guns and advisers were on the way (Paterson 1992, 11). Meanwhile Gairy addressed the NJM's infiltration of organized labor; some of their leadership held elected executive positions in Grenada's major labor unions and strongly challenged the GMMWU's domination of organized labor. Not only was Gairy—the GMMWU—concerned about the domination of organized labor by the NJM, but these unions also had an extremely strong anti-Gairy outlook. In other words, Gairy had largely lost the political support of organized labor by 1978 (Brizan 1998, 386–87). The GMMWU withdrew its membership in the Grenada Trade Union Council on April 25, 1978 (*Grenada Newsletter*, May 6, 1978, 8).

In February 1978 the government passed the Essential Services (Amendment) Act 1978, and the Grenada Port Authority (Amendment) Act 1978. The latter affected the nature and settlement of industrial disputes involving the Seamen and Waterfront Workers' Trade Union (SWWTU) and the Grenada Shipping Agents and considerably weakened the strike weapon previously used on the docks. The Essential Services Act made provision for the settlement of disputes in essential services solely by arbitration, rendering illegal strike action in the essential services (Brizan 1998, 387). This was a complete turnaround from 1951, when the colonial government enacted legislation to neutralize the worker militancy that Gairy's rise engendered. In 1978, Gairy used the identical strategy to maintain his political power (387–88).

On Sunday, June 19, 1977, a violent confrontation arose between the armed forces, the Green Beasts, and unarmed, peaceful demonstrators led by the People's Alliance in St. George's, during which the soldiers fired automatic weapons in the air and drove people off the streets.[7] The incident occurred at Market Square, then Grenada's most important public space. Bishop Sidney Charles, head of the Roman Catholic Church in Grenada, strongly condemned the action of the Green Beasts. He refused to retract the statement, but Charles was supported by the Caribbean Conference of Churches.[8]

All of this occurred during the seventh session of the Organization of American States (OAS), held from June 14 to June 22 at the six-hundred-seat geodesic dome constructed on the grounds of the Holiday Inn Hotel, Grand Anse.[9] This must have embarrassed both Gairy and his government.

The House of Representatives was reduced to a rubber stamp for Gairy's plans. Bishop himself was elected Leader of the Opposition over elder statesman H. A. Blaize. Neither Blaize nor Bishop was able to influence the proceedings of the Parliament, which became a theatrical one-man, one-party affair, with Gairy always the leading actor. There was little or no debate; the members of the ruling party laughed and said aye. The Opposition voted the expected no. The 1976 Parliament was a grotesque, deformed version of the Westminster model.

Another important development took place not in Grenada but in Kew, London, in June 1978, where Paul Scoon, deputy director of the Commonwealth Foundation, accepted Gairy's invitation to be Grenada's second governor-general (Scoon 2003, 3). Scoon accepted. The director, John Chadwick, warmly congratulated him and advised Scoon that he should prepare himself for a coup in Grenada, an eventuality that Scoon sharply refuted (3–4).

Between late 1978 and early 1979, the revolutionaries became increasingly self-confident. Gairy had become a pariah among leaders of the Anglophone Caribbean (Steele 2003, 376). Despite this, he had secured a knighthood from Queen Elizabeth II in 1977.

In September 1978 the official parliamentary opposition became officially unstuck. The non-NJM members of the People's Alliance broke rank and met with Gairy on "a plan put forward for the industrialisation of the island."[10] This was Gairy's final major policy initiative, called "Project Industrialisation and Employment Bootstring," and he even engaged the business community (*Grenada Newsletter*, August 26, 1978, 1). On September 20, 1978, Gairy also announced the granting of free secondary education by 1981 (*Grenada Newsletter*, November 11, 1978, 6).

Gairy then showed open favor to the GNP in permitting their use of public address systems while denying their use to the NJM.[11] He then began to publicly toy with the idea of snap general elections.

The newspapers from January 1978 to March 1979 show references to clandestine activities and condemnation of the relationships between the government of Cuba and groups in Grenada itself. The Grenada-Cuba Friendly Society was established on October 7, 1978 (*Grenada Newsletter*, October 7, 1978, 3). The *Torchlight* was almost equal in its criticisms of both Gairy and the NJM.[12] There were rumors of arms being smuggled into the country in barrels of grease and weapons purloined from government forces.

In November 1978, Gairy addressed students of the St. George's University School of Medicine, where he said that "in moving around Grenada, they would find the 'odd man or woman' who does not support his Government. There had been political troubles in the island 4 years ago but they had been 'straightened out.' 'We are not soft,' he said, 'but we stick to human rights.'"[13] Gairy also announced his "honorary membership" in the Human Rights Organization of Latin America.[14]

A controversy arose over the NJM's observation of the Bloody Sunday incident. A rally, originally scheduled to take place on November 19, 1978, was canceled by government proclamation on November 18.[15]

In early 1979, the government discovered evidence that arms were being smuggled into the country. On February 27, 1979, Reverend Leopold Bain, a Vincentian-born Anglican priest, had his car searched by party of uniformed and plainclothes policemen. Nothing illegal was found.[16]

Then, in February 1979, two Grenadians named Humphrey and Wardally were arrested by the U.S. Federal Bureau of Investigation for allegedly exporting arms or conspiring to export arms to Grenada in containers marked "Grease." They were released on US$10,000 bail each.[17] It is believed that bail was met by a Grenada-born mathematics professor at a prestigious, historically black University in Washington, D.C., who, on an auspicious occasion in 1994, would be acknowledged by Sir Eric Gairy as his son.

The accused were identified as "actively connected with the radical New Jewel Movement," and there was "an uncomfortable silence from all quarters which has been providing unhealthy suspicions as to the intended use of the guns."[18]

On February 15, the seventy-five-year-old Mrs. Louisa Whiteman, mother of NJM member of Parliament Unison Whiteman, had her home and premises searched by some one hundred armed policemen, in a vain search for illegal literature and arms.[19] Then the automobiles of Coard, Whiteman, and Radix were searched at Gouyave after a meeting at Sauteurs. Nothing illegal was found.[20]

The *West Indian* of February 28, 1979, reported the expulsion of five Dominican priests from Grenada. According to the report, Gairy had identified five priests who were known to be "actively associated with Communist opposition groups in to-date futile but nonetheless violent efforts to overthrow the government."[21] The *West Indian* quoted Gairy as calling the priests "communists. . . . They want to get me out, but we will see who goes; whether I or they go."

On March 10, police raided the homes of Bishop, Coard, Whiteman, Radix, Hudson Austin, and Vincent Noel for arms but found none. For those who were not at home, their whereabouts could not be ascertained. For those who were at home when the police arrived, they disappeared soon after the police left.[22] Several NJM leaders were in a multistoried building on Lucas Street, St. George's examining electoral lists in anticipation of a snap election, when they received word that instructions were issued for their arrest. They went into hiding.

Gairy had left for the United States and was believed to have ordered the detention of the eight top leaders of the NJM and the construction of special cells at Richmond Hill Prison. On March 7, Bishop, Strachan, Whiteman, and Coard met and decided that Strachan should attend the Latin American and Caribbean Continental Association of Students (OCLAE) meeting in Cuba. The real objective is believed to have been to request Cuba's assistance in the armed overthrow of the Gairy government, as the Grenadians believed that their present resources were insufficient.

Gairy left for the United States a day or two after Strachan left Grenada for Cuba. It is believed that Gairy was heard to say that upon his return, he was to be shown either their cells—or their graves. Even after Gairy's departure, the government had no strong evidence of what was afoot. Sir Paul Scoon, governor-general of Grenada, during an interview with acting prime minister George Hosten, was told: "Your Excellency, we have those boys well covered. They cannot try anything funny" (Scoon 2003, 32). Around March 11, Bishop, Coard, and Whiteman assembled in a safe house in Mt. Parnassus and awaited word from Cuba while expecting to be arrested at any moment. Coard said that they should strike immediately, using their available resources, but Bishop and Whiteman preferred to wait until word came from Cuba. This situation continued until March 12, when George Louison and Hudson Austin arrived. George Louison cast the deciding vote to strike (Paterson 1992, 14–15). The Grenadians had decided that their own resources were enough to topple Gairy's government.

The military chiefs assembled at True Blue Hill (today called Freedom Hill) overlooking the True Blue barracks, while the political leaders group went to the radio station. Bishop had closed the meeting with an address that ended with the reflective words "Well, comrades, history is in your hands now" (Paterson 1992, 9). It was.

March 12, 1979, marked the end of a pivotal period in Grenada's modern contemporary history, which began with Gairy's arrival in December 1949 and ended with his departure from Grenada in March 1979. After his overthrow, he never again held public office in Grenada. By 1951, Gairy had emerged from humble origins to become the embodiment of the dreams and aspirations of Grenada's masses, trapped in the aftermath of colonialism and slavery. Even as he became the hero of the lower classes and anathema to the colonial authorities and their favored hangers-on, and even as his career promised to advance the cause of the class that had produced him, he was either unable or unwilling to continue the social revolution that his emergence promised. He spent so much time and energy using the state apparatus to settle his political vendettas, and—in later years—for his personal enrichment, that he lost sight of what he was elected for in the first place.

By using the structural violence resident in the state apparatus to address political discontent, Gairy opened the door to his being toppled from office by the very methods that he used to maintain his rule. The events of March 13, 1979, overthrew the dictatorship of one man and replaced it with the dictatorship of an intellectual elite (Brizan 1998, 393).

Notes

1. *West India Royal Commission Report Presented by the Secretary of State for the Colonies in Parliament by Command of His Majesty* (with an introduction by Denis Benn), London: His Majesty's Stationery Office, Cmd. 6607, July 1945 (Jamaica: Ian Randle, 2011), 373.

2. T. A. Marryshow (1887–1958) used the pages of his newspaper, the *West Indian*, to popularize the causes of representative government, self-government, and the British West Indies Federation. C. L. R. James published the essay "The Case for West Indies self-government" in 1933; see Anna Grimshaw, ed., *The C. L. R. James Reader* (Oxford: Blackwell, 1992), 49–62.

3. Alfred Thayer Mahan was an American military historian who gained much influence with American policy makers toward the end of the nineteenth century. He stressed the importance of naval power as a prerequisite for the United States to become a great nation. Once the Americans adopted this idea, then the security of the borders and the approaches to the United States became dominant strategic considerations. He is also acknowledged to be the originator of the term "the Middle East."

4. Dame Hilda Bynoe, personal communication with the author, circa June 1996.

5. Personal communication with Selwyn Strachan, 2013.

6. Lord Brownlow was also a close friend of the Duke of Windsor, uncle of Queen Elizabeth II, who had abdicated and made way for her father, George VI, to become king in 1936, thus making way for her succession on February 6, 1952.

7. *Grenada Newsletter* 5, no. 24 (week ending July 2, 1977): 1.

8. Ibid., 8.

9. *Grenada Newsletter*, Special OAS issue, June 29, 1977.

10. "No Alliance Solution Yet," *Grenada Newsletter* 6, no. 27 (week ending November 4, 1978): 1.

11. *Grenada Newsletter* 6, no. 27 (week ending November 4, 1978): 4.

12. The *Grenada Newsletter* 6, no. 27 (week ending November 4, 1978): 2, reported that the managing director and the editor of the *Torchlight* were then prominent members of the UPP.

13. *Grenada Newsletter* 6, no. 28 (week ending November 11, 1978): 16.

14. *Grenada Newsletter* 6, no. 28 (week ending November 11, 1978): 16.

15. *Grenada Newsletter* 6, no. 29 (week ending November 18, 1978): 11.

16. *Grenada Newsletter* 7, no. 1 (week ending February 3, 1979): 12.

17. *Grenada Newsletter* 7, no. 3 (week ending February 17, 1979): 1–2.
18. *Grenada Newsletter* 7, no. 3 (week ending February 17, 1979): 1–2.
19. *Grenada Newsletter* 7, no. 3 (week ending February 17, 1979): 3.
20. *Grenada Newsletter* 7, no. 4 (week ending February 24, 1979): 10.
21. *Grenada Newsletter* 7, no. 5 (week ending March 3, 1979): 7.
22. *Grenada Newsletter* 7, no. 6 (week ending March 10, 1979): 1–2.

References

Besson, G., and B. Brereton. 1991. *The Book of Trinidad*. Newtown, Port-of-Spain, Trinidad and Tobago: Paria Publishing.
Brizan, B. I. 1998. *Grenada: Island of Conflict*. London: Macmillan Education.
———. 2002. *Brave Young Grenadians: Loyal British Subjects; Our People in the First and Second World Wars*. St. George's, Grenada: George Brizan.
Douglas, C. 2003. *When the Village Was an Extended Family in Grenada*. Paradise, St. Andrew, Grenada: Maryzoon Press.
Franklyn, O. D. 1999. *Bridging the Two Grenadas*. St. George's, Grenada: Talented House Publications.
Grimshaw, A. 1992. *The C. L. R. James Reader*. Oxford: Blackwell.
Jacobs, C. 2002. "The Fédons of Grenada, 1763–1814." Paper presented at the University of the West Indies School of Continuing Studies Grenada Country Conference. St. George's, Grenada, January.
Jacobs, W. R., and Ian Jacobs. 1980. *Grenada: The Route to Revolution*. Cuidad La Habana, Cuba: Casa de los Americas.
Kissinger, H. 1979. *White House Years*. Boston: Little, Brown.
Mendes, J. 2003. *Cote ci Cote la Trinidad and Tobago Dictionary*. Port-of-Spain: Medianet.
Nyack Compton, S. 2004. *Gertrude Protain: Glimpses into the Life of a Great Grenadian*. Belmont Estate Heritage Foundation, Great Grenadians Series.
Paterson, M. 1992. *Big Sky/Little Bullet*. St. George's, Grenada: Maurice Paterson.
Ryan, S. 1974. Introduction to *Independence for Grenada: Myth or Reality?* Proceedings of a Conference on the Implications of Independence for Grenada by the Conference Committee, Institute for International Relations, University of the West Indies, St. Augustine, Trinidad and Tobago.
Scoon, P. 2003. *Survival for Service: My Experiences as Governor General of Grenada*. Oxford: Macmillan.
Sheppard, J. 1987. *Marryshow of Grenada: An Introduction*. Barbados, West Indies: Letchworth Press.
Singham, A. W. 1966. *The Hero and the Crowd in a Colonial Polity*. New Haven: Yale University Press.
Steele, B. A. 2003. *Grenada: A History of Its People*. London: Macmillan Educational.
———. 2011. *Grenada in Wartime: The Tragic Loss of the "Island Queen" and Other Memories of World War II*. Grenada: Beverley A. Steele.

West India Royal Commission Report Presented by the Secretary of State for the Colonies in Parliament by Command of His Majesty. London: His Majesty's Stationery Office, Cmd. 6607, July 1945. Jamaica: Ian Randle, 2011.

3. Grenada: Socioeconomic Overview, 1960–2012

Kari H. I. Grenade

This chapter provides a socioeconomic overview of Grenada from 1960 to 2012, paying special attention to economic performance in the era of the People's Revolutionary Government (PRG) from 1979 to 1983. It starts with a brief overview of the economic environment during the Gairy era (specifically 1960–78) to help explain some of the possible antecedents (from an economic perspective) of the PRG's insurrection in October 1979 and why they would have pursued economic development differently from Gairy. Next it examines several aspects of development planning and policy, as well as the performance of the four key economic sectors (real, fiscal, monetary, and external) from 1979 to 1983. The chapter then provides a brief socioeconomic overview of Grenada (focusing primarily on economic growth performance) since the collapse of the Grenada Revolution through to the end of 2012.

Economic Context: 1960–1978

The Development Plan of 1960 defined the long-term development policy of Grenada as "the promotion of self-sustained growth and the generation of sufficient domestic savings, to allow the country to become independent of external development aid" (Governments of Grenada and Trinidad and Tobago 1965, 31). During the 1960s, the groundwork for political independence was being laid, and the Gairy administration's policies and programs were geared toward the attainment of self-governance. The administration subscribed to the tenets of the free market, with strategic involvement in the economy that cohered with its long-term development vision for the country.

Fortuitous economic circumstances made preparations for self-governance easy. Benefiting from guaranteed prices and secured markets, the agricultural sector buoyed economic growth. Real gross domestic product (GDP) grew at an annual average rate of 5 percent from 1960 to 1970. Sugar was the dominant export. However, in a bid to diversify the agricultural sector (consistent with the long-term development vision for the country), there was a gradual shift, beginning in the early 1960s, from sugar production to production of banana, cocoa, nutmeg, and mace. Focus was also given to developing the tourism and manufacturing sectors. However, tourism expansion was constrained by limited room stock. Manufacturing was done on a relatively small scale and focused on the processing of sugarcane into syrup and molasses, which were refined into sugar and rum. By 1970 the Grenadian economy had not transformed structurally and, though agriculturally diversified, was still in essence a one-sector economy.

The early 1970s were a tumulus period for Grenada not only economically but also socially and politically. On the economic front, a series of internal and external events buffeted the economy. Starting in 1970, the suspension of aid by the British government in that year significantly affected public finances, leading to contractions in public services. In 1973 adverse weather devastated the agricultural sector, which negatively impacted export earnings and government revenue. The year 1974—a watershed year for Grenada—was marked by an outright economic crisis. The escalation in international oil prices (oil shock), coupled with the closure of the port (due to strike actions that lasted for the entire first quarter) portended severe socioeconomic hardship for Grenadians; prices skyrocketed, economic activity fell owing to the suspension of imports and exports and the reduction in tourist arrivals, unemployment rose, and uncertainty increased. These events exacerbated Grenada's fiscal problems as tax revenue plummeted because of the contraction in economic activity and the suspension in trade. Political instability and social unrest compounded the economic situation. Grenada was faced with a fiscal and external balance-of-payments crisis, as well as a social crisis.

Grenada's economic fortunes turned around somewhat from 1975 to 1978, underlying which were increases in international commodity prices, which buoyed agricultural exports. Additionally, the tourism sector recovered, and the construction sector expanded with the building of a medical school in 1977. Ancillary services also benefited from the expansion of the construction sector. It is estimated that real GDP grew at an annual average rate of 5 percent during from 1975 to 1978. However, the introduction of new taxes (including stamp duties, tax on the interest on deposits, and a telecommunications tax) and the welcomed turnaround in economic activity did not ease the fiscal pressure. The growth in revenue was outpaced by that of expenditure, especially current expenditure (wages and salaries and subsidies to state enterprises).

Overall, Gairy's economic policies were largely supportive of the inherent capitalist structure of the economy. According to Watson (1984), the capitalists and the proletarians were the main economic classes. The capitalist class dominated the tourism, agriculture, and light manufacturing sectors, while the proletariats made up the urban working class employed by the private sector. Watson argued that this economic class structure remained largely unchanged throughout Gairy's era, even with increasing levels of foreign capital into tourism and light manufacturing and the presence of black petite bourgeoisie engaged in commercial activities. The structure of the economy (particularly but not exclusively the agricultural sector) was such that there was a small number of big capitalist producers and a large number of small, inefficient producers (Jacobs and Jacobs 1980). While Gairy's development policies were broadly supportive of a market economy model, Watson contended that some of the policies were destabilizing; for example, the victimization of certain capitalists and the expropriation of their properties. According to Brizan (1998), "The Gairy Government of 1970–1979 used a combination of fear, terror, force, and patronage to govern" (392). Indeed, protracted political repression and an economic and social crisis in 1974 and 1975 culminated in the insurrectionary seizure of power in March 1979 by the PRG.

Economic Context: 1979–1983

Economic Policy

The PRG faced a difficult economic environment when it seized political power. As described in the previous section, the economy was challenged by internal issues (class struggle and political repression) under Gairy, and particularly during the 1970s, the economy had been buffeted by a series of natural and economic shocks. The PRG's challenge was not only to remedy the ailing economy but to transform it (as promised) given inherent structural weaknesses that characterize small, open, dependent economies like that of Grenada. In 1981, Bernard Coard, the minister for finance, planning, and trade, in presenting the economic plan for 1982, remarked, "For years in our country there was no serious planning, our people had experienced corrupt and inefficient leaders making haphazard decisions which left our country and its people underdeveloped and poor" (PRG 1981, 43). Coard further articulated the PRG's avowed intention of pursuing systematic development planning and building on the strengths of Grenadians to make the country self-sufficient.

To this end, the government undertook a mass organization of skills, talents, and efforts to strategically exploit the potentials of agriculture, agro-processing, manufacturing, fishing, and tourism. Moreover, there were different approaches to the organization of work, the motivation of workers, and the mobilization of creative talent. For example, an education committee was responsible for trade union and worker education classes, and a creative ideas committee was charged with developing better production methods. A disciplinary committee dealt with raising standards and discipline in the workplace. All established committees were accountable to the overarching production committee. The production committee was responsible for ensuring that every aspect of work became better organized for broad-based enhancement of productivity and efficiency. According to Coard, there was to be a "systematic attack on any form of corruption, waste, inefficiency, unpunctuality or laziness" (PRG 1981, 68).

The process of economic development was to evolve in an organized and orderly manner that made the most efficient use of scarce resources. The PRG aimed to set targets, prioritize goals, and inspire workers to be efficient and productive so as to promote nation building. The PRG was determined to reverse years of an ad hoc, unorganized, and market-oriented approach to economic development by planning the economy and ordering its development. Though the PRG's political philosophy was socialist in orientation, the government adopted a mixed-economy approach. Accordingly, a mixed-economy system that comprised the state, the private sector, and the cooperative sector, with the state being the dominant sector, was the underpinning economic edifice. The economic development model was deemed feasible and realistic to underpin real progress and achieve meaningful development results. The development model was to deliver dividends in terms of improved living standards and quality of life by mobilizing resources and using them efficiently, strengthening human capacity and productivity, and boosting quality investment. People were placed at the center of development, and as such, the mass organizations, the cooperative sector, and the private sector each played integral roles throughout the development planning process—from the preparatory stage to the implementation stage.

The PRG took a hands-on and practical approach in planning the economy, with a view to meeting its objective of fundamentally improving the quality of life of all Grenadians. In its "Report on the National Economy" (PRG 1981), the PRG expressed its willingness to work with the private sector, whether local or foreign, so long as private investments were in keeping with the PRG's economic development vision for Grenada. As cited by Watson (1984), the International Monetary Fund (IMF), in its review of the economy in early 1983, noted that the PRG had encouraged private-sector confidence in many ways, through regular consultations that aimed to solicit private-sector responses to proposed government policies. The IMF report concluded, "In general, the relationship between the government and the private sector has improved consistently during 1982" (cited in Watson 1984, 33). Payne, Sutton, and Thorndike (1984) noted the PRG's declaration that the economics of the market were to be respected except where the public's interest was threatened. The PRG also worked closely with the cooperative sector with the aim of further diversifying the agriculture, agro-processing, forestry, fishing, manufacturing, and tourism sectors.

On the socioeconomic front, it is safe to argue that Grenadians' quality of life might have improved because of the myriad social services that were provided free of cost. Income tax was abolished for 30 percent of the lowest-paid workers (Watson 1984). Grenadian citizens also benefited from a "social wage," which was described in the "National Report on the Economy" (PRG 1981) as those benefits that were provided to Grenadians for which they did not have to pay, for example, medical (dental, optical, and general) and education services. University scholarships were offered in areas that were consistent with the country's economic development thrust, school uniforms and books were free, and a literacy/adult education program and a teacher in-service program were introduced. Further, the Housing Repair and Construction Programme led to improved housing quality and access. Still further, no interest was paid on loans for house repairs. Payne, Sutton, and Thorndike (1984) reported that more than two thousand houses were repaired during the PRG's four-year rule. Additionally, prices of several items (including food and fuel) were controlled by the state, and equal pay for women became law. The social system, like the economic system, was ordered and geared toward the benefit of all Grenadians. According to Payne, Sutton, and Thorndike (1984), GDP per capita (the most common proxy for economic well-being) almost doubled to US$870 in 1983 from US450 in 1978.

The next section delves deeper into the economic aspect of the PRG's reign by examining the performances of the main economic sectors (real, fiscal, monetary, and external) under the mixed-economy approach to development.

Economic Performance

Economic growth averaged 3.0 percent from 1979 to 1983; however, growth over the period was by no means smooth. The economy grew by 6.0 percent in 1979, contracted by 0.4 percent in 1980, rebounded in 1981 (2.0 percent), accelerated in 1982 (4.9 percent), and decelerated in 1983 (2.9 percent). Underlying overall economic performance were activities in the key productive sectors, which varied from year to year throughout the entire period.

In the agriculture sector, production of some crops fell, while the output of others either stagnated or grew marginally. For example, whereas the output of fruits and vegetables grew significantly (buoyed by strong demand by Trinidad and Tobago), production of bananas fell sharply, and yields from cocoa, nutmeg, and mace fluctuated or declined marginally. In the specific case of cocoa—the leading export crop, which according to the World Bank (1985) accounted for 30 percent of total agricultural exports—production was particularly affected by volatile international price movements from 1979 to 1983. On the whole, agricultural output was affected by problems of predial larceny, pest and diseases, and inadequate supporting infrastructure (Joefield-Napier 1986). Natural disasters also affected the sector. According to Payne, Sutton, and Thorndike (1984), the disasters of August 1979 and January 1980 resulted in damages totaling US$27 million, destroying 40 percent and 27 percent of banana and nutmeg production respectively. The effect of these events on the agriculture sector continued to be felt up to 1983, especially the destruction of nutmegs, given the length of time it took for new plants to mature.

Performance of the other key productive sectors was mixed. Activity in the construction sector was robust, imbued with a few large public-sector investments, particularly the Point Salines International Airport, feeder roads, and water enhancement projects. Indeed, 1982 was called "the year of construction" (PRG 1981, 1). By 1983 the construction sector was the fastest-growing sector in the economy, with growth averaging 35.0 percent from 1980 to 1983. Activity in the manufacturing sector was hampered by several factors, including high tariffs, high corporate tax rates, inferior product quality, lack of aggressive export promotion, and price controls. In 1983 the sector suffered a significant blow when clothing exports to Trinidad and Tobago were reduced following that country's imposition of exchange controls and ceilings on clothing imports from all trading partners. On the whole, manufacturing output declined at an annual average rate of 1.3 percent during the period. According to Brizan (1998), the manufacturing sector did not have the economic impact envisaged.

Growth in the tourism sector was constrained by weak external demand owing to recession in the United States and Western Europe in the early 1980s. Additionally, limited availability of accommodations, negative publicity abroad (given the socialist orientation of the PRG and the realities of the Cold War), and inadequate flight capacity significantly curtailed visitor arrivals. Total arrivals declined from 175,012 in 1980 to 102,668 in 1981, falling further to 82,672 in 1983. Total tourist expenditure dropped to US$11.6 million in 1983 from US$17.5 million in 1980. Tourism performance was also adversely affected by internal inefficiencies of the sector. The amalgamation of five state-owned hotels, operating as the Grenada Resort Corporation, suffered from weak management and an inefficient, bloated staff complement (World Bank 1985). Notwithstanding the decline in the tourism sector, it accounted for about 50 percent of the country's foreign exchange receipts in 1981 (Brizan 1998).

The inflation rate averaged 20.3 percent between 1980 and 1981, owing to rising international prices for fuel, which fed into the domestic prices of household supplies, transport, and food. Rising domestic prices prompted the PRG to impose tighter price controls, which in Joefield-Napier's (1986) view accentuated distortions in the market by slowing the responsiveness of supply. A retreat in international prices resulted in a plummeting of the inflation rate to an average of 5.5 percent between 1982 and 1983.

With respect to the labor force, while information is scanty, the World Bank (1985) noted that the unemployment rate was estimated at 17.4 percent based on the 1981 census. According to Brizan's (1998) estimations, employees of state-owned enterprises and the public services accounted for around 30 percent of the workforce (about 10,000) in 1982. It is possible that the unemployment rate may have been reduced somewhat by 1983, due to increased migration of both skilled and unskilled workers. According to Joefield-Napier (1986), net migration averaged 1,584 during from 1979 to 1983, compared with the average of 1,408 from 1975 to 1978. Payne, Sutton, and Thorndike (1984) estimated that the rate fell to 10 percent by 1983, mainly benefiting youth and women. According to these authors, more than 3,500 jobs were created during the PRG's reign, mainly in the areas of public works and construction.

Information on wages is also scanty; however, based on the "Report on the National Economy" (PRG 1981), average public- and private-sector wages increased by 17.3 percent and 11.5 percent respectively in 1981. Brizan reported that public servants received wage increases of 10 percent and 12.5 percent in 1982 and 1983 respectively. While there were increases in wages, Joefield-Napier contended that on the whole, the labor market was a tight one during the PRG's reign, and the rate at which productive jobs were created lagged the number of new entrants to the labor force.

Overall, when compared with the rest of the countries in the Organisation of Eastern Caribbean States (OECS), Grenada's average economic growth of 3.0 percent from 1979 to 1983 was on par with that of its peers, where growth within the subregional group averaged 2.8 percent, ranging from 1.7 percent in Saint Lucia to 5.5 percent in Saint Vincent and the Grenadines.

Public spending expanded rapidly, consistent with the heavy involvement of the PRG in the economy. Total government expenditure climbed from 38.7 percent of GDP in 1979 to 52.7 percent of GDP in 1982 (the largest ratio since compilation of records started), before falling to 47.9 percent in 1983. The significant increase in total public-sector expenditure was underpinned largely by strong growth in capital expenditure, which rose from 12.1 percent of GDP in 1979 to 22.5 percent of GDP in 1983. The expansion in capital spending reflected the accelerated Public Sector Investment Programme, in support of the development of critical social and economic infrastructure, for example, the construction of the international airport, road networks, and low-cost housing. Watson (1984) noted that the airport project absorbed 42 percent of total public investment during the PRG era, while investment in road infrastructure accounted for 20 percent, and other projects made up the remainder.

In contrast, expenditure on goods and services (current expenditure) fell during the PRG's reign, moving from 22.5 percent of GDP in 1979 to 18.8 percent of GDP in 1983. Subsidies to loss-making state-owned enterprises also made up a large part of current expenditure. A close examination of the current expenditure components shows that spending on a few critical areas of social services (housing and health particularly) was lower from 1979 to 1983 than from 1975 to 1978. Joefield-Napier (1986) reasoned that this seemingly paradoxical outcome suggested that welfare gains were not as widely distributed as one would have expected, given the socialist political regime.

Generally, current expenditure was aligned with current revenue, keeping the current account balance in surplus for much of the period, except for 1980 and 1981, when there were small deficits of 1.2 percent and 1.0 percent of GDP respectively. Due to the rapid and significant expansion of capital expenditure, the government's overall fiscal deficit (after grants) deteriorated markedly throughout the period, increasing to 54.3 percent of GDP in 1982, an almost twofold increase relative to the ratio in 1980. A drop in capital spending in 1983, mainly on account of the completion of the international airport, helped to narrow the overall fiscal deficit to 46.4 percent of GDP in that year.

Public revenue increased during the early period of the PRG era on account of measures introduced as part of the IMF program that was entered into in August 1979. Measures included increased rates for stamp duty on imports, consumption duty on gasoline, a company tax, and an international airport levy on the value of imports. By the end of 1983, public revenue as a share of GDP had risen to 31.4 percent from 25.5 percent in 1981 (World Bank 1985). By 1982, total revenue was estimated at US$27.4 million compared with US$20.3 million in 1979 (Brizan 1998).

Throughout the PRG era, fiscal deficits, which averaged around 28 percent of GDP from 1979 to 1983, were financed mainly by external capital grants, which accounted for 20 percent of GDP on average during the same period. However, as the fiscal financing gap became larger with increasing deficits over the period, loan financing (both external and domestic) became important. Net external borrowing rose from 0.8 percent of GDP in 1980 to 8.3 percent in 1983. Domestic commercial banks were required to make special deposits to the government's account, which was tantamount to providing an interest-free loan to the PRG. Overall, total outstanding debt surged almost threefold to 63.6 percent of GDP in 1983 relative to the ratio in 1980. In an effort to restore fiscal stability, the PRG entered into another financing arrangement with the IMF in August 1983. However, the IMF arrangement was short-lived given the demise of the Grenada Revolution in October of that year.

When compared with the other member countries of the OECS, Grenada's expenditure share to GDP (29 percent) was just below the average for the OECS of 30.1 percent from 1980 to 1983. While Grenada's average expenditure to GDP ratio was below that of its peers, the ratio represented a 3 percent increase relative to the average ratio from 1975 to 1978. The increase in the expenditure ratio was consistent with the PRG's heavy involvement in the economy and society.

Monetary developments reflected activities in both the real and fiscal sectors. Weak economic activity constrained deposit growth, while increased borrowing by the PRG from commercial banks resulted in tight liquidity of the banking system. Moreover, the PRG required all commercial banks to make deposits to its accounts above that which was stipulated by the Monetary Authority of the OECS; this also contributed to the liquidity squeeze in the banking sector. The loans to deposit ratio (liquidity ratio) increased from 68.7 percent in 1980 to 74.5 percent in 1983, signifying a tight liquidity position as a greater share of deposits was being extended in loans. The liquidity squeeze hampered growth in credit to the private sector, which increased by a mere 9.0 percent between 1980 and 1983. The focus on public-sector investment might also have constrained growth in credit to the private sector. Despite the tight liquidity situation, interest rates remained broadly stable throughout the period. Deposit rates ranging from 2.5 percent to 4.5 percent were well below the inflation rate, which meant that savings rates were negative in real terms. Lending rates ranged between 9.0 percent and 10.5 percent and were set by the PRG. Grenada's banking system comprised five commercial banks, two of which were indigenous banks established during the period of the revolution (the National Commercial Bank and the Grenada Bank of Commerce).

The United Kingdom was Grenada's main export market. However, the PRG developed strong trading ties with other socialist regimes, in particular Cuba and the Soviet Union. Exports to the Soviet Union expanded from 3.6 percent of total exports in 1982 to 9.3 percent in 1983. Trinidad and Tobago also became an important trading partner, accounting for 31 percent of Grenada's exports of fruits and vegetables by 1982 (Payne, Sutton, and Thorndike 1984). However, on the whole, earnings from the export sector declined at an annual average rate of 2.5 percent during the period. Traditional agricultural exports were significantly affected by declining international prices and falling volumes (arising from factors such as pest and disease, as well as an inadequate supporting infrastructure and shrinking markets). The combined receipts from the top three exports (cocoa, nutmeg, and bananas) fell from US$18.4 million in 1979 to US$10.5 million in 1983. Overall, the export sector was challenged by unfavorable prices, rising costs of imported inputs, and declining sales because of restricted markets.

While export earnings sagged, imports, especially relating to the PRG's Public Sector Investment Programme, surged. Consequently, the external current account deficit increased twofold from 20 percent of GDP in 1980 to 42 percent of GDP in 1982. The external deficit narrowed to 35 percent of GDP in 1983, largely because of a reduction in construction-related imports as a result of the completion of the international airport. The external deficit was financed by concessionary loans to the government and large inflows of external grants, at least until 1982. Official grants rose from US$34.3 million in 1979 to US$45.1 million in 1982, while the ratio of external debt to total exports grew from 36 percent in 1980 to 124 percent in 1983.

In summary, while a critical assessment of the PRG's economic record is beyond the scope of this chapter, the following observations are noteworthy. First, the pursuit of an orderly and systematic approach to development did not automatically translate into significant economic gains, judging from the modest economic growth, which averaged 3 percent from 1979 to 1983. Indeed, from the examination of sectoral performance, it is evident that growth was not broad based. Apart from the construction of the international airport, feeder roads, and low-cost houses, there were few other major capital investments. Industrial development on the whole was not immediately visible. The enterprise sector remained small, and there was little structural transformation of the economy.

Second, the socioeconomic outcomes suggest that the focus on "planning the economy" rather than coherent and sound "economic planning" did little to significantly promote the kind of fundamental structural transformation that is required to propel and sustain development. Moreover, institutional fragilities hampered the PRG's ability to effectively execute its development policies and programs. Joefield-Napier (1986) opined that the economy remained underdeveloped, and the growth process was "grossly unbalanced" (52). Joefield-Napier asserted that the less-than-sanguine economic outcomes were associated with inadequacies in the PRG's planning architecture. One such inadequacy was the lack of human capacity to effectively steer the transition from a market-oriented approach to development to one of a central planned mixed-economy model. Joefield-Napier remarked, "The persistent inability of the PRG to implement a satisfactory central planning mechanism to replace the market mechanism seriously impaired the functioning of the economic system" (4).

Consistent with Joefield-Naiper's view, Brizan (1998) contended that Grenada's rate of economic growth "did not have a significant impact on people's living standards" (401). Brizan noted that even if the PRG's management and planning were incomparable, the government was constrained in its ability to sustain economic growth because of the volatility of exports, given the economy's inherent structural vulnerabilities of a narrow production base, small size, and heavy external dependency. Nonetheless Brizan duly acknowledged the PRG's limited time frame and also recognized the improvements in some social indicators. For example, Brizan drew attention to the following statistics: (1) the literacy rate increased to 90 percent in 1981 from 85 percent in 1978; (2) students in university on scholarships rose to 250 from 35 during the same interval; and (3) infant mortality per 1,000 fell from 29 to 14.8. According to Brizan, the successes in the social and infrastructural areas were negated by the poor performance of the major economic sectors. This, Brizan argued, "helped to undermine the regime and create the conditions for internal dissatisfaction and internecine party rivalry and conflict" (411).

While the macroeconomic and social policies of the PRG were not all ill designed, implementation of most were frustrated by the harsh external circumstances of global price volatility and weaknesses in the economies of the country's major trading partners. Indeed, Payne, Sutton, and Thorndike (1984) recognized the human and physical resource constraints that Grenada faced given its heavy external dependence, and correctly pointed out that diversifying the economy away from the export of raw products was a daunting, if not an impossible, task. Lewis (1987), while also acknowledging this reality, lauded the efforts and commitment of the PRG to transforming Grenada's economy and society, calling the four years of the revolution "a heroic effort in social and economic reconstruction and at times, transformation"

(26). Brizan (1998) took a more balanced view and, while praising the PRG's efforts at transforming Grenada's economy, argued strongly that those efforts were negated by "blind adherence to the theory and practice of Scientific Socialism" (399). According to Brizan, "The Government failed to recognise that successful export promotion is private-sector led and not public-sector led" (399). Brizan correctly pointed out that in a highly open economy with a fixed exchange rate, economic growth is driven by exports and the accumulation of foreign exchange. Overall, the economic record of the PRG was mixed.

Brief Socioeconomic Overview: 1985–2012

After the collapse of the Grenada Revolution in October 1983 and the subsequent U.S. invasion of Grenada, the country's economic orientation shifted from a mixed-economy approach to a more market-based one. The services sector rose in prominence, and its earnings aided the transformation of both the economy and society.

Nongovernment services accounted for an average of 72 percent of the country's GDP from 2000 to 2012, up from averages of 59 percent in the 1980s and 65 percent in the 1990s. Activity in the tourism sector, as represented by hotels and restaurants, generated the bulk of the country's foreign exchange earnings. Agriculture's contribution to GDP fell from an average of 20 percent during the 1980s to averages of 10 percent in the 1990s and 6.9 percent from 2000 to 2012. Manufacturing's contribution to GDP averaged 5.6 percent during the same period, the same as the average in the 1980s, but 1 percent below the average in the 1990s.

Similar to other small island developing states in the Caribbean, Grenada's economic structure and, by extension, its economic performance over the review period were influenced by the following inherent features: dependence on external trade, lack of diversification, limited private-sector capacity, narrow production base, limited infrastructural development, diseconomies of scale, inadequate human resources, and insufficient institutional capacity, among other constraints.

From 1985 to 2012, real economic growth averaged 3.2 percent, but economic growth was by no means smooth, as evidenced by the standard deviation of 5.0 percent over the period. Volatility in output growth is a distinct feature of the Grenadian economy, a reflection of its vulnerabilities to the vagaries of the international economy on which it depends. Table 3.1 shows robust growth averaging 6.7 percent from 1985 to 1989, well above the Caribbean's average of 4.5 percent. Underpinning Grenada's growth in that period

Table 3.1

Real GDP Growth: Grenada and Peers

	1985–89			1990–99			2000–2012		
	Av.	SD	Yr.	Av.	SD	Yr.	Av.	SD	Yr.
Antigua and Barbuda	7.7	1.4	5	3.4	3.4	9	1.6	6.5	9
The Bahamas	3.0	0.9	5	2.7	4.9	8	1.2	2.5	10
Barbados	3.2	1.5	4	0.5	3.6	7	1.2	2.6	10
Belize	10.8	8.8	4	5.9	4.7	10	4.4	3.4	12
Dominica	4.3	3.8	5	2.6	1.4	10	1.7	3.0	10
Grenada	**6.7**	**3.0**	**5**	**4.4**	**4.0**	**9**	**1.0**	**5.4**	**7**
Guyana	−2.2	3.0	1	4.8	4.1	8	2.4	2.6	10
Jamaica	2.9	5.1	3	1.3	1.9	7	0.8	1.7	10
St. Kitts and Nevis	8.0	1.8	5	4.1	1.9	10	2.0	4.4	9
St. Lucia	10.0	5.8	5	3.5	3.5	9	1.6	3.6	9
St. Vincent and Grenadines	6.8	4.7	5	3.6	3.4	9	2.3	3.1	9
Suriname	0.2	7.2	1	0.6	3.5	6	4.4	1.8	12
Trinidad and Tobago	−3.3	1.5	0	3.9	3.7	8	5.1	5.3	10
Caribbean	4.5	1.2	5	3.2	0.9	10	2.3	2.2	11

Source: World Development Indicators 2012

Notes

Av. = average

SD = standard deviation

Yr. = number of years of growth

was buoyant construction activity associated with several infrastructure projects including the international airport. Growth remained relatively robust in the 1990s, averaging 4.4 percent, mainly reflecting strong tourism activity. Additionally, sound macroeconomic policies pursued in the context of structural reforms also helped to buoy private-sector confidence, which augured well for overall economic performance. The first decade of the twenty-first century was particularly challenging for Grenada's economy, as evidenced by the average growth of a mere 1 percent during the period, the second-lowest average in the Caribbean after Jamaica. In addition to the attacks on the United States on September 11, 2001, and the global economic and financial crisis of 2007 and 2008 that buffeted all Caribbean economies, Grenada also suffered devastation from two hurricanes in 2004 and 2005.

The 9/11 attacks in the United States significantly affected Grenada's tourism sector. Value added in the sector contracted by 4.5 percent and 6.1 percent respectively in 2001 and 2002, resulting in an average contraction in GDP growth of 0.7 percent over the two-year period. Growth rebounded in 2003 but was short-lived owing to the devastation wrought by Hurricane Ivan in 2004. The damages from the hurricane exceeded 200 percent of GDP (EC$2.4 billion or US$0.8 million). Virtually every house on the island was affected, with 30 percent completely destroyed; schools and universities suffered extensive damage, as did hospitals and shelters. Productive sectors were severely affected; the hurricane affected close to 90 percent of the tourist plant. In agriculture, the nutmeg sector was decimated. Grenada was the world's second-largest producer of nutmegs, and the sector employed an estimated 30 percent of the population directly or indirectly. The entire population was without water and electricity in the immediate aftermath of the hurricane (OECS 2004). According to the IMF (2005), before Hurricane Ivan, the government was making progress to restore fiscal sustainability and spur growth. To compound the problem, in July 2005, Hurricane Emily bashed Grenada while the country was still recovering from the impact of Hurricane Ivan.

Hurricane rehabilitation spending, coupled with tourism and construction activities associated with World Cup Cricket in 2007, buoyed economic activity, with growth averaging 4.5 percent from 2005 to 2007. Grenada's economic fortunes began to turn in 2008 with the onset of the global economic and financial crisis, and by 2009 the economy suffered its worst contraction (7.7 percent) since 1984. As observed by the IMF (2010), Grenada's economic challenge has become more daunting in the wake of the global economic crisis that started in 2007 and intensified in 2008. The Grenadian economy was buffeted by the global crisis; in particular, the inflows of tourism receipts, external investments, and remittances were significantly curtailed in 2008 and 2009 (IMF 2010). Because of the economic contraction, Grenada's fiscal situation deteriorated significantly, triggering a fiscal crisis by 2010 that saw an accumulation of domestic payment arrears, difficulties in meeting public-sector salaries and other expenses, and difficulties in servicing the public debt. The IMF program that was entered into in 2006 was suspended in 2011 as the government missed all the agreed fiscal targets. Indeed, Grenada's fiscal crisis deepened so much that it defaulted on some of its external debt in 2012. In that year, the ratio of public debt to GDP reached 105 percent, the highest in the country's history: an almost threefold increase relative to the ratio in 1999. In 2012 the IMF reported:

Following two years of consecutive decline, there are signs that a fragile recovery may be underway. Real GDP grew by 1.1 percent in 2011 and is expected to reach 1½ percent in 2012, on the back of a continued growth in agriculture and a gradual recovery in tourism stay-over arrivals. Inflation is expected to stay broadly stable at about 3 percent in 2012. However, the fiscal situation deteriorated in 2011, in part, reflecting revenue shortfalls due to the extension of various temporary tax exemptions. Private sector credit growth remains sluggish as banks continue to remain cautious and tighten lending standards given the increase of nonperforming loans. The current account deficit is expected to remain around 25 percent of GDP, reflecting high food and fuel prices. Looking ahead, significant downside risks remain. These include the high public sector debt level and budget financing constraints, high current account deficits and net external liabilities, and financial sector vulnerabilities, including potential spillovers from the region. (IMF 2012, online version)

Growth since 2009 has been weak, averaging –0.7 percent, associated with economic contractions in 2010 and 2012. Grenada's economic realities are not dissimilar to those of its peers. Indeed, given the Caribbean's overdependence on tourism and foreign direct investment and remittances, the Caribbean was one of the hardest-hit regions in the world, and it is undergoing the most sluggish recovery. The Caribbean Development Bank (CDB) reported that the context framing regional prospects remains one of limited fiscal space and an uncertain global outlook, with additional downside risks relating specifically to the region's vulnerability to natural hazards and climate change impacts (CDB 2011). The Commonwealth Secretariat observed that Caribbean economies were demonstrating unsustainable development or "brown growth." They were suffering from high debt-to-GDP ratios; they were relatively undiversified; and tourism inflows were slowing after the global financial crisis (Grenade and Skeete 2012, 4). The IMF reported that the Eastern Caribbean Currency Union (ECCU), of which Grenada is a member, had been hard hit by the global economic downturn and was faced with a protracted recovery. Moreover, a heavy focus on debt management and debt servicing detracts from efforts that could otherwise be channeled to pursuing regional development goals.

Grenada's economic activity has been insufficient to allow the country to match economic performance levels of some of its counterparts in the Caribbean, as indicated by the level of GDP per capita. Grenada's GDP per capita income (in constant prices) was US$5,831 in 2012, the fifth-lowest level among thirteen Caribbean countries and below the Caribbean average of US$7,654. Grenada's average level of GDP per capita in each of the three decades starting

Table 3.2

Human Development Index (HDI) Rankings, CARICOM (2007–11)

Country	2007	2007/8	2009	2010	2011
Antigua and Barbuda	59	57	47	n.a.	60
Bahamas	52	49	52	43	53
Barbados	31	31	37	42	47
Belize	95	80	93	78	93
Dominica	68	71	73	n.a.	81
Grenada	85	82	74	n.a.	67
Guyana	103	97	114	104	117
Haiti	154	146	149	145	158
Jamaica	104	101	100	80	79
St. Kitts and Nevis	51	54	62	n.a.	72
St. Lucia	71	72	69	n.a.	82
St. Vincent and the Grenadines	88	93	91	n.a.	85
Suriname	89	85	97	94	104
Trinidad and Tobago	87	59	64	59	62

Source: United Nations Development Programme 2012

Notes

n.a. = not available

in 1980 has been consistently less than that of the Caribbean average, though the average rate of per capita growth has been relatively robust, averaging 6.8 percent over the period from 1985 to 2012.

The economic challenges that the country faces underscore the need for policies to reinvigorate economic growth to address two key imperatives: reducing poverty and creating jobs. The following discussion deals with Grenada's social context, in particular, the social implications of constrained economic growth.

Social Context

Grenada's modest economic performance, especially during the early years of the twenty-first century, has been accompanied by rising poverty and unemployment. Based on the most recent country poverty assessment by KAIRI Consultants (2008), 37.7 percent of the population was estimated to be living below the poverty line of US$2,163.71 per annum, per adult, in 2008, up from

32.1 percent in 1999. The unemployment rate was estimated at 24.9 percent in 2008, up from 14 percent in 1999, with the rate being higher for women (31.8 percent) than for men (17.9 percent). Nearly 8 percent of the labor force was displaced from their jobs in the immediate aftermath of Hurricane Ivan, raising the unemployment rate to over 20 percent. Poverty levels reportedly rose sharply, particularly among farmers and women (see IMF 2005 and OECS 2004).

According to the CDB (2009), rural-to-urban migration creates housing demand, resulting in the development of unplanned and informal settlements. Additionally, limited public resources, generated from low levels of economic activity, hamper critical interventions to improve economic development. Moreover, because of inadequate investment in education, the quality of education is compromised (CDB 2009). Although Grenada has attained almost universal school access, significant gaps exist above the primary level. Regarding health, noncommunicable diseases are a major health problem (Delegation of the European Union 2009). According to the United Nations Development Programme's Human Development Report (2012), the Human Development Index (HDI) for Grenada was 0.748 in 2011, which gave the country a rank of 67 out of 182 countries (table 3.2).

Conclusion

This chapter has provided a socioeconomic overview of Grenada from 1979 to 2012. It started with a brief overview of the socioeconomic context under the Gairy regime to explain some of the possible causal antecedents (from an economic perspective) of the PRG's insurrection and why they would have pursued economic development differently. The chapter then delved into the economic aspects of the PRG era by reviewing development policy and planning, as well as economic management and performance. Based on the economic review, one key conclusion emerges, which is that the PRG had a coherent vision for economic development; policies were well defined, but institutional and human capabilities were inadequate to effectively implement the policies. Moreover, the misalignment between the political and economic realms seemed to have undermined development efforts. Notwithstanding extensive social programs, the pursuit of a mixed-economy approach to development in an inherently and deeply entrenched global capitalist economic system mitigated the attainment of meaningful development results. One of the five lessons that this review has distilled from the PRG era is that there must be a mutually reinforcing political and economic framework to underpin economic governance.

Glaring differences set apart the era from 1979 to 1983 and the three decades after the demise of the Grenada Revolution. First, whereas the PRG adopted a mixed-economy approach, subsequent governments pursued a more market-based approach to development. This was due in large measure to transformation in the global political economy and a new ideological focus. Second, the PRG placed serious emphasis on agriculture and agro-processing. However, there has been a general decline in the agriculture sector and greater emphasis on the services sector. Again, this is a consequence of changing global trends toward services. For the last three decades, the Grenadian economy was buffeted by natural disasters and other exogenous shocks. What appears to be constant throughout the revolutionary and postrevolutionary eras is economic volatility, high public debt, dependency, and exposure to external shocks.

References

Brizan, G. 1998. *Grenada: Island of Conflict*. London: Macmillan Education.

Caribbean Development Bank [CDB]. 2009. *Country Strategy for Grenada*. Report No. 24/09-BD. http://www.caribank.org (accessed July 13, 2013).

———. 2011. "Annual Report 2011." Caribbean Development Bank: Barbados.

Commonwealth Secretariat and World Bank. 2000. *Small States: Meeting Challenges in the Global Economy*. Report of the Commonwealth Secretariat and World Bank Joint Task Force on Small States. London: Commonwealth Secretariat.

Delegation of the European Union. 2009. *Grenada-European Community Country Strategy Paper and National Indicative Programme for the Period 2008–2013 (10th EDF)*. http://www.llec.europa.eu (accessed July 13, 2013).

Governments of Grenada and Trinidad and Tobago. 1965. "Report on the Economic Commission of Grenada and Trinidad and Tobago." St. George's, Grenada, and Port-of-Spain, Trinidad and Tobago. January.

Grenade, W. C., and K. Skeete. 2012. "Regional Integration in Small States: The Case of the Caribbean Community." Report submitted to the Commonwealth Secretariat. July 15.

International Monetary Fund [IMF]. 2005. "Grenada: 2005 Article IV Consultation—Staff Report; and Public Information Notice on the Executive Board Discussion." IMF Country Report No. 05/290. Washington, DC: International Monetary Fund.

———. 2010. "Grenada: Fifth review under the Extended Credit Facility, request for waivers of nonobservance of performance criteria and request for a three-year arrangement under the Extended Credit Facility, and financing assurance review." IMF Country Report No. 10/139. http://www.imf.org/external/pubs/cat/longres.aspx?sk=23888.0.

———. 2011. "Eastern Caribbean Currency Union Staff Report for the 2010 Discussion on Common Policies for Member Countries." IMF Country Report No. 11/30. Washington,

DC: International Monetary Fund. http://www.imf.org/external/pubs/ft/scr/2011/cr1130 .pdf (accessed July 13, 2013).

———. 2012. "Statement by the IMF Mission to Grenada." Press Release No. 12/198. May 30.

Jacobs, W. R., and B. I. Jacobs. 1980. *Grenada: The Route to Revolution*. Havana, Cuba: Casa De Las Americas.

Joefield-Napier, W. 1986. "Macroeconomic Growth during the People's Revolutionary Government's Regime: An Assessment." Caribbean Development Bank, Bridgetown, Barbados.

KAIRI Consultants Limited. 2008. *Final Report, Country Poverty Assessment: Grenada, Carriacou, and Petit Martinique*. http://www.caribank.org.

Lewis, G. 1987. *Grenada: The Jewel Despoiled*. Baltimore, MD: John Hopkins University Press.

Organization of Eastern Caribbean States [OECS]. 2004. "Grenada: Macro-socio-economic Assessment of the Damages Caused by Hurricane Ivan, September 7, 2004." Saint Lucia: Organization of Eastern Caribbean States.

Payne, A., P. Sutton, and T. Thorndike. 1984. *Grenada: Revolution and Invasion*. London: Croom Helm.

People's Revolutionary Government of Grenada [PRG]. 1981. "Report on the National Economy for 1981 and Prospects for 1982." St. George's, Grenada: Government Printing Office.

United Nations Development Programme. 2012. *Grenada: The Human Development Index; Going beyond Income*. http://www.hdr.undp.org/en/reports/global/hdr2009.

Watson, H. 1984. "Grenada: Non-capitalist Path and the Derailment of a Populist Revolution." Paper presented to the 9th Annual Conference of the Caribbean Studies Association, Saint Kitts and Nevis. May 29–June 2.

World Bank. 1985. "Economic Memorandum Grenada." Report No. 5606-GRD. Washington, DC: World Bank.

———. 2005. *Organization of Eastern Caribbean States: Towards a New Agenda for Growth*. Report No. 31863-LAC. http://www.worldbank.org/info.worldbank.org/etools/wti/docs/ wti2008/brief177.pdf.

World Development Indicators. 2012. World Development Indicators Data Bank. Data file. http://data.worldbank.org/data-catalog/world-development-indicators.

PART II
Insiders' Perspectives on the Grenada Revolution

4. A Retrospective View from Richmond Hill: An Interview with Bernard Coard

Wendy C. Grenade

What follows is an interview that I conducted with Bernard Coard, former deputy prime minister of the People's Revolutionary Government (PRG), on October 17, 2008, at Richmond Hill Prison before his release on September 5, 2009.

The Grenada Revolution in Historical Perspective

WENDY GRENADE: Today is October 17, 2008, almost twenty-five years to the day since the implosion of the Grenada Revolution. What do you want a twenty-five-year-old Grenadian and Caribbean son or daughter to know about the Grenada Revolution?

BERNARD COARD: First, it must be seen within the context of the many revolutionary upsurges of the Grenadian people over centuries. There are links between the Fédon Revolution, the slave revolts, the ex-servicemen's revolt in 1920, the 1951 Gairy revolutionary upsurge, the 1973–74 revolutionary upsurges, and the Grenada Revolution in 1979–83. The Grenada Revolution should be appreciated within its historical depth, that is, at the level of Grenada; but also laterally or horizontally, as part of a Caribbean and wider anticolonial struggle.

Second, in terms of the actual experience of the Grenada Revolution, we have to see that the principal goal of the Grenada Revolution was economic, social, and political transformation of the life circumstances of the vast majority of people. In my booklet "Grenada: 1951–83" (Coard 2003), I outline the two main achievements of the Grenada Revolution: first, defeating Gairy and Gairyism, which I defined; and second, transforming Grenada. The four main transformational goals of the revolution were transforming the physical infrastructure of the country; developing the human resources of the country; developing direct productive enterprises, and mobilizing the people. There is significant evidence of all this, so that one can read the goals as well as the achievements and shortcomings of the revolution in the programs undertaken. Twenty-five years later, the impact of the revolution in Grenada is quite clear. The vast majority of our doctors, dentists, veterinary surgeons, economists, engineers, qualified teachers, and most other professionals were trained in Cuba, Eastern Europe, North America, Mexico, Australia, Kenya, Tanzania, France, or Britain because we had scholarships from forty or fifty different countries. We also see it in the role of women in the society today, their confidence. The signs were clear during the revolution. This was the era when women came into their own. We also see the legacy of the revolution in the patriotism of Grenadians—their strong sense of "Grenadianness," which they had during the revolution and never lost.

The Economic Model

WG: What was the thinking behind the economic model you adopted?

BC: I remember lectures I used to give in Wednesday night classes, and I used to say to comrades, "I studied bourgeois economics in Brandeis in America and at Sussex in England, and I studied Marxist economics, and if I ever made the mistake of running the Grenada economy with either strict bourgeois economics or Marxist economics, the economy would mash up in five minutes." I told all comrades all the time, "Do not bother with them books; be pragmatic (or) our economics must serve our own situation!"

In this context, I followed the market mechanism and encouraged competition. When I wanted to control the merchants who were overcharging farmers for fertilizers and ripping off customers for basic necessities, I set up the Marketing and National Importing Board (MNIB) in competition with the private sector to bring overcharging down to a controlled price. The MNIB would make a profit and yet charge so much less. I also set up the National Transport Service (NTS). When gas prices went up by ten cents, bus drivers put up bus prices by twenty cents. I tried to keep price rises at a certain rate, so that everyone could make a reasonable profit. Yet with the state-owned NTS, customers had transport in the night, on weekends, and so on, which private bus owners were not offering. I also set up the state-owned National Commercial Bank (NCB) to compete with the foreign banks. When the Royal Bank decided that it wanted to sell out because they were moving out of several countries, I bought it, but I did not incorporate it with NCB as one state bank, because they would have had 50 percent of all deposits in Grenada. I wanted competition, so I set up two separate state banks: NCB and Grenada Bank of Commerce (GBC), with separate boards of directors and management, competing with each other, and with Scotia and Barclays and so on. I also set up the Grenada Resorts Corporation (GRC), which created competition within the hotel sector. In every sector of the economy, both in wholesaling and retailing, banking, public transportation, hotels, farms, everywhere, *the model was to compete in order to achieve maximum efficiency*, so that we could speedily deliver benefits to the Grenadian people. And every year, the World Bank and the International Monetary Fund (IMF) praised me for how I ran the economy—and this is despite the fact that I accepted none of their usual conditions! (On this subject, see H. A. Bartilow, "IMF Financing in Grenada: Defending Revolutionary Socialism," chap. 4 in *The Debt Dilemma: IMF Negotiations in Jamaica, Grenada, and Guyana*, 80–103 [London: Macmillan Education, 1997]. The four agreements we signed with the IMF were all on *our* terms.)

WG: What are some of the concrete economic achievements of the revolution?

BC: The Point Salines International Airport has transformed the tourism sector. Given that agriculture had totally collapsed for many years and we never really had a manufacturing sector to talk about, the international airport is one of the major accomplishments of the PRG. The National Insurance Scheme (NIS) is another major achievement. NIS has already raised over half a billion dollars, and it has paid out tens of millions of dollars in benefits long before it started paying pensions; and, of course, as I mentioned, there were the NCB, GBC, and MNIB. So we have those concrete institutions, projects, and programs, which are still alive today and still serving the country. This is apart from bringing electricity to Petit Martinique and half of Carriacou, building over fifty miles of farm and feeder roads, and well over two hundred other infrastructure projects to considerably increase the productive capacity of the country.

We increased, moderately, real wages each year, and household income massively, by reducing unemployment from 49 percent to 12 percent, thereby having more breadwinners in every family. We also expanded the social wage substantially; that is, the number of goods and services that were provided entirely free, or at heavily subsidized prices for working people. At a time when the world was gripped in what was then considered the worst recession since 1929–33, we had positive economic growth in each year of the revolution while other countries experienced zero or negative growth.

Ideological Influences

WG: What were the forces that influenced your worldview?

BC: There were several overlapping forces. I grew up in a context where my parents had absolutely no interest in boxing, yet whenever Joe Louis, the

Brown Bomber, was in a world heavyweight championship fight, my father and mother would stay up late in the night with their old transistor radio, listening to the fight. Clearly, this is cultural nationalism going on here. Whenever I went to spend time with family on the West Coast, they would be talking about Julien Fédon (1795–96) as if it were something that happened last year. My mother and father also spoke of Toussaint-Louverture and Henri Christophe, Jacques Dessalines, and the Haitian Revolution. My mother and father never went to secondary school; my mother never finished primary school. Yet they spoke of Nkrumah, young Kenyatta—the early African leaders. They spoke of Marcus Garvey and Paul Robeson. So clearly I came from a family rooted, without realizing it, in cultural nationalism. And this was true, I think, of all the leadership of the New Jewel Movement (NJM).

WG: What influenced your Marxism?

BC: Julius Nyerere was famous for UJAMAA, African socialism. Now once you are talking about socialism, you are talking about some Marxist influence, but here it is mediated, filtered through an African cultural perspective. His work where he set out the principles was a very big influence on all of us in those days. Then the Cuban Revolution was also a very big influence, not in the sense of Marxism-Leninism but in the sense of it being a Caribbean country. And, of course, as Fidel once put it at the time of the Angolan crisis with South Africa, "(Cuba is) Latin Africa, a Caribbean African country." But throughout that whole period, including even when I returned and I was teaching at the University of the West Indies in St. Augustine, Trinidad, from 1972 to 1974, I was still anti-Soviet in outlook. (People don't know that—you know, propaganda is a hell of a thing!) In fact, I remember being part of a panel at UWI St. Augustine, speaking to a body of students one night, and Winston Suite, the student leader of URO, the United Revolutionary Organisation—what in ideological terms was the equivalent of the Workers Party of Jamaica (WPJ)—gave me what you would call an extremely tactful tongue-lashing over that! Anyhow, in that sense, my thoughts and my conception of revolution would have been broadly in keeping with all those above influences.

WG: What changed your anti-Soviet outlook?

BC: I guess it was studying the Russian revolutions of 1905 and 1917, and several of the writings of Lenin. Unlike Stalin, Lenin was extraordinarily creative and practical in his application of Marxist economic principles. How many realize, for example, that Lenin repeatedly wrote and spoke these words in trying to change the thinking of his party and government: "*Russia suffers not from too much but from too little capitalism*"? It is Lenin who implemented what he called the New Economic Policy, or NEP. The Chinese Communist

Party today asserts that they are implementing their version of NEP. Stalin, of course, reversed all of Lenin's economic policies, which in my opinion laid the basis, decades later, for the Soviet Union's demise. Significantly, the leaders of the Soviet Union during our time (1979–83) fully supported our approach of *not* following their path!

The New Jewel Movement: Early Beginnings

WG: Some observers have argued that you influenced the OREL[1] faction of the NJM and thus greatly shaped the political outlook and the policies of both the NJM and the People's Revolutionary Government (PRG). Do you agree with this observation?

BC: That is not an accurate observation. Two groups came together to form the NJM. On March 11, 1973, MAP[2] and Jewel[3] had a joint convention, and the two joint leaders were elected then, Maurice Bishop and Unison Whiteman.

WG: So are you saying that OREL was not a part of NJM?

BC: It was that Ewart Layne, Leon Cornwall, and I cannot remember the name of the other person, were the leaders of OREL, and they were the ones responsible for the whole implosion of the revolution. Ewart Layne was never a member of OREL. Leon Cornwall asked to join OREL days before OREL was disbanded. So he was a member for what, ten days, two weeks, whatever, some small period of time. But according to these experts, Layne, Cornwall, and the other one were the leaders of OREL.

When OREL was formed, I was teaching in Jamaica at the time. When I was based in Trinidad from September 1972 to September 1974, there was no OREL. OREL did not exist. If I remember correctly, it was formed in the first half of 1975. The founder and leader of it was Liam James ("Owusu"), who was a dockworker and trade unionist—Seamen and Waterfront Workers Union. He had gone to the Presentation Brothers' College (PBC), and he was one of the leaders of the youth movement based in PBC. There were a number of youth movements at the time, and so some members of these youth movements were loosely allied to the NJM in the mass-party kind of way, not in a structured way, and so on. Some of them, just a few of them, decided to form OREL, and it had two objectives. One, to study Marxism-Leninism, especially its organizational aspects, with a view to transforming the organizational state of NJM so that they could succeed in fighting Gairy; and two, they got a piece of land that they used to work. Anyhow, all of these guys were individually members of NJM, in the loose kind of way in which anyone became a member in those days—NJM did not have membership lists. If you were an activist on a day-to-day basis, everyone knew you were a member. That was the kind of structure we had. By that time all the leaders, Maurice, Uni, all of them, were into reading Marx and Lenin. They read individually, and occasionally they met in groups to study it. The leadership was very casual at the time.

What changed the leadership's attitude was the defeat of 1973–74. That was the turning point. Once that happened, Maurice, Uni, Kenrick, everyone now said, "We have to study this thing, and we have to study especially Lenin's work—'What Is to Be Done?'" So they began to study in a serious way. This is why by the very end of 1976, and if I am wrong, certainly by the first half of 1977, OREL was disbanded precisely because it was no longer required. The entire party now had organized weekly study. Maurice himself was the ideological guide for one study group, Unison Whiteman for another one, and so on. The top leaders were academically trained, had degrees, and so on, so they were now ideological study guides of different groups of members.

WG: What was your role in those early days?

BC: When I was in Trinidad, all my lectures were on two days, and I often came home five days a week. When I was in Jamaica, however, I came home five times in those two years. And each time I came home, it was either for one week, or if it were summertime, I would have had one or two weeks. Sometimes, if there was a meeting of lecturers at the Trinidad campus or at Cave Hill, I would take a trip over to Grenada. And on those occasions, OREL asked me to be the study guide for them during those sessions, but when I was not there, they had their own study sessions.

WG: Why did Marxism-Leninism become important to the NJM?

BC: It became important when we came to the conclusion that Gairy would not permit the holding of free elections. That he was becoming ever more violent, through his "Green Beasts" (i.e., his army), his Mongoose Gang, his secret police, his Rural Constables (GVC), his Voluntary Intelligence Unit for the Protection of Private Property (VIUPPP), and other bodies. The beating of students on their way home after studying in school in the evenings and all the other things that were happening, like the Duffus Commission (1975) and all of that. Even the killing of Rupert Bishop in broad daylight on January 21, 1974—that was just the most high-profile example of what was happening. What really increased the Marxist-Leninist perspective of all of us was the defeat in 1973–74. We had the upsurge. We had 10,000 to 15,000 people marching in the streets for weeks. We had a general strike from January to March of 1974; electricity blackouts; nothing coming in or going out of the port because the dockworkers were on strike; the whole country was locked down. And at the end of that, Eric Pierre, one individual, leader of the

Dock Workers' Union, apparently held meetings with representatives from the Gairy government and then ordered the workers back to work. And that was the end of it.

What we had shown in 1973–74 was the capacity to mobilize the people, over a period of six weeks, by holding village meetings. We would hold six, seven, eight political meetings simultaneously in different villages, splitting up the leadership. So in that way we covered the one hundred and thirty or so villages in Grenada in the space of a few weeks. We did this from the time we were formed on March 11, 1973, to May 6, which was the first big mass rally in Seamoon, which was called "The People's Convention on Independence." The theme for that was "Meaningful versus Meaningless Independence." So we spent the six weeks leading up to May 6 holding these meetings, explaining to people what we meant by meaningful versus meaningless independence.

We recognized that through independence Gairy wanted more power. We argued: "Look at what he is doing without independence, God help us if we get independence under his rule, without checks and balances!" So we organized this mass rally in Seamoon on May 6, and over 10,000 people attended. When the brutality became greater, we had another one on November 4. This one was called "The People's Convention to Decide the Fate of the Gairy Regime." Again, for the six or eight weeks leading up to it, we had mass mobilization with a lot of drama and melodrama associated. The evening before the rally, he picked up several of the leaders. I flew in the night before, from Trinidad. When I came in, they had people there waiting to arrest me, but one of the Immigration men organized a taxi, and by the time they realized it, I was out of there. We had to go into hiding. They had police everywhere, and we had to get a second rung of the leadership to start the meeting; and when the police got tired and thought we were not coming, then we showed up.

At the November 4 rally we brought twenty-seven indictments against Gairy, and the counts were read out, and the people voted for all of them. We set up an Interim Council, and we gave him until November 18 to resign, and on the 18 was when he brutalized six of the leaders in Grenville. Therefore the first general strike and mass protest started the very next day, Monday, November 19, 1973. It went on for a while, then it was halted to give him a chance to do something. He did nothing. It was resumed in January and continued to March 1974.

The NJM had demonstrated its mass popularity and eclipsed the Grenada National Party (GNP) as the main opposition force. It had the capacity, given a few weeks, to do mass mobilization. It had the capacity to bring together 10,000 to 15,000 people into one venue. But this is the critical point: we had no organized, continuous, sustained, day-by-day relationship with the people.

So that one man could simply order the workers back to work because he was the trade union leader, and that was that. So the 1973–74 upsurge and general strike were defeated by backroom deals. So we recognized that we did not have the organizational capacity. That is why I say the Marxist-Leninist style was really organizational more than anything else; certainly at that time.

WG: Elaborate on this.

BC: We recognized that we needed to have an organized relationship with the people. That is why a lot of the NJM activist leaders and subleaders, who were already workers, began to contest for positions in their unions. That is why some of the women formed the National Women's Organization (NWO). That's why youth, who did have youth movements before, decided to organize in more serious ways. It was decided in late 1974 or early '75 but was implemented in 1976—NJM's Women's Arm, Youth Arm, Workers' Arm, Farmers' Arm, Fishermen's Arm, Publications' Arm. The idea was to organize the masses in their areas of work, in their gender, in their age group, as the case may be. So that on a day-to-day basis we had organized relationships with the people. We followed both the Marxist-Leninist ideology and the methodology. The need for one influenced the other.

I should emphasize that we embraced the overall ideology of Marxism-Leninism, not just its organizational aspects, even though the initial impetus may have been organizational because of the defeat in 1974.

However, in retrospect, it is clear that our Marxism-Leninism was infused with heavy doses of cultural nationalism, and Grenadian nationalism. It was, as we intimated earlier, also extremely pragmatic and flexible in the areas of economic and social policy. Even in the area of domestic politics and international relations, we showed a streak of pragmatism, even as we revealed our inexperience and immaturity in some areas. For example, as I will discuss later, we retained the queen of England as head of state, not just for the early days and weeks so as to gain quick international recognition but throughout the revolution. We desired a strategic partnership with Britain. Likewise, we retained Gairy's appointed governor-general throughout. We appointed six nonparty individuals, mostly businesspeople, to our twenty-two-person People's Revolutionary Government (PRG), and two leading businessmen, one a former president of the Chamber of Industry and Commerce, to our eleven-person cabinet. We had excellent relations with Canada, Britain, and the European Community. Indeed, they all voted with us in the IMF board so that we got the funds, when the United States had launched a major campaign to block us. Prime Minister Thatcher provided us with the loan guarantee of EC$28 million so that we could purchase all the equipment for our international airport, at a time when Ronald Reagan was calling it a Soviet MiG fighter base in construction.

Our blind spot was the United States, most especially the United States under Reagan. This was motivated less by Marxist ideology than by our profound antagonism toward bullies. But I have strayed a little from an examination of the organizational imperatives that stimulated our more systematic embrace of Marxism-Leninism.

WG: What led to the vanguard party?

BC: We needed to because of the circumstances in which we operated. We formed a vanguard party following the defeat of 1973–74 so as to have a tightly knit, disciplined, efficient, highly effective organization, capable of operating clandestinely. In light of the Duffus Commission of Enquiry, in light of the kind of regime Gairy was running, which was becoming worse and worse with every passing day, any other model for getting rid of Gairy, if we had continued having a loose mass party to do that, would not have come off. We had a mass party in 1973–74; what good did that do?

Before March 13, 1979, we had planned to move on Gairy. That was right after 1974. It would be during the days or two weeks after the killing of Rupert Bishop, the brutalization of people on the Carenage, and the attempted killing of schoolchildren. People were in a state. The guys decided—I was in Trinidad at the time—to move on three targets: the police headquarters, Gairy, and the army. They had three people assigned to lead each unit and so on, and you'll be surprised at some of the people who were involved. (I cannot call their names because some of them are still involved in our society.) The Political Bureau was split on the decision. At that time we did not have a central committee. The bureau was eight members, including myself, and three voted for, three against, and one abstained. This decision fell in the two days that I was teaching in Trinidad. So Maurice sent a message to me through an air hostess—we did not want to use the telephone. Just "SOS"; that is all it said. I rearranged my lectures and flew up. "This is the situation," they told me. "You have to cast your vote. You have to make the casting vote."

So we discussed the proposal that the following day was when we would move against Gairy. The plan was to move at midnight. They took me to a building somewhere in the Tempe–Mt. Parnassus area; they had about fifty guys there cleaning weapons and all kinds of things. I observed, I saw some characters, and I said to myself, "Boy, some of these guys will be talking, boasting to the fellas on the block, and who would be telling their girlfriends because they want to big-up in front their girlfriends, and so on." I thought, "This cannot work; this is crazy." I started asking some logistical questions. I did not get satisfactory answers, so I voted against moving, and we abandoned the plan on that basis. That night I went to a fete down in Beverley Flats, Maurice's father's place. And at the fete there was this Grenadian guy, he was an engineer in Trinidad, and he said to me, "All you moving tomorrow then?" I said to myself, "What the hell is going on here? Thank God I made the right decision, right decision." . . . That was what the NJM was like as a mass party.

So the taking power from Gairy on March 13, 1979, was made possible, among other factors, by the fact that we had a highly effective and efficient vanguard party. We had about forty-six men ready for the assault, a sort of underground army: a wing of the party. We had this kind of tightness because everything was vanguard. And they would go out and do training, military training, in the bushes and hills, in other areas. Other people did not realize what they were doing. . . . But our failure to transform NJM back into a mass party (but a properly organized and structured one this time) after March 13, 1979, contributed to the fatal implosion of the revolution.

WG: I will get to the implosion shortly, but explain what eventually led to March 13, 1979.

BC: In the weeks leading up to March 13, 1979, we had to ask, "Is Grenada ready for revolution?" "Does it meet the criteria for making a revolution?" By studying Marxism, we knew that if you are a leader, you should be in front of the people. But if you are too far in front of the people, you are not leading anyone. And if you are behind them, they are leading you. So it is a delicate balancing. You cannot be so far in front that when you look back, you are not seeing anybody; neither can you be marking time and the people are ahead of you. Now, for many years, between 1973 and 1978, all kinds of people would meet us and say, "What all yuh doing with the man?" "Why all yuh ain't overthrow the man?" "Why all yuh don't pick up arms and deal with the man?" On one famous occasion, Maurice and I were at a conference in Barbados, and a group of businessmen actually left Grenada and came all the way to Barbados and met us in a hotel room, pressing us to move on Gairy. They did not want to discuss such matters in Grenada. Now, come the very end of 1978 and the first two months of 1979, people started to say to us, "Give us the arms and let us do it." Instead of "all yuh," it was now "we." In other words, this was a dramatic shift.

WG: But you were part of the parliamentary opposition; were you not preparing for upcoming elections?

BC: We were on a two-track approach. If the elections were held, we would take part, even though we realized they would be rigged. We had six seats in Parliament, and we needed two more to form the government. On the other hand, there was no way we would be permitted to form the government. The level of violence was growing, so we had to prepare for armed struggle as well.

But we couldn't tell anybody about that. So I'm saying that Lenin has a famous definition for "when the conditions are right for revolution." This really captured the Grenada situation. It is an extraordinarily large paragraph where he listed all the different ingredients, the different elements that make for a revolutionary situation. It was as if it were literally written for the Grenada situation of early 1979.

WG: How was the decision made to overthrow Gairy?

BC: To explain March 1979, I have to again go back to our initial plan to overthrow him in 1973–74. Kenrick Radix was a member of the Political Bureau at that time. He figured that I was coming up from Trinidad and I would vote in favor of moving against Gairy. So he warned some close members of his family, who then warned certain members of one of the other leaders' family. These two sets of family members then left for Trinidad hurriedly. Now that caused such a scandal, though only the top leadership knew about it. That was the point at which we set up the Security and Defense Committee. It comprised four out of the eight members of the bureau. We decided that all military and security decisions would be taken by that four-man committee from henceforth, for security reasons, because the alternative to that was to throw Kenrick Radix out of the bureau, which at that time was not considered necessary or required, but certainly he had to be kept out of certain decisions.

In 1973–74 Gairy was waiting for us. So in 1979 the four of us went into hiding: Maurice, Uni, G-man (Austin), and I. Three of us went one place; one of us went another place. Three of us debated, and one joined the others on March 12. Four of us, now together on March 12, asked, "Do we move?" We looked at all the factors. We had forty-six men, twenty-one weapons. The rest had to go with some bottles, some gasoline, oil, and pieces of rag, make them into Molotov cocktails, homemade style. So that kind of puny force faced Gairy's armed forces of 1,350 men: 200 army with weapons from the Chilean Pinochet, army officers trained by Pinochet, and 36 police stations around the island. Altogether, between all of them, 1,350 men formed the army, armed police, secret police, and Mongoose Gang.

Here was the plan. We wanted an element of surprise. We planned to move at 4:00 a.m. We planned how to take the most important target, the army. This would be psychologically demoralizing to Gairy's forces. Concentrate all your forces on Gairy's army, instead of trying to take three and four targets at one time. Then you move from one to the next to the next to the next. And you take the radio station. So we would mobilize the masses to come out and support. The masses would surround the police stations and force the police to surrender, put up the white flag, and so on. The whole model was worked out. So we came to the vote. Maurice and Uni said, "We have to move, but when the timing is right." In other words, no disagreement about the fact that we needed armed struggle; the question is, do we move now, can we move now, is it realistic? Hudson Austin and myself said, "No, we should move, and we can succeed, and this is why we can succeed." So the vote was two to two. We had to bring in the other four. (At this time, Kenrick Radix was still a member of the bureau.)

Things were getting hot; we had to go underground because Gairy had sent army and police to get us from our homes. That was one reason why we were pushed into the situation. We had been informed by a reliable police source that there were plans to put us in underground cells, these were just being completed, then they would pretend that we tried to escape and wipe us out. Kenrick was in a lawyers' conference in Barbados; we did not want him around because of what had happened in 1974. Selwyn Strachan was in Cuba at the time, and Vincent Noel, who was on the bureau at the time, had been picked up on the Saturday at 1:00 p.m. when they swept our homes; he was the only one who was home at the time, so he was picked up. The rest of us were in a meeting at the party secretariat, planning a voter registration drive, so we went underground and did not emerge again until March 13. One man was left, George Louison, so we called him in. Both sides explained all our arguments to him; he asked all the questions he wanted to, and he voted with the two of us who had said to move. So anyhow he broke the tie, and that is the irony of the situation. I tell you that to say this: Maurice and Uni, by their actions two seconds after that decision was taken and right throughout, no one would have imagined that they had voted against making the revolution on March 13, 1979. That is how we operated: you close ranks, people would have no idea who voted how because everyone respected the majority decision.

Democracy and Human Rights

WG: Although general elections were promised in the early days of the revolution, that promise was never kept. What was your thinking on elections during the period 1979–83?

BC: We were all of the view in the leadership that we would proceed to hold elections within a matter of months, so much so that we actually appointed someone, a senior civil servant, to start organizing a proper voters' list, et cetera. We inherited a flawed system from Gairy. There were no identification cards in those days; some people were registered to vote seven, eight, and nine times in different polling divisions. So immediately after the revolution there were negotiations taking place with people like Tom Adams and others in the region to work out some sort of a compromise, in terms of getting Gairy and several of his ministers to resign from Parliament, use a kind of a by-election model, as proposed by Tom Adams. There were a lot of different models being looked at. The truth is that this was happening five, six days after March 13, 1979, by phone and with people flying in and so on, to the point that the leadership was exhausted. We had not slept, and imagine we had a million things to do, so we were just in a state where we were not able to think clearly about this. We had two lawyers from Trinidad; they were not on the left or right; they were center and broadly progressive in their politics. They said to us, "Are you mad? You have a situation where Gairy has been dominating the country for twenty-eight years. While 70 percent of the people are anti-Gairy, 30 percent are Gairyites, and the possibilities for mischief and destabilization are there. You have inherited a bureaucracy, a complex situation, and you need a clean break. You need to establish your own institutions. You need to be able to start delivering benefits to the people and showing them what you can do, including the Gairyites. . . . Hold on, and when you have some sleep, do some more thinking on this, don't rush into any of these arrangements."

So that advice played an important part in our holding off on elections in the early days of the revolution. We finally came to the position that we should take the equivalent of a term. The issue was never one of the popularity of the revolution. It was universally recognized that we would have swept the polls. So it was a question of building new structures and establishing the imprint of the revolution, because a revolution is more than just simply changing the people who sit in chairs. We are talking about economic, political, and social transformation. And what they were raising—as I told you, these were not left-wingers, most interestingly, but they were mature people. What they were raising was, "How do you achieve that transformation with inherited structures set up by a repressive regime? How do you start developing new structures, new thinking, new programs, new projects, and new ways of doing things? How do you start impacting people's lives in a transformational way, both at the psychological level and at the practical, down-to-earth level, if you simply operate within the confines of old, traditional structures?" I am putting all of this in my own words; these are not the words they would have used. But their advice is what guided our thinking then.

WG: Was all the leadership of the PRG comfortable with this advice?

BC: The truth is, we needed to have thought that out for ourselves; we were not thinking clearly. But that was the advice, and we all agreed with it. In fact, one of the striking things about the revolution and about the NJM: both in the years when we were fighting Gairy and in the years we were in power, there was very, very little upon which we disagreed in terms of tactics, but we disagreed not one bit on strategy.

WG: I will come back to the question of party cohesion later on, but comment further on elections. As the revolution progressed, were there any plans to hold elections?

BC: Having decided to take four years to address the issues I just outlined, we went for a new constitution. The idea then was to set up a constitutional commission, which we established in June 1983. Selwyn Strachan and I were mandated to make the arrangements, and a number of persons were appointed to the commission. Alan Alexander, senior counsel from Trinidad, was the chairman; and Richard Hart, the famous Jamaican trade unionist, lawyer, and historian, was also a member. There were representatives of the trade union movement and others. So there were about five to seven representatives on the commission. I think they met a couple of times before the crisis and invasion. Their mandate was in fact to examine relevant constitutions worldwide for ideas, taking into account the specific history of Grenada and the region, and in particular seek to incorporate appropriately the organs of popular democracy that had sprung up within the country—zonal and parish councils, the national conference on the economy, and things like that—so that they would become institutionalized as part of the constitutional framework. The idea was that they would report and there would then be national consultations and discussions on the report, then a referendum and the new elections under the new constitution as approved in such a referendum within twenty-four months. So that would have been within twenty-four months of June 1983, so we would have been somewhere around June 1985. As you know, we suspended the old constitution in the first phase, and we gradually brought back many sections of it, but not all of it.

WG: Twenty-five years later, what are your views on those decisions?

BC: In retrospect, I think we took the wrong decision. It was a strategic error, and I'll come to that later. I'm just letting you know what our thinking was and what guided it, as opposed to whether it was right or wrong in retrospect.

WG: From your own writings and evidence from our history, the revolution chose to defend itself at the expense of civil liberties. What was the thinking behind this?

BC: That is a correct characterization of the situation, in my view. I think it was misguided in retrospect and ultimately unnecessary—a strategic error. The reasoning behind it was a generally held one, albeit misguided. Iran 1953, Guatemala 1954, Guyana in the 1960s, Chile in the 1970 to '73 period, Jamaica leading up to and during the 1976 elections: all of these and others were uppermost in our thinking when we took that course of action. Imperialism, using its intelligence arms, as well as its more normal diplomatic and economic sanctions mechanisms, had a track record of seeking to determine the composition, the shape, and the direction of governments in the Third World by the use of destabilization methods if they were unhappy with the domestic and/or foreign policies being pursued by any Third World government. And, of course, they used existing opposition forces, traditional opposition forces like media outlets.

WG: In retrospect, despite the threats, were the detentions justified?

BC: There were one or two genuine cases of violent plotting. For example, the bombing in Queen's Park, the killing of the five people up in Plains in St. Patrick's, and one or two things like that. But the vast majority of detentions were unjustified. Sometimes, in situations like that, neighbors who have feuds would bring false reports, and people get detained unnecessarily. This happens in many parts of the world. These are all of the risks whenever you have a system without checks and balances. We were young, immature, and inexperienced. It was wrong.

Foreign Policy

WG: How would you describe the thinking behind the PRGs foreign policy?

BC: We were independent thinkers. We were not following the Russian model or the Cuban model; we were not following any centrally planned economy; we were not following any Communist International. We did not take power and declare ourselves a republic; we still had the queen of England as the head of state. As I mentioned earlier, we were thinking both strategically and tactically when we did that. We wanted to develop ever closer relations with Britain, even as we had close relations with Cuba and the Soviet Union and others. We saw Britain in a different way altogether from the United States. We saw Canada too in a different way than we saw the United States. We made grave errors with the United States, do not get me wrong, but we had it right with the others. We had it wrong with Cuba for different reasons.

WG: If you are saying that the revolutionary leadership was made up of independent thinkers, why, in the United Nations, did the PRG vote to support the Soviet Union's invasion of Afghanistan?

BC: I will give you an answer in two words: "temporary insanity." We were blinded by our hostility to the United States as a result of its seeking to dictate (and even threaten) us, and also by its breathtaking hypocrisy on the question of military invasion of other countries to safeguard or promote its perceived interests. Its squealing "foul" over the Soviet Union's doing likewise in Afghanistan prompted us—in an act of immaturity and craziness—not to vote *for* the Soviet Union but to stand up to U.S. pressure by voting *against* the U.S.-sponsored resolution on the issue.

WG: What are your views on the role Cuba played in the Grenada Revolution?

BC: Leaving aside for the moment the negative and ultimately fatal aspects of their role, the Cubans played a vital role in assisting us in the transformation of Grenada's physical and human infrastructure, and in building our national security capacity.

WG: You mentioned some of the grave errors that were made in relation to the United States. What were some of those errors?

BC: Our revolutionary process was unfolding in the context of the Cold War at its height, and with the most right-wing government to that point in time, the Reagan administration, in power in the United States. We failed to adequately appreciate just how "ballistic" the United States would become as a result of our ever-closer ties with Cuba (and by Cold War extension, the Soviet Union).

We saw ever closer ties with Cuba (and therefore the Soviet Union) as vital for the success, and the defense, of the revolution from external aggression. Such ties, however, the United States perceived as a strategic threat to its hegemony in the region, requiring, therefore, the revolution's overthrow by military invasion, since such seemed the only way to dislodge the deeply entrenched revolutionary process and its growing international communist links.

We believed fervently in "the equality of all nations regardless of size." Each time the United States did or said something displeasing to us, we pounced on it and launched powerful verbal counterattacks. In effect, we baited the United States. Each time the lion growled at us, we pulled its tail or its whiskers. This made us immensely popular among many Third World nations and their peoples—including those too scared (too wise?) to themselves bait the lion.

U.S. foreign policy (including its use of military action) is driven by more than just cold, calculating, rational considerations. Pride and other "irrational" considerations do enter into its decision-making mix from time to time. After all, it is a country of proud people, not machines, people with a fervent belief in their manifest destiny to tell others how they should live; what is and is not acceptable. Many countries have learned how to keep a low profile, maintain good diplomatic relations with the United States, but pursue—quietly—their own chosen domestic and foreign policy agenda. We in the Grenada Revolution knew not how to do this. We shouted from the rooftops at every opportunity.

If there was any chance of the United States believing it could influence our behavior through diplomatic channels and efforts, we told them, with an international megaphone to our lips, that this was just not on. In effect, we told them that short of massive military invasion, they could do us nothing, exert zero influence on us, and moreover, we would continue to thumb our noses publicly at them. Our naïveté, our immaturity, in dealing with the greatest threat that we faced, was, in retrospect, staggering.

Implosion of the Revolution

WG: You were very close to Maurice Bishop. You were both political and personal friends. Do you believe both of you shared similar political philosophies?
BC: First of all, read Maurice's "Line of March" speech (of August 1981). I did not write it; I was not even in Grenada when it was delivered or when it was written. I heard about it afterward. I received a copy of it with the minutes, on my return to Grenada. So to anybody who sees an ideological difference between Maurice and me, I would reply, "The only ideological difference is if he were to the left of me, if you read his 'Line of March' speech." Then I also draw your attention to the State Department/Department of Defense joint document they put out called the Blue Book. Some of it is a bit doctored, but let us forget that point for now. I am dealing now with their introductory statement. They said that their experts examined tons of our documents: minutes of meetings, these are all confidential documents, minutes, position papers, you name it, diaries, the works, and what was the conclusion they came to? They could spot no substantial ideological differences within the leadership emerging from any of these documents. So that is not Bernard Coard saying that. So that answers all this thing about political philosophy. There really, genuinely, was no difference there.
WG: Why the call for joint leadership in 1983?
BC: The joint leadership decision came out of a three-day meeting of the Central Committee (CC), September 14 to 16, 1983. The CC comprised fifteen members at the time. One member was abroad on an official trip; another was ill; thirteen attended the meeting. The decision was nine in favor, one against—George Louison the one—and three abstentions: Maurice abstained, Unison abstained, and Hudson Austin abstained because he was on a visit to Vietnam and North Korea throughout and had just returned literally one hour before the meeting ended, so he had not heard any of the arguments. He did not know what was happening, so he said, "I cannot make a decision." Maurice abstained because he said, "Look, my concern is really about whether this is about 'no confidence in me.' That's my concern." He was not opposed to it; neither could he say that he was in favor. So he abstained on that basis. So did Unison. Always before, the most important decisions were

by majority vote. Because he was the leader; we were not removing him, but we were establishing a joint leadership, which, by the way, was how the party was founded, and also that was the reality of how we functioned until the Cuban influence.

So we said, let's put it to a general meeting of all members, all full members on the 25th and of all candidate members on the 26th of September. One thing I am really happy about is that every committee of our party had a secretary. They sat in at our meetings; they were not members but secretaries, and they recorded who was present, who was absent, the proposals, the decisions taken, et cetera; so we had minutes. The minutes were then typed up, reproduced, and circulated within days of the meeting so that at the next meeting one week later the minutes could be confirmed. Those controlling Grenada after the invasion chose not to hand them over for their kangaroo trial of us, but the bottom line is that they exist. So sooner or later, all the so-called experts who have chosen to hide the truth would be exposed. For instance, everybody knows about the meeting of the CC on September 14–16, but somehow, conveniently, nobody knows about the general meeting of full members on September 25 and of all candidate members on September 26. At the meeting on the 25th, every single member of the party spoke. The meeting started at 9:00 a.m. and ended at exactly midnight—fifteen hours. That meeting is when every member said, "Hey, Maurice, we love you, the revolution cannot do without you, and these are the reasons why it can't, but at the same time organization is not your strong point, there are different areas where you are strong, we need to return to what we had before." I have put this in my own words. The bottom line is, that is when he said yes, and he voted in favor of joint leadership. So did Unison Whiteman. Everybody except one individual, George Louison's first cousin from Concord, I forget his name, but he abstained. (George Louison himself was out of the country on September 25–26.)

WG: But why joint leadership?

BC: The joint leadership proposal was part of a package of measures to reverse system overload/system breakdown in the party. During the four and a half years of the revolution, people worked extremely hard. The party moved from a vanguard initially of only about 51 to somewhere around 450 to 500 members, but we needed 2,000 to 3,000. The failure to move there meant that these 400 or 500 people had to do everything, all the work—what we inherited, the new state bodies, all the programs that had to be delivered, the mass organizations, everything. So each individual was involved in five, six major areas of work. People were working twenty hours a day, seven days a week, so there was breakdown. And this stress affected our judgment and decision making.

The vanguard party just could not cope. A mass party brings mass opinion within the bowels of the party and creates a framework where the leadership has more of a check on it and a better framework, perhaps, for conflict resolution within the party, and so on. That is a maybe position; I cannot say definitely.

WG: What was your role in the party and government as outlined in the joint leadership proposal?

BC: Let's start by being clear about one thing. The joint leadership proposal was strictly for the party and how it would organize its affairs. It explicitly excluded the state or government. Maurice would have remained prime minister and leader of the revolution. In fact, on April 5, 1981, the Central Committee had accepted unanimously a proposal I put forward that all those of us in the Political Bureau, including myself (but excluding Maurice), who held ministerial or state positions would permanently resign these positions within five years, to be replaced by younger comrades with appropriate qualifications and experience relevant to the specific ministries, and groomed in advance to take over. We would then focus all our future work on building the country's mass organizations and organs of popular democracy. This is why, for example, a young, brilliant economist who had been tapped years earlier by Maurice and myself to succeed me was able to take over the reins of the Ministry of Finance, Trade, and Planning on October 14, 1983, just twenty-four hours after I resigned all state positions.

The Central Committee identified Maurice's areas of strength—charisma, a special connection with the people, oratorical skills, extraordinary communication skills, and an ability to motivate the people to work and build the revolution—as my areas of weakness. It assessed my areas of strength as vision, organization, personal discipline, and work ethic. It concluded—as did Maurice himself—that these were Maurice's areas of weakness. The division of work between us was therefore designed with this in mind, and was spelled out in both the Central Committee minutes and in writing for the fifteen-hour general meeting of party members on September 25, 1983, to consider the proposal. I cannot give you all its precise provisions off the top of my head, but these are in the Central Committee minutes of September 14–16, 1983.

WG: How did the proposal for joint leadership affect the party?

BC: The proposal for joint leadership led to a grave split within the party. What is important for analysts to observe is that this proposal was intended to effectively restore the de facto management model of joint leadership between Maurice and myself that had served the party well over the years, since about 1976, in resisting the Gairy dictatorship, overthrowing that dictatorship, and building the revolution during its first vital two to two and a half years before the Cuban influence and other factors began to shake it. The joint leadership proposal merely spelled out, in a formal, written decision, the actual division of responsibilities and authority that had existed in the party for several years. It was also an implicit rejection of the "maximum leader" model that had crept up on the party leadership under Cuban influence and, at times, insistence. However, much as it was in keeping with the party's very origins and internal historical political decision-making culture; and despite its overwhelming endorsement by the party's membership, it was the wrong decision. It was a fatal mistake. It was profoundly naive to believe that the clock could be turned back, given all that had already taken place.

WG: In retrospect, why was the proposal for joint leadership a wrong decision?

BC: There are at least three reasons for saying that in retrospect joint leadership was doomed to failure: First, it failed to take into account the human element, in terms of how Maurice would see a downgrading of the new role he had gradually acquired, with Cuban help, over the previous two or so years of the revolutionary process. Questions not just of power sharing but of personal pride were involved. Naively, the party leadership—and membership—generally saw decisions in terms of how they would improve things and serve the interests of the party and the process, never in terms of how the individuals affected would view the decisions.

Second, it also failed to take into account the reaction of a small group of party members—a half dozen—who were very influential with Maurice and who saw themselves as losing status and power should the CC's decision on joint leadership be implemented. George Louison (Political Bureau member) led this trend, supported by Unison Whiteman (also Political Bureau member), Vincent Noel (former Political Bureau member), Kenrick Radix (former Political Bureau member), and Louison's younger brother, Einstein (the chief of staff of the army).

Finally, the party leadership totally underestimated—in fact, completely failed to consider—the reaction of the Cubans to the party's decision on joint leadership. In retrospect, this was extraordinary, given Cuba's behavior with respect to key party decisions in the past. Certainly, to the extent that some party leaders thought that Cuba would strongly disapprove of the party's decision on joint leadership, none of them considered, at the time the decision was made, that Cuba would energetically intervene to persuade Maurice to reject and defy what was now a decision of the entire party membership—and for which *he* also voted, at the end of that famous meeting.

WG: Elaborate on the role of the Cuban government in the implosion of the Grenada Revolution.

BC: I deal with this issue in some detail in my "Summary Analysis" (Coard 2002). John Ventour's "The Missing Link" (1988) provides considerable concrete evidence of Cuban interference, even imposition of decisions on the party and PRG, playing on our growing economic and military dependence on them; and of the fatal consequences of these actions for the revolution. Finally, for a comprehensive treatment of Cuban-Grenadian relations in that period, there is Ewart Layne's "Cuba-Grenada Relations and the October Tragedy" (1988a). Layne's "The Making of the Grenada Revolution" (1988b) provides detailed, wide-ranging evidence of the way decisions of all kinds were taken within the NJM before Cuba's entry onto the Grenada stage.

Let me therefore just say the following: countries have models of decision making that are derived from a combination of their history, culture, concrete political circumstances, and the personalities shaping and leading their struggles. The *caudillismo* model was the dominant model in most of Latin America for centuries. The Cuban Revolution had, from its inception, a left-wing "maximum leader" version of this. The Grenada Revolution, in contrast, had a collective leadership model from the day that the NJM was formed on March 11, 1973. All important decisions were taken not by even the party's joint leaders acting by themselves but by the entire leadership after discussion. This, as we saw earlier, was true of even potentially life-and-death decisions regarding when to launch the armed struggle to remove the Gairy dictatorship.

The Cubans, who played absolutely no role in making the Grenada Revolution, then entered the picture through their substantial economic and military assistance. They were appalled by our decision-making model, which they simply could not understand or accept. From Fidel Castro personally, right down the line, they consciously and actively encouraged—and, at certain crucial moments, literally imposed—the "maximum leader" model on our party and process. They sent high emissaries (on one occasion, General Ochoa himself, then one of the most decorated army generals in Cuba, the hero of the Cuban battles in Angola and Ethiopia, which he led, and a senior member of Cuba's Central Committee) to persuade and then insist to Maurice that he and he alone could take certain types of decisions—not the Central Committee, not the Political Bureau, not the Security and Defense Committee, not even the general meeting of the party. That "the leader" was in effect not subject to party rules, procedures, and discipline; that "the leader" was above this.

This is the context in which one can see Maurice, having accepted and indeed voted in favor of the joint leadership decision at the general meeting of September 25, 1983, reversing his position on October 8, 1983, on returning to Grenada after spending three days in Cuba on his way back from a trip to Eastern Europe. Moreover, on the fateful day of October 19, 1983, despite a sizable crowd waiting to hear him speak in the market square following his release from effective house arrest by demonstrators, he instead went with a large section of those demonstrators to army headquarters, where his first phone call was to the Cuban ambassador in Grenada, Julian Rizo. According to Fidel Castro himself, Maurice requested Cuban military intervention to crush the party and army of the Grenada Revolution [see Castro 1986]. Frankly, I cannot conceive of Maurice leading a crowd to seize the army HQ, disarming all the soldiers there and their officers, arming the civilian crowd, and then phoning for Cuban military help, unless he felt totally confident that this assistance would be forthcoming. These acts constituted the final twists in a series of events that spun completely out of control and ended in catastrophe on that terrible day.

WG: Did you seek the assistance of any mediators?

BC: Both Maurice and I asked Trevor Munroe to come in to help us sort out the situation, because I remember I rang him and said, "Both Maurice and I want you to come in," and he said, "I am willing to, but I want to hear it from Maurice as well." So he rang Maurice and Maurice told him, "We want you to come." That was in September, before the thing got really out of hand. He did not stay long. The bottom line is, his role was a mediating role. Other people have their own views. I do not know what he might have said when he went back to Jamaica; he may have said, Look, I agree with this side or the other. But while he was in Grenada, he was a mediator.

WG: From your perspective, why did the revolution implode?

BC: There are ten factors that I believe were critical in the implosion of the revolution and invasion that followed, including pressures we came under that would have contributed.

1. The manner of taking power. Armed overthrow meant the emergence of armed forces controlled by the ruling party, not by law or the constitution.
2. The absence of checks and balances within the party, the government, and the society. The absence of checks and balances at all three levels. And you see the link with the vanguard party in that regard.
3. The failure to hold elections and to restore in full the constitution within the first six to twelve months of taking power by armed overthrow.
4. The continuation of a political culture of suppression by force of opposing views of individuals, political parties, and the media, inherited from the colonial and Gairy eras.
5. The emergence of a culture of political fratricide from the earliest days and throughout the life of the revolution. To explain this point would

require far more time than is available now, so I'm simply stating it here for completeness and truthfulness.

6. The development of military rules of engagement from the earliest days and throughout the process of "take no prisoners" once anyone took up arms to challenge the revolution or its leadership. Once anyone took up arms to challenge the revolution or its leadership, our position was to militarily defeat such a person or forces rather than seek to identify their underlying concerns with a view to arriving at a compromise where possible. In this way we failed to practice the art of compromise, something that would later come back to haunt us.

7. The making of fundamental strategic errors in internal party structures and operations in the context of what was required to run the country and transform its economic and social circumstances. Internal party structures were far too top-down. This is a feature of vanguardism, but I must say it is also a feature of mass parties of the traditional political types in the region, let's be frank. The party had no internal capacity to resolve conflicts at the level of its top leadership. And there were no "outside forces," meaning at state or civil society level (not outside in the sense of outside Grenada), to rein in or constrain the party's actions. Also, failure to move quickly, meaning within twelve to twenty-four months from March 13, 1979, from a vanguard to a mass party. It is my considered view that power could hardly have been taken by means of armed overthrow of the Gairy regime without a tightly knit, well-trained, and disciplined vanguard party. However, the success of the revolutionary process, the effective control and operation of all arms of the government, the success of mass organizations and organs of popular democracy, and the delivery of the many and multifaceted programs and projects of the revolution to all the population mandated the need for a mass political party. To sum it up, too few were being asked to do too much in far too little time. Our goals and time frames were utterly unrealistic: a product of both our passion to transform society as quickly as possible, and our inexperience.

8. The encouragement and facilitation of personality cultism and the failure to institutionalize, constitutionalize, and give legal teeth to the organs of mass popular democracy that emerged and grew during the life of the revolution, making their abandonment, instead of their use, possible during the gravest crisis faced by the revolution and the country.

9. The making of fatal errors by the revolutionary leadership in its relations with the United States, born of inexperience and immaturity.

10. The making of quite different but equally fatal errors in the revolution's relations with Cuba.

In my "Summary Analysis" paper (Coard 2002), I explain how the interplay of all these factors, and their cumulative effect over the four and a half years of the process, led inexorably to the October 1983 crisis and tragedy.

WG: In response to your critics, you argue that "non-'ideological' factors (i.e., factors unrelated to hastening 'socialist construction'): Altruism, idealism, perfectionist personality traits, etc., explain The Reality of what happened far better than the outside experts' determination to fit everything into ideological boxes" (Coard 2002, 11). While nonideological factors were important, explain the role that ideological differences played in the implosion of the revolution.

BC: That presupposes a premise that is false. That is why in my "Summary Analysis" I pulled together all the factors, the who, the what, the when, that were at play, that led to the tragedy—a genuine tragedy that included the following:

1. The Cold War context.
2. A right-wing government in Washington, DC—the most right-wing to that date (replacing Jimmy Carter's administration).
3. Incorrect foreign policy—both in substance and in rhetoric—by the PRG, especially close military, political, and diplomatic ties with Cuba and the Soviet Union. This incorrect foreign policy was in turn caused by the PRG's fatal underestimation of U.S. imperialism's hostility to the Cuba-Soviet link and indeed its determination to smash such a link, which, in turn, was a product of the leadership's political immaturity and inexperience, and the PRG's belief that the Cuban-Soviet link was necessary for its defense against external aggression.
4. Incorrect domestic policy in one crucial area: the failure to hold multiparty elections to determine and renew, periodically, the government of Grenada, which would have offered U.S. imperialism an opportunity to remove a government whose policies the United States strongly disapproved of by nonmilitary means, as they did in Jamaica in 1980, Nicaragua in the late '80s, and so on. Propaganda, the financing of opposition parties, et cetera, were its tools, instead of military invasion. It was precisely this fear on the part of the PRG's leadership that led to its postponing for five years the holding of such elections. However, it can be argued that that very fact made U.S. imperialism's only option for getting its way that of direct military invasion, especially given the PRG's

military and other support from Cuba. In other words, yet again: a policy aimed at preventing overthrow, leading to precisely that outcome.

WG: What were some of the errors that you personally made?

BC: See all the things I listed in my "Summary Analysis." These were fundamental errors that were made. Apart from my responsibility, along with other party leaders, for many of the errors of commission and omission, my specific mistakes included: not going to the airport on October 8 to meet Maurice on his return from abroad; my failure, during the October 8–11 period, to take the initiative and go next door, to Maurice's home, and talk things out with him; my failure to propose, much earlier than the night of October 18, the abandonment of the party's decision on joint leadership, given what was happening inside and outside the country; my failure to foresee the likely consequences of the house arrest of Maurice—the single gravest error of the crisis before October 19 itself—despite his spreading of the rumor. I should have led energetic efforts to reconcile with Maurice and defuse the dangerous situation.[4]

Hindsight is twenty-twenty vision; with perfect vision I can see these errors now. The truth of the matter is that many things were done that proved flawed, and some proved fatal. We did a great many things that were highly successful, as I pointed out at the beginning of the interview. The spark of the revolution is still found in Grenada. The fact that people came out spontaneously all over Grenada in the last several Sundays (of 2008) to do community work: that is the collective memory of the revolution triggered twenty-five years later. That is a concrete manifestation. Not just the dentists and the economists and the engineers we spoke of earlier and the various institutions, like the National Insurance Scheme (NIS) and the banks, the Marketing and National Importing Board (MNIB), the international airport, and so on. The revolution has placed its stamp that is as indelible as it is permanent. But at the same time, we made many errors.

WG: If the revolution was about the political, economic, and social transformation of the country, there was a real pragmatism in the economic realm that was not matched by similar pragmatism in the political realm. Why?

BC: Absolutely. I believe this was linked to our preoccupation, even paranoia, over imperialism's likely use of the destabilization tactics it had so successfully used in so many countries from the 1950s to the 1980s, discussed earlier. Early signs of this within Grenada, in late 1979 and in 1980, only reinforced us in our strategically fatal path of inflexibility in political matters, even as we proved highly flexible on the economic and social fronts.

WG: The revolution lasted a mere four and a half years. Do you think there was too much haste to build the revolution?

BC: In the minutes, you would see that time and time again, I kept saying, "Don't go too fast," "We are going too fast," "Slow it down." In fact, in a lecture I gave in London to the Caribbean Association of Teachers, I said then, and it was later published, "We must not adopt an instant Nescafé revolutionary approach." Yet all I am reading about me is that I am this hard-line communist who thought we were not going fast enough.

WG: How would you summarize the main lessons to be learned from the Grenada experience?

BC: I like how I sum it up in this booklet I wrote for O-level students:

> We as Grenadians can learn even from the NJM/PRG's greatest catastrophe: the events of October, 1983. By far the most important lesson to be learned from this ghastly tragedy is the fundamental importance of a society having structures:
> (a) Which ensure CHECKS AND BALANCES, in terms of the exercise of power;
> (b) Which provide for effective mechanisms of PEACEFUL CONFLICT RESOLUTION;
> (c) And, in order to achieve "(a)" and "(b)", which provide for an OPEN, VIBRANT, MULTI-PARTY DEMOCRACY. This, in turn requires, for its achievement, AN EDUCATED, AND TOLERANT POPULATION, AND, MOST DECISIVELY, A DEVELOPED CIVIL SOCIETY. (Coard 2003)

WG: What do you want to say to people who do not know the real Bernard Coard?

BC: Talk to people who have known me for many years, without the horns that have been put on by the Americans and George and Kenrick and their self-serving propaganda. Judge me by what you see me do, not by what you heard I did.

WG: How do you want to be remembered?

BC: I never thought about that, to be honest. During my whole life—I take no credit for it, my parents, if you want to call it my parents' indoctrination, was: "Anybody who is in need and you are in a position to help, help them without thought of reward." That is where I am coming from. Money means nothing to me. Material things mean nothing. Power and prestige, status, fancy house and fancy car, fancy clothes, and all these things, the same. My parents taught me to think that way. They were my role models. Right now I am in a situation where I have no pension. I paid social security in several countries, England, America, and elsewhere, but not long enough to earn a pension. I set up NIS here; I paid contributions, but not enough. I have no pension, I have no funds, I have no savings, I have no insurance policy, and I am sixty-four and I am not worried. Because material things do not matter much to me; once I have a roof over my head and some food on the table, I am good. That has always been my outlook. Wherever I am, my task is to help those in need. This is the essence of who I am. I did this when I lived in the United States, and when I lived in the UK. I did it during the revolution, and I have done it during the last twenty-five years of my time in prison at Richmond Hill. In this regard, I cannot change. I've learned a number of things in life. I have been in the armchair, the field, in government, on the streets, and I have been in prison. I have learned from all these different perspectives.

WG: If you had to do it all over again, what would you do differently?

BC: I would do it all differently.

WG: Why?

BC: I refer, of course, to the many, many errors that we made throughout the period of revolutionary struggle and revolutionary power. We achieved many outstanding things. As I mentioned earlier, the positive legacy of the revolution can be seen to this day in the considerable physical and, even more importantly, human infrastructure and economic institutions developed in that period. But the cumulative effect of our errors over that same period led inexorably to the catastrophe of October 1983. Obviously, then, I would want to do everything that led to that differently, if I could start all over. That, of course, is impossible. What is possible, however, is that others learn from our mistakes and thus avoid them.

WG: I thank you very much.

BC: Keep up the good work, Wendy.

Notes

1. The Organisation for Revolutionary Education and Liberation.
2. Movement for Assemblies of the People.
3. Joint Endeavour for Welfare, Education, and Liberation.
4. See Coard 2002, 72–73.

References

Bartilow, H. A. 1997. *The Debt Dilemma: IMF Negotiations in Jamaica, Grenada, and Guyana.* London: Macmillan Education.

Castro, F. 1986. *Nothing Can Stop the Course of History: Interview by Jeffrey M. Elliot and Mervyn M. Dymally.* New York: Pathfinder.

Coard, B. 2002. "Summary Analysis of the October 1983 Catastrophe in Grenada." Unpublished manuscript. St. George's, Grenada.

———. 2003. "Grenada: 1951–1983; Notes for CXC/O-Level Students of History and Social Studies." Unpublished paper. St. George's, Grenada.

Government of Grenada. 1975. "Report of the Duffus Commission of Inquiry into the Breakdown of Law and Order, and Police Brutality in Grenada." St. George's, Grenada: Government of Grenada.

Layne, E. 1988a. "Cuba-Grenada Relations and the October Tragedy." Unpublished manuscript. St. George's, Grenada.

———. 1988b. "The Making of the Grenada Revolution." Unpublished manuscript. St. George's, Grenada.

Ventour, J. 1988. "The Missing Link." Unpublished manuscript. St. George's, Grenada.

5. Grenada Once Again: Revisiting the 1983 Crisis and Collapse of the Grenada Revolution

Brian Meeks

> If old truths are to retain their hold on men's minds, they must be restated in the language and concepts of successive generations.
>
> —**Friedrich Hayek**, *The Constitution of Liberty*

Remembering Grenada

The twenty-fifth anniversary in October 2008 of the tragic killing of Maurice Bishop and his associates and the subsequent invasion of Grenada, followed closely by the release on September 5, 2009, of Bernard Coard and the six remaining prisoners convicted of his murder, has been cause for a flurry of new conferences, papers, letters, and communiqués on the Grenada Revolution and its tragic demise.[1] Among the most outstanding were the conference and remembrance activities on the twenty-fifth anniversary at the University of Toronto;[2] the April 2009 conference on the legacies of radical politics in the Caribbean at Pittsburgh University; Rupert Roopnaraine's reflective paper delivered at the Pittsburgh event;[3] and Shalini Puri's panel at the 2009 Caribbean Studies Association (CSA) conference, along with her graphic presentation of memory and the revolution first presented in Toronto.[4] Then, after the September release of the seven, things picked up pace. Thankfully, many of the letters on the ubiquitous websites and e-mail circuits, particularly those written by Grenadians, suggested wariness with the recriminatory monologues that have been typical of many reflections on the tragedy. Wendy Grenade's "Beyond the Legal Chapter: An Opportunity for Rebirth in Grenada," for instance, suggests that the release of the seven provides the opportunity for a genuine and open discussion on the strengths and weaknesses of the revolutionary period and calls for the assertion of humanitarian, socialist, and democratic principles for the future.[5] Patsy Lewis's intervention, in similar vein, distinguishes the reaction of Grenadians as opposed to those of other West Indian nationals who attended the 2009 CSA panel. She suggests that Grenadians have moved farther along the road of reconciliation, while others seem to have been suspended at the traumatic moment of crisis in 1983.[6] Most tellingly, layperson Randal Robinson's letter to the Methodist Church's newsletter, suggesting genuine happiness over the release of the seven, strengthens Lewis's conviction of a deep current of reconciliation on the island: "This day will be a bittersweet one for us Grenadians, but if we don't learn to forgive we will all perish through hate and there is no place in Heaven for haters."[7]

Countering Conventional Wisdom

Understandably, all commentaries did not comply with this tone. Jorge Heine, for instance, who had written one of the early forensic studies of the collapse of the revolution, wrote in his short piece "The Return of Bernard Coard"[8] that the "dual leadership" formula of the Central Committee (CC) was "utterly impractical and unworkable" and, inter alia, opposed to the common perspective that Coard and Bishop held distinct and contradictory ideological perspectives that "no differences existed among the party leadership as to the pace or general direction of 'The Revo.'" These observations I entirely agree with and shall return to look at in more detail anon, but I part company with Heine's substantial claim as to the fundamental cause of the crisis. He suggests that the entire joint leadership proposal was merely a ploy, as he puts it, "merely one additional move in Bernard Coard's long-term strategy to gain full control of the party and state."[9] In relation to the underlying causes—the impetus for Coard's actions—Heine proposes a "feeling of resentment" that the young Bernard had inherited from his father. Coard's father, Frederick, had written a book titled *Bittersweet and Spice: Those Things I Remember*, in which he reflected on the fact that as a civil servant he was subordinate to people less qualified than himself. This led to resentment, and by a process of transference, Heine proposes that the son came to feel the same way about his seemingly perpetual number two position in revolutionary Grenada:

> The son identified with the father. Both bureaucrats to the core, who loved statistics and files, the colonial civil service was to the father what the party was to the son. The complaints by father and son about their fellow clerks or party comrades are also similar. The father's frustration is that he never made it to the very top

of the colonial civil service, the officer of comptroller of income tax. Thirty years later, for Bernard Coard, the prospect of spending the rest of his professional life in the relative obscurity below the very top of the political structure, doing the legwork for somebody else, was surely unbearable. To live in the shadow of Maurice Bishop, whose father was a martyr of the anti-Gairy struggle and who had once employed Bernard's father as a clerk, was unacceptable, as was working under somebody he considered his intellectual inferior.[10]

Heine's proposal is highly tendentious and eminently contestable. I am not equipped to delve into the claims of inherited psychological states and thus will leave that aspect of his argument for the experts to consider. However, the equation of the elder Coard's lowly status in the civil service with his son's number two position in the New Jewel Movement (NJM) begs an immediate response. From his return from Jamaica in 1976 until his resignation from the CC in 1982, Coard enjoyed inordinate influence in the party and, after the March 13, 1979, revolution, in the state. This was in part the result of a special and peculiar symbiotic relationship between Maurice and Bernard, which was palpable and noted often in various commentaries. In what was a de facto form of joint leadership, they divided labor according to their respective talents and maintained a genuinely fraternal relationship between each other. Thus Roopnaraine in his paper recollects speaking with Maurice at the first conference in solidarity with Grenada in St. George's in November 1981. Just before leaving the event, Maurice pulled him aside and said: "If ever you come and I am not on the island, talk with Bernard. Talking to Bernard is the same as talking to me."[11] Claremont Kirton, then a senior economist with the People's Revolutionary Government's Ministry of Finance, told me in an interview in the 1980s, "I worked with both of them, and each used to tell me, if I submitted documents to one, then ensure that the other had a copy. I had no reason to believe on the basis of what I could see that there was any kind of tension at all between them."[12]

I recall meeting Maurice for the first time in Jamaica in 1977 when he and Bernard were seeking support from the Jamaican government and subsequently, though without any success, from the Cubans. They were ebullient and almost romantically optimistic about their hopes for success in their struggle against Eric Gairy. What was most evident, though, was the closeness between them. There was a distinct casualness that suggested friendship in their conversation and a naive willingness to share what seemed to me at the time very dangerous details of the covert aspects of the anti-Gairy struggle. Coard evidently was no bureaucratic subordinate to Maurice. On the crucial decision to strike on March 13, Maurice was against it, but when the majority of the Political Bureau (PB), including Coard, voted in favor, he supported the action wholeheartedly.[13] Maurice accepted Bernard's fine eye for detail, superior grasp of economics, and, for the most part, political judgment. Bernard and, indeed, the entire party understood equally that Maurice, while considered weak from organizational and theoretical perspectives, possessed a quality that was more valuable than any of these. He was the person with the common touch, the ability to move crowds, to convert the PRG's policies into words that everyone could grasp, and the timing to use them appropriately. He was the charismatic leader, and everyone seemed to understand this. Both men enjoyed tremendous prestige within the ranks of the NJM, but if one were asked who in 1983 commanded the greater respect, I would have to conclude that it was Coard. This in some respects was inevitable. After March 13, Maurice had an immense responsibility for state and diplomatic work. Bernard had the Ministry of Finance, but with his meticulous organizational abilities, he was able to manage this and also play the leading role in party organizing and building. Thus Coard's popularity grew among party cadres while Maurice's consolidated and blossomed in Grenada as a whole and beyond.

On the question of long-standing conspiracy, I suggest that the Achilles' heel in Heine's and most of the conspiracy-based arguments is exposed when asked to explain how Maurice became so marginalized within his own party. One school, led by Fidel Castro, proposes that Coard and his clique were able, by subtlety and subterfuge, to eke out majorities in the CC and in the military leadership, and this is how they eventually ousted Bishop.[14] This notion of a narrow majority primarily at the level of the leadership is a misrepresentation. In reality, when the crisis ripened, the overwhelming majority of the NJM was opposed to Maurice, as was the leadership of the People's Revolutionary Army (PRA) and also the rank and file. This, I suggest, is because they, unlike the rest of the population, were privy to the twists and turns of the joint leadership discussions; had voted, in the main, in favor of it; and had collectively come to the conclusion that it was Maurice who had disrespected the party by breaching a solemn promise. Herein lay the root of the tragedy of October 19; for if the NJM had been divided and the PRA split, Maurice would have rallied the "loyal" sections to his side, and with the populace overwhelmingly in his favor, the jig would immediately have been up for Coard and the recalcitrant minority. But with a united party and behind them a united army facing the largely unarmed and now hostile population, the door was open for dangerous and deadly solutions.

As an aside to the notion of conspiracy, I recall an incident in August 1983 during my stint with the Ministry of Mobilization after Maurice's return from what would be his final visit to the United States. He had given a triumphant anti-imperialist speech to an adoring Brooklyn crowd at CUNY's Hunter College,[15] belying the view expressed by many subsequent commentators that his trip to the United States represented some sort of attempt to modify the PRG's previously uncompromising approach to the Reagan regime. Selwyn Strachan, who at the time was minister of mobilization, on the instruction of the PB, called on me as coordinator of worker education classes to play the hour-long videotape of Maurice's Hunter speech at every class, as it was an excellent speech in defense of the revolution and showed the comrade leader at his best. A month later, divisions would become apparent; two months later, Bishop would be killed. This directive, however, suggests that in August, Strachan, arguably at the time the third most powerful man in the country and someone who would spend the next twenty-six years of his life in prison, convicted and accused of killing Maurice Bishop, was in August 1983 actively promoting him. This is a powerful piece of evidence, and I am remiss, out of a desire to take my own story out of the narrative,[16] in not having used it in previous writings, for it throws significant amounts of sand in the engine of the conspiracy idea.

In preliminary summary, then, in response to Heine's contention that Coard resented his second-best status as deputy leader, I advance the simple contention that significant evidence points to a very comfortable and, one might argue, fulfilling relation of mutual sharing of leadership between both men, certainly until late 1982. This questions, though in itself cannot dismiss, the notion of a power grab based on venal, long-term, psychologically fueled factors. In relation to conspiracy, I advance the evidence of Strachan's position on promoting Maurice in August and ask for consideration whether the entire party, bar a handful, was duped by Bernard Coard's magic, or whether the overwhelming suit of majority votes in the party opposing Maurice on pivotal decisions suggests a different, more complex story that needs to be told, beyond the tattered notion of a long-standing conspiracy based on the will to power.

The second comment that I wish to contest is that of the Barbadian lawyer and political activist Robert "Bobby" Clarke. In a sketchy letter,[17] though significant for its reflection of commonly held perspectives, Clarke makes a number of assertions, three of which are worth mentioning:

1. *Bernard Coard was made deputy prime minister not by Maurice Bishop's government but by an announcement made by his wife Phyllis on the radio.* This argument is new to me, and I cannot recall seeing evidence of it in any of the numerous Grenada documents stolen from

the country as spoils of war by the U.S. military in 1983. Taken on its own, the claim is preposterous. The NJM was an aspiring Leninist party, which, as tragic events would prove, actually believed in the notion of democratic centralism as the best way to organize a party to lead a revolution. Phyllis Coard was on the CC, but she was not a member of the all-powerful Political Bureau (PB) and as such simply did not have the kind of influence to get away with such a maneuver. She would have been roundly condemned, and the results of the inquiry would have surfaced in the captured and extensive party minutes.

2. *The OREL conspiracy proposition.* The pre-party Organization for Revolutionary Education and Liberation (OREL), which Bernard Coard helped to guide before the revolution and included key proponents of joint leadership like Liam "Owusu" James and Ewart "Headache" Layne, was never dissolved into the NJM but remained as a conspiratorial clique, guiding the plot and eventually displacing Bishop for Coard. This is also part of Fidel Castro's argument, but it is equally fallacious.[18] Again, there is simply no evidence of OREL in any of the minutes or the numerous microfiche documents. Elsewhere I have argued that on Grenada's physical and demographic scale, it is impossible to hide a conspiratorial organization for four and a half years of revolution in which virtually everything was public and social. Inhabitants of larger small countries like Jamaica or Trinidad, with populations in excess of a million, are beyond a certain minimal threshold for an easy grasp of the phenomenon that it is impossible to keep an organization secret for very long in a microstate with roughly 100,000 inhabitants. This applies not only to the OREL contention but to the general theory of a long-standing conspiracy. Moreover, the overwhelming demand on time that the party and revolution imposed on leading individuals would have made it virtually impossible for frontline cadres like Coard, Ewart Layne, Leon Cornwall, Owusu James, and John Ventour to maintain a parallel set of meetings, minutes, and so on. The OREL argument, I suggest, is simply not true.

The subset of this contention, however—that Coard maneuvered people onto the CC so that in the end, his people were on board and Maurice's were ousted—needs also to be addressed. The pattern of promotions and demotions, while at first glance persuasive, ultimately belies this argument. Layne, James, and Ventour, formerly members of OREL, all found their way onto the PB after the revolution, while long-standing militants like Kenrick Radix and Vince Noel were demoted. But on closer examination, it was the chairman of the PB—Maurice Bishop himself—who was in charge, and he never once expressed doubts about this process. Indeed, on closer examination, the pattern is simply not consistent. George Louison, who had risen fastest in terms of state and party responsibilities, was never a member of OREL and ended up on Maurice's side in the final dispute; among the members of the PB who had been severely reprimanded by Coard at an earlier date for showing militaristic tendencies was Ewart Layne, a former OREL member and one of the final seven convicts; and also among the seven and in favor of joint leadership in the crucial September meetings were Selwyn Strachan and Hudson Austin, who were with Maurice from the founding of the NJM and definitely not part of the OREL group.[19] Louison himself, hostile to Coard and the other prisoners until his death, in an interview with me in the 1980s, put the nail into the coffin of this argument when he said, "I think that over the years there were certain people who earned their position on the CC, and there were certain people who could not function or pull their weight in the last days."[20]

3. *Bishop was ideologically different from Coard.* Clarke asserts that Maurice's position "differed completely in that the Grenada Revolution should take the path of a combination of Marxist economics and Caribbean based cultural philosophy."[21] Bernard Coard, on the other hand, "was influenced by his mentor Dr. Trevor Monroe (Munroe) of the Workers Party of Jamaica, a devout Stalinist at the time,"[22] and "he advised (Coard) on all the actions he should take to bring about a USSR style government."[23] My own residency in Grenada between 1981 and 1983, consultations with Maurice Bishop on the editing of the weekly newspaper the *Free West Indian*, meetings with Bishop, Coard, and Strachan on planning the worker education classes, and subsequent extensive reading for my doctoral thesis of many of the available documents on the Grenada Revolution lead me to the conclusion that there were few if any substantial differences on critical ideological matters between the two. Both had been nurtured in the Black Power and antiwar movements of the sixties—Coard and Bishop in Britain, Coard subsequently in Trinidad and Jamaica, and Bishop in the cockpit of action in Grenada itself. Both had subsequently passed through that transitional phase between 1970 and 1975 when a significant part of a generation of radical intellectuals shifted from various Black Power streams to an equally varied potpourri of "Marxisms."[24] Both had settled on a particular version of the doctrine that we might call, for want of a better coinage, "Caribbean Marxism-Leninism," and the available evidence suggests that on the key markers of ideology, theory, party

strategy, and government policy, no discernible differences existed between them before 1983. Caribbean Marxist-Leninists cannot simply be folded into "Stalinists," though they were subject to potentially dangerous authoritarian tendencies that derived in part from ideology but also from indigenous regional traditions of authoritarianism. From this perspective, to describe Trevor Munroe as a "Stalinist" or, even more startling, a "Pol Potist" is as wrong and equally mechanical as was Munroe's highly flawed praxis as applied by the WPJ. Stalin was a product of one of the worst forms of state oppression in the nineteenth and twentieth centuries—czarist Russia—and he became its even more terrible alter ego. Despite the WPJ's propensity for dogmatic interpretations of Marx and its failure to gain political traction in Jamaica, to equate Munroe with Stalin is a travesty and a failure of imagination in not sufficiently understanding Caribbean politics and its inhabitants on their own historical foundations. The irony is that Coard, Bishop, and Munroe were all part of the same postindependence, radical Caribbean middle-class intellectual stream. Neophytes in Marxism, the overarching problem is that they had all launched into the big league of revolution while attempting to master instruments that they had barely begun to comprehend. When crises overtook them, rather than seeking creative solutions, they looked for the answer in exegesis—the doctrinaire adherence to scripture. The peculiarity of the Caribbean turn to Marxism of the intellectual generation of the early seventies, then, is its immaturity and the dangerous implications that this held for popular movements that were advancing at a faster pace than were their intellectual leaders. This approach, I think, offers more fertile ground for an inquiry of the collapse than the worn notion of a "moderate" or "cultural" Bishop versus a "Stalinist" Coard.

Much work, however, still needs to be done on the WPJ's involvement in the Grenada events. There is a view held in Jamaica and elsewhere and evident in Clarke's comments that the WPJ was the intellectual and ideological mentor—the éminence grise—of the NJM. This was not the case, but there was WPJ involvement, and again, a more complex picture needs to be painted. Coard had read Marxism-Leninism with a Workers Liberation League (WLL)[25] study group during his sojourn in Jamaica from 1973 to 1976 and was therefore very close to the Jamaican party. An interesting footnote to this is that when Trevor Munroe, who was seeking to win port workers away from the traditional unions and organize them in the University and Allied Workers Union (UAWU) was attacked and seriously injured along with a group of students and union workers on the Kingston waterfront in 1974, Bernard Coard was physically present. He narrowly escaped injury by being farther away from Trevor, who was the main focus of the attack. This story, to my knowledge, has never been told, and I speak from personal experience. I traveled to Grenada for the first time in July 1981 at the request of the PRG to help build the media there. After the 1980 Jamaican elections, the entire News and Current Affairs Department at the Jamaica Broadcasting Corporation had been made redundant by the newly elected right-wing Jamaica Labour Party (JLP) government, which had considered us adversaries in the hotly contested 1980 election campaign. George Louison visited Jamaica in March 1981, and among his requests was that Maurice and Bernard wanted me to come and work. I packed my bags and left in July, without a contract and quite willing to work for free if that were the arrangement. I was somewhat surprised to discover that I had a rented house that I shared with another WPJ comrade *and* a salary. This was a far cry from the bleak future that I faced in Jamaica as an unemployed television producer in a country with one government-owned television station and a hostile government that had just kicked us out of work. There were seven WPJ comrades in Grenada when I arrived, with an additional two coming sometime after. Four of us worked in the media, two in the commercial sector, and one in the Ministry of Justice. Aside from the Cubans, whose numbers, boosted by hundreds of construction workers on the airport, far exceeded other international workers, WPJ comrades were the largest group and the only one to my knowledge with an organized cell. We participated fully in the life of the Revo, attending rallies, conferences, budget debates, and so on, and all members of the group interacted regularly with the leadership of the PRG, though this was more in the nature of tiny Grenada than any special favor extended to us.

What was immediately evident was that the Grenadians had their own distinct organizational standards and a keen sense of national pride. During the Julien Fédon maneuver, a friend had loaned me a green army jacket, which I was wearing with some pride on the steps of Butler House when I was spotted by Ewart "Headache" Layne, then a colonel in the PRA. He approached me discreetly and indicated that as an international comrade it would be damaging to the revolution if I were photographed in even a partial army uniform. I removed the jacket immediately. It is difficult to know the details of party-to-party relations beyond the material in the minutes reproduced in the Grenada Documents, Grenada Papers,[26] and the original papers and microfiche documents in the National Archives in Washington, DC. However, this much is evident: In the weeks leading up to the October crisis, Trevor Munroe did visit Grenada, as did leaders of other "fraternal" parties, including Michael Als from Trinidad and Rupert Roopnaraine from Guyana. What Munroe said and what effect this might have had on the NJM leaders is difficult to discern, but I suggest that the crisis had its own dynamic, rooted in the tension between the two logics mentioned earlier. The WPJ almost certainly supported the idea of joint leadership, but it was not their invention, and any notion of the WPJ giving directions to the NJM simply fails to understand Grenadians in general and the enhanced sense of pride and self-determination that blossomed with the revolution.

As to which side the WPJ stood with in the end, I recall a poignant moment on October 19—the day of the killings on the fort. I had returned to Jamaica to pursue doctoral work at the University of the West Indies on the political economy of the revolution. News of the crisis had traumatized the entire country, but it was particularly acute for me and the few Grenadians on campus, including my close friend and later wife Patsy Lewis. I had gone down to the WPJ office on Lady Musgrave Road, because I knew that there would be a close monitoring of events. News of Maurice's death was not yet confirmed when a female comrade on the WPJ Central Committee emerged and said quietly, "Maurice is dead. The CC is in charge." For my part, there was just a deep and bottomless sadness. For at least a year, I was unable to put pen to paper to write about Grenada. Gradually, with Patsy's help, I emerged from depression. Over time, I started to do research, and the act of writing became cathartic. I finally finished my thesis, "Social Formation and People's Revolution: A Grenadian Study," in 1988.[27]

In summary, then, in 1983 the WPJ sided with the NJM's Central Committee on the matter of joint leadership, though its influence on the peculiar dynamic of events was, I suggest, limited. In the sweep of history, however, it paid the price for this position, as the party and many of the other left-leaning groups in the Caribbean failed to survive. I propose that while the WPJ did not instigate the joint leadership proposal, the WPJ's support for the majority on the NJM's Central Committee gave the CC greater confidence in the decisions that had been taken and thus contributed significantly to the hardening of positions and the slide that eventually led to the collapse of the revolution and the discrediting of radical politics in the Caribbean for a generation or more.

Alternative Explanations

Since I have tried to counter some of the flaws that seem to be reemerging in the new round of debate, it is only reasonable to propose even the outlines of an alternative explanation. If Coard was not power hungry, whether via Freudian or Nietzschean explanations; if OREL was not planning to overthrow Bishop; if Bishop and Coard did not have measurable ideological differences; then why was he placed under house arrest and subsequently executed in the most brutal, militaristic manner? I have tried to explain this twice before, in my doctoral thesis and in my book on Caribbean revolutions, but time provides new information, and as Hayek's epigraph suggests, a new generation demands that old truths be restated. I restate my argument as a series of theses.

Authoritarian Social Formation

At its fundamental level, the crisis of 1983 was rooted in traditions of authoritarianism and arbitrary rule that the Grenadian revolutionaries inherited from Eric Gairy and the colonial regime that preceded independence. Gairy, in his hostility to the local elites and desire for effective power, abandoned many of the tenets of liberal democracy, including notions of habeas corpus, individual security, and free and fair elections. The British, despite the active opposition of tens of thousands of citizens, granted independence in 1973 in the full knowledge of Gairy's predatory capabilities and what he was likely to do if given greater autonomy. Indeed, it was Gairy's arbitrary rule, fixing of elections, and terror, particularly from 1972 to 1979, that undermined his initial legitimacy and laid the foundation for popular support of extraconstitutional activity.[28] The NJM therefore came to power with an ideological predisposition that disparaged bourgeois constitutional electoral government, but also in a social and political moment in which these forms had already been savaged by Eric Gairy. Nonetheless, it was the failure of the imagination[29] of the NJM leaders as a whole not to recognize that, after having promised early elections at the birth of the Revo, the longer they held on to power without restoring democratic rights and freedoms, the more they came to mirror the regime that they had toiled so hard to overthrow. An early election, say in 1981, when anti-Gairy feelings still ran high, would undoubtedly have been won by the NJM, would have undermined the internal opposition to the regime, would have blunted the effectiveness of the U.S. and regional conservative opposition to the process, and would have given the PRG breathing space to consolidate its authority as it strove to complete the program of infrastructural development. Elections, however, are uncertain things and hold, inevitably, the possibility of defeat. The straightforward lesson derived from the Grenada tragedy must be that revolutionary and reforming regimes must be prepared to lose. If democrats believe that the people ultimately are sovereign, then they must be willing to concede governmental power when the voters are fed up with them, return to the hustings, and live to fight another day.

This, some might argue by quoting Lenin perhaps, is a form of parliamentary cretinism and fails to take into account the overwhelming power of capital, the poisonous nature of the media, the machinations of the CIA, and so on. These factors, as in Allende's Chile in 1973 or Sandinista Nicaragua, all work together to ensure that reforming regimes are isolated, excoriated, and never able to return to power. All of these are substantial points, but the stark alternative is to hold on to power in the absence of the perceived wishes of the majority, and this must, in the end, lead to the erosion and destruction of any notion of popular rule.

The Role of Vanguardism

The vanguard party, the "small group of highly trained and committed comrades leading and guiding,"[30] was a critical element in the success of the March 13 overthrow but became its dialectical opposite afterward. In 1973 and 1974, when the newly formed NJM was able to put a significant part of the population on the streets and help shut down the country in opposition to independence under Gairy, it was still unable to remove him from power. The party was capable of bringing people into the streets, but it did not possess the capacity for clandestine work, nor did it have a military capability. In the new, more repressive conditions that emerged after independence, both of these were critical requirements for political survival and, with the erosion of free and fair elections, were vital for possible military victory over the regime.[31] Both of these features were incorporated after 1975 and served the party well as it built a small but effective armed force and planned for the possibility of insurrection. At the same time, NJM vanguardism led to a rapid fall in the number of active cadres and a highly hierarchical top-down system of command, both inimical to popular democracy and empowerment. Inevitably, too, the NJM became a somewhat schizophrenic organization, with the full members reading Marx and seeking to build a "real" Marxist-Leninist party, while the popular base remained largely ignorant of all this, supporting the party mainly because of its history of standing for popular causes.[32] In hindsight, the best solution after 1979 would have been a rapid transition from a clandestine vanguard structure to a mass organization, allowing all supporters with minimal requirements to join. This would naturally have to be accompanied by elections to posts in the party at all levels, conventions, and all the paraphernalia of democratic mass parties. To the Grenadian "Leninists" and their wider Caribbean compatriots, this was heresy; but consider what would have been the result of a joint leadership dispute that went before a convention with—based on the crowds the NJM was able to mobilize from its birth—ten thousand party members. Coard would have had his fulsome say, and so would Bishop. Which one of them could oppose a decision for joint leadership, carefully considered, if the vast majority of that ten thousand supported it? Which one could even have considered calling on the PRA for support if the overwhelming majority of the ten thousand party members and quite likely the majority of the soldiers felt that it was a bad idea? This, of course, is wishful thinking, but it is sobering to consider that such a discussion was entirely off the agenda of the party for four and a half years, only to be raised by Bernard Coard in the dying weeks of the revolution, when he proposed that there should be popular involvement in the selection and promotion of members to the party.[33] Finally, the small and narrowly constituted nature of the NJM was taking a terrible toll on the health of its membership. Faced with the daunting task of running a state, maintaining an army, building a revolution, projecting tiny Grenada onto the diplomatic stage, and building the party, by 1983, most of the leadership and many of the members were groggy, sick, or demoralized from overwork and sheer exhaustion. This as a factor in the final demise cannot be overstated, for it undergirds the evident lack of judgment that prevailed among all the leadership in the final days.

Rethinking the Cuban Connection

What brought Grenada sharply into the crosshairs of the United States was its extraordinarily close relationship with Cuba. The Cubans played a central role in the building of the airport, new housing construction facilities, medical care, and the education of hundreds of Grenadian professionals, among many other gestures that went far beyond the boundaries of generosity.[34] Most urgently, the Cubans provided critical military support in the form of small arms and equipment in the uncertain days after Gairy's overthrow and the months and years that followed. In exchange, Grenada gave Cuba and her strategic ally the Soviet Union diplomatic solidarity, most egregiously by supporting the Soviets in voting against the condemnatory UN resolution surrounding the 1979 Soviet invasion of Afghanistan.[35] This was a dangerous game, as it served to focus unnecessary attention on Grenada and strengthen the view of the hawks in Washington that in a military standoff, Grenada would be a reliable and valuable asset for the Soviets in the middle of a presumed American sphere of influence. To the resurgent Right under Ronald Reagan, this situation was intolerable and underlined their expressed fears about what the airport meant. As assistant undersecretary of defense Dov Zakheim said after the invasion: "It mattered little whether the airport at Point Salines would be used primarily as a tourist facility, as the NJM claimed. It was the potential that the airport offered to the Soviets that worried American analysts."[36] In retrospect, it is difficult to see how the PRG would have survived without a modicum of military assistance, and Cuba was the only regional force able to provide it. But a more tactical diplomatic relationship with Cuba might have blunted the arguments of the U.S. policy hawks. The vote on Afghanistan certainly was entirely unnecessary. Would the Cubans have stopped assistance to Grenada because of an abstention on this issue? It is unlikely. In the end, this is a moot question, as the murder of Bishop so egregiously tore down the last defenses against invasion that the subtleties of diplomatic maneuvering were made redundant.

Crisis and Collapse: Coard's Resignation from the Central Committee

If long-standing conspiracy, secret cells, and ideological differences are to be ruled out of the equation, then the crisis of 1983 can best be understood as a series of vignettes, each causally connected to the previous and each contributing to an accumulation of uncertainty and misunderstanding that was eventually irrecoverable.

The first stage was the resignation in October 1982 of Bernard Coard from the Political Bureau, Central Committee, and Organizing Committee (OC), though he retained his public positions as minister of finance and deputy prime minister. Coard claimed that he was tired, that his influence had intimidated other comrades, and that they would now have a chance to develop. More pointedly, he said that the CC was "slack,"[37] and so as not to have personality clashes with its chairman, Maurice Bishop, Coard would rather resign. What had undermined the carefully developed synergy between Coard and Bishop to the point that Coard felt he would rather withdraw than clash with the leader? I suggest elsewhere that this was part of a divergence that had been present from the taking of power in 1979, in which two logics competed against each other.[38] One was the logic of the vanguard party, in which collective CC decisions, arrived at by democratic discussion and then applied downward in an authoritarian manner (democratic centralism), prevailed. The other logic was that of the charismatic national leader, in which, typically, the leader is responsible only to himself and the crowd. Bishop through the years in opposition adhered faithfully to the notion of democratic centralism, as most strikingly illustrated in the previously mentioned decision to seize power. But as the months and years wore on, the influence of the second logic became overwhelming. It was he and not the NJM whom the crowds saw as the embodiment of the Revo. He was the individual who more often than not interfaced with heads of state and prime ministers. While the party remained the creaky, increasingly overworked, but necessary instrument that held everything together, outwardly, to the general population of Grenada, it barely existed. The very exclusivity, clandestine nature, and secrecy that had served it well in the preparation for insurrection was returning to haunt it. Bishop was also prompted by his new Cuban associates, particularly in the diplomatic and military spheres, who, in elevating their own particular experience of a single powerful leader almost to a law, encouraged him to act independently without reference to the party. This was the cause of the clear spat—to my knowledge, the first between Coard and Bishop—in mid-1982, when military comrades who should have attended an OC meeting chaired by Coard were told that they were instead to attend an army meeting under Bishop's direction.[39] Yet Coard's absence from the leadership in this period seemed to have done nothing to assuage the tension between these two competing logics. Faced with his resignation, the CC, now entirely under Bishop's leadership, in conceding to Coard's reference to slackness, sought not to rapidly increase membership by loosening entry requirements but to place the party on a more rigid Leninist footing by increasing study times, tightening membership requirements, and intensifying disciplinary measures for supposedly recalcitrant comrades. Alongside these actions, plans were also put in place to project the image of the leader more effectively in public events and in the media—undoubtedly the basis for the aforementioned directive to use Maurice's Hunter College speech in worker education classes. Thus in late 1982, notably under Bishop's sole leadership, but with the full assent of all the CC members, vanguardism was intensified while simultaneously the tendency to imbue the leader with a heroic national profile was accelerated by the party itself.

The Nature of the Crisis

The revolution was approaching a crisis, which became evident in early 1983. The U.S. military maneuvers of March 1983, in which elements of the U.S. fleet carried out activities in the Atlantic off the coast of Barbados, were for the first time met with a lukewarm response from Grenadians. A subsequent party survey of support for the NJM and PRG in some workplaces came out with frighteningly low figures,[40] which suggested significant disenchantment with the process. My own experience in teaching worker education (primarily

Caribbean and Grenadian history)[41] classes in a number of workplaces in this period supports the contention that support was tepid, though I had no basis to assess whether it had decreased over time or had always been low. I taught classes in the nutmeg factory in Grenville, to the road-building crew on the Eastern Main Road, the Grenada Electricity Company workers, and civil servants in the Ministry of Finance. In all instances, attendees were polite, and over time I developed an easy camaraderie with many of the participants. But many others, particularly in the ministry, did not attend, and among those that did, a handful were clearly hostile to the idea of spending an hour each week talking about Caribbean history and politics. At the time, it struck me that, for a country in the midst of revolution, the atmosphere was far less militant than I had expected, indeed, far less militant than the average trade union meeting that I remembered in Jamaica. My own perceptions, blurred by the intercession of a quarter century, may be skewed, but they are echoed in the documents of the CC, where the dominant opinion, including that of Maurice himself, felt that the party had come close to losing its mass base.

This perspective was conveyed to a meeting of the entire party in July, in which the state of the deteriorating links with the people was raised.[42] The CC, in keeping with its earlier positions, used the opportunity to blame party comrades for indiscipline and called again for a further intensification of Leninism as the only required solution. This time they were met with solid opposition from the members, led by the women, who argued that they were doing the best for the party and sacrificing care and attention to their children in the process. Members demanded and succeeded in getting the CC to reconvene and review its assessment. When the CC reconvened on August 26, extensive debate was followed by the sobering conclusion enunciated by chairman Maurice Bishop and noteworthy for its effect on the course of subsequent events. He said, in concluding, "We are faced with the threat of disintegration."[43] Jorge Heine, Gordon Lewis,[44] and others have argued in effect that the revolution was going well in 1983 and that elements in the CC argued that it was doing badly so as to promote their solution of joint leadership, effectively to elevate Coard and demote Bishop. This argument is predicated on the notion that Grenada had recently obtained IMF loans, many of the infrastructural programs were advancing, and when the Point Salines airport was completed, it would have led to significant improvements in the country's economy. This assessment is largely true, though it misses the effects of the international economic downturn of 1982–83 and the resultant fallout of loans, which even then had started to adversely affect employment. However, the cutting edge of the crisis was not the economy but the effective collapse of the party and the implications therein for the collapse of popular support and the revolutionary base. This was a point understood by the entire leadership and enunciated by Bishop, above all. It required creative solutions, but the one that was eventually sought was fatally flawed, exacerbated the latent tension between the dual logics of the party and of the leader, and eventually contributed to the catastrophe of October 1983.

The Joint Leadership Debates

On September 16, 1983, the Central Committee of the NJM reconvened to consider the crisis that, under the chairmanship of Maurice Bishop, it had previously recognized in August. Liam "Owusu" James started the meeting by criticizing Maurice's leadership style and calling for a new model of joint leadership, marrying the qualities of the two men, Coard and Bishop. Unlike in the earlier meeting, there was no unanimity. After much discussion, nine voted in favor; Bishop, Unison Whiteman, and Hudson Austin, who had arrived late, abstained; and George Louison voted against.[45] Bishop was obviously wavering and expressed the view that the masses might interpret this as a power struggle in the revolution. Despite the vote, however, he was asked for time and granted it to consider the implications. Nine crucial days elapsed until the party general meeting on September 25. What happened in that period is difficult to piece together. I recall being asked seemingly out of the blue by two party comrades in the corridors of the Ministry of Mobilization on Lucas Street what I thought were the qualities of a leader. I found it odd and do not recall what my answer was, except that they seemed pleased with whatever it was I had said. I was preparing to head back to Jamaica at the time of the full party meeting on September 25 and recall hearing from my house next to the St. George's lagoon muffled sounds from the gathering farther up the hill in Butler House.

The meeting itself appeared to be a decisive turning point. Bishop at first expressed his reservations, couched in the notion that there was a distinction between the Party's Leninist perceptions of what a leader should be and that of the masses, who, he argued, tended to build up a cult around a single individual. In this, he was expressing in his way the tension between the two logics of the party and of the leader. Then member after member spoke from the floor, overwhelmingly expressing support for joint leadership, but also love and respect for Bishop and Coard. Maurice was clearly overwhelmed and conceded to the views of the majority. The meeting ended with embraces between the two now joint leaders and the singing of "The Internationale." Later, members of the CC gathered at Maurice's house for what seemed like completely convivial drinks and reflection.[46]

It is important to pause for a moment and take stock of the events up to this point. Only Louison and Whiteman aside from Maurice Bishop on the CC had expressed reservations about the policy of joint leadership. The party members were overwhelmingly in favor, and Bishop himself was genuinely swayed by the show of solidarity. Had he not been scheduled to travel the next day to Hungary with both Whiteman and Louison—the two leaders most opposed to the proposal—as part of his entourage, things might have turned out differently. I am certain that both worked to convince him that he should change his mind. However, the decisive moments occurred on his way back from Hungary, when the plane stopped over unexpectedly in Cuba. Maurice met with Fidel Castro, and something emerged from that meeting that changed the mood entirely. Bishop's personal security chief, Cletus St. Paul, is reputed to have called Grenada and threatened the overall head of security that blood would flow on their October 8 return.[47] In response to this ominous threat, Coard did not go to the airport to meet Bishop, as was the custom, and indeed did not see him for four crucial intervening days.

Then on October 12 rumor hit the street that Phyllis Coard and Bernard[48] (in that order) were trying to kill Bishop, heightening tensions and leading to the first physical clash when a militia group in Bishop's community, St. Paul's, sought to mobilize in defense of their leader and one member was shot. When the party, now in full emergency mode, met on October 13 to consider the source of this damaging rumor, Bishop denied knowing anything about it. He was immediately followed on the floor by Errol George, the second person in his security unit, who testified that the rumor had been given to him by none other than Bishop himself. When asked to respond to George's report, Maurice refused to answer. There was deep emotional distress, and many comrades started to cry.[49] It was at this moment on October 13 when the integument between Maurice and the party was severed. From that point onward, the overwhelming majority of the vanguard were convinced that their adored if still only human leader, who had despite his reservations stuck with the party over its desire to improve the profile and substance of leadership, had betrayed them in the worst possible way. Not only had he seemed to be retreating from the joint leadership agreement, but he had opened the door to division and actually caused bloodshed by what they perceived to be his dangerous and unprecedented rumormongering. This is the setting within which the CC took the precipitous measure of detaining Bishop, which brought the inner party conflict—without any prior warning—to the people for the first time and rang the death knell of the revolution. The critical factor at this juncture, I underline once more, is not the overwhelming support of the masses for Bishop; this was a relative constant throughout the process. He was the leader and was revered then as he is in death today by many Grenadians of a certain age and beyond. Who, after all, to the man in the street, were these interlopers who were mere shadows in the wake of the great leader? What is critically new is the unity that now prevailed in the party and by extension the PRA, whose officer corps was composed almost entirely of party members and candidates. Without the people, the NJM could not rule, but Maurice equally could not easily assume power in the face of a fully mobilized PRA and a party convinced that he had betrayed their trust by reneging on his own solemn commitment of September 25. This is what I have referred to as the "gridlock of events"[50] with each in its own moment contributing to a traffic jam of consequences, leading beyond these to his release on October 19, the decision to capture the fort, the clash with the troops sent to retake it, the capture of Maurice and his small contingent, and then their bloody execution.

Conclusion

To attempt, therefore, to move beyond conventional wisdom and try to understand the crisis, I suggest that three critical decisions need to be brought to the fore:

1. *The fatal choice of joint leadership.* Joint leadership was not something entirely alien to Grenadians. Bishop and Unison Whiteman had been joint leaders when the two movements JEWEL and MAP merged in 1973 to form the NJM. Coard and Bishop were in effect joint leaders, though informally so, at the time of Gairy's overthrow. There were therefore some resonances in recent Grenadian history, but the time for such an approach had been eclipsed by the transformation in Bishop's role and standing after the seizure of power and the very nature of the NJM, which in its mechanical approach to the vanguard severely restricted membership and thus damaged its organic connections with the people. The average Grenadian who revered Maurice but knew little or nothing about the party could not be expected to understand that out of the blue, for no apparent reason, Coard was now to be elevated to equal rank with Bishop. This, some have argued disingenuously, was an internal party matter and did not affect the profile of the state. Such a fine distinction could only be expected from persons who were fully aware of the party and its relationship to the state, and this was by definition only known to senior party members. In the end, the perception

was inevitable that Coard was being promoted, while Bishop's sole leadership of both party and state was being reduced.

2. *Reneging on joint leadership.* Those responsible for opening up suspicions and hostilities on the trip to Hungary and on the way back in Cuba must take their full share of the blame. Whether it was Fidel Castro, George Louison, or Unison Whiteman, or all three and others unnamed, the question, in retrospect, must be asked: what were they thinking? Anyone who attended or was given reports of the September 25 meeting, the show of solidarity and the sense of relief when Bishop consented to the sentiments of the majority, should have thought twice about the implications of convincing Maurice to renege on his initial agreement. This could only have been met by hostility and the closing of ranks, which is exactly what eventually happened. Was the plan to execute a military coup with the support of Cuban construction worker and militia-trained contingents, as Ventour and Coard,[51] writing from behind bars, intimate? This is a possibility, but would a seasoned tactician like Fidel Castro and the other members of the Cuban leadership have advised Bishop to resist the agreement on joint leadership if they knew exactly how united and determined the party was at this moment? I suspect not, supported by the fact that at best lightly armed Cuban construction workers would have been heavily outgunned by the PRA with their artillery, light armored vehicles (BTRs), and heavy machine guns. The only feasible context for a military victory by Maurice, supported by the Cubans, over the Central Committee would be a situation where the party was divided and a significant section of its members and their comrades in the military had supported or been won over to Bishop's side, and this was never the case. One distinct possibility, then, is that Whiteman and Louison convinced the Cuban leadership that the party was an insignificant force or that support among its membership, and crucially in the military, was split. This is a consideration, as it would have been a means of boosting their own image, when the alternative point is argued that they had no support whatsoever in the party beyond their own small contingent. I return to this argument in the postscript.

3. *The decision to hold power after the popular rebellion.* The CC had one final option when they became aware that the crowd had freed Maurice from house arrest. They could have called it a day. Indeed, Bernard Coard had made it clear that he was packing and preparing to leave. This would effectively have ended NJM rule in Grenada, though whether Bishop would have been able to piece together a new party

and resume power in the fluid situation in which the United States had already begun to mobilize its assets in and around Grenada is moot. It might, however, have avoided the worst possible outcome, the terrible events on Fort Rupert. Had Maurice headed to the Market Square, mobilized a general strike, cut off power, and called for the resignation of the entire leadership, this new Maurice without the party might have had a fighting chance to succeed. But when the crowd headed for the fort, entered the compound, stripped female soldiers of their clothes and weapons, and threatened NJM members present, the die was cast for a military confrontation.

Over the past thirty years, I have thought long and hard about the Grenada Revolution, about my time in that wonderful little island, and about those sad and tragic days of October. I stand in utter revulsion of the all too real image of soldiers putting Maurice Bishop, Jacqueline Creft, Fitzroy Bain, Norris Bain, and their supporters up against the wall and riddling them with bullets. Whether Maurice's supporters had fired first and were responsible for the deaths of the four soldiers who were killed in the approaching BTRs or not, all conventions of war assert that combatants, once hostilities have ceased, have the right to be treated humanely. The execution of Maurice Bishop thus put the final nail in the coffin of the Grenadian Revolution. The U.S. invasion, despite the fierce resistance from the PRA and elements of the militia,[52] was its inevitable reprise. The story of what happened, however, is still to be fully told, and as a partial result, what I consider to be old misunderstandings keep recurring. I have tried to address these and to rethink and restate what I know to the best of my ability for a new generation and a completely different world.

Postscript: The Turn to Fort Rupert

Much has been made by the many commentators on the events of October 19, including myself on the crowd's decision on the way to the Market Square to turn toward Fort Rupert.[53] The common wisdom as intimated here is that had Maurice and the group who freed him gone to the square to meet the very large throng waiting there, he would have lived. The military would have found it difficult to fire on an unarmed crowd, as was the case when they had come to force his release only moments before at his home in Mt. Wheldale. From this tactical place amid his natural mass support base, he would have been able to follow a variety of tactics, including, most potently, calling for a general strike, as was the case against Gairy in 1974. Why the decision to confront the military by going to the fort? Did Bishop, Vince Noel, Unison Whiteman, Einstein Louison, and the others who led the group (Einstein in particular, George's brother and the only senior PRA officer to break with the CC) expect that the show of popular force would divide the army and give them at least a fighting chance of success? If this were the case, the tactics followed once the fort was occupied should surely have been aimed at appeasement, discussion, and an attempt to win over potential converts who were wavering among the troops, militia, and party cadres who were present. Instead the opposite was the case. Soldiers were forcibly disarmed, female soldiers in particular were treated badly, and at least two were stripped.[54] Party comrades who were present were forced to lie prostrate and were told that they would soon be "dealt with." Meanwhile a small contingent of armed men led by his press secretary Don Rojas had traveled the short distance to Grentel, the telephone company located on the Carenage, and gave instructions that all telephone lines to the homes of CC members and the other St. George's military installation at Fort Frederick be cut.

This is powerful evidence to suggest that Bishop and his closest supporters had made the clear decision that a military solution was the only possibility. The implications of this are clear. The party and PRA in turn were fully aware of the events on the fort, and it was now a matter of survival. Having conceded to the crowd at Mt. Wheldale, they were unlikely to concede again, as in their minds it was a matter of life and death. But did Maurice genuinely think that a largely untrained group of people off the streets of St. George's could bring the small but reasonably well-trained PRA, with its BTRs and light artillery, to its knees? Bernard Coard and John Ventour, writing from their time in prison, suggest that at this stage Bishop and his supporters were depending on Cuban support. The some eight hundred Cuban construction workers—a sizable counterforce by any measure—in typical Cuban fashion were all trained militia and were prepared to be mobilized into a battalion led by Cuban officers who were present in Grenada to train the PRA. If, indeed, the Bishop-led group expected such a force to rally to their side, then it would explain not only the turn to the fort but also the uncompromising behavior once it was occupied. It might also explain the fact that once crowds had started to come on to the streets before October 19 and the CC sought to negotiate terms with Unison Whiteman, they were met with the sole response "no compromise."[55] So why in the end didn't the Cubans mobilize? I suspect, to return to a point made earlier in the chapter, that whatever discussions occurred in Cuba (vehemently denied with regard to any Cuban participation by the Cubans to this day) were predicated on a split party, or at minimum a split army. The Cubans understood that the united PRA was a small but committed force and certainly a match for a lightly armed Cuban militia. The likelihood of the decimation of their own units when it was known that they would face the PRA at full strength would have given the Cubans pause, thus settling the balance of military forces for the tragedy that was about to unfold.

Notes

This paper is dedicated to Richard Hart, in honor of his indomitable spirit and lifelong struggle on behalf of the working people of the Caribbean at home and abroad; and for being one of the few voices to mine below the surface in seeking to understand the reasons for the fall of the Grenada Revolution. An earlier version was published in *Caribbean Political Activism: Essays in Honor of Richard Hart*, ed. Rupert Lewis (Kingston and Miami: Ian Randle, 2012), 199–226.

1. I use Hayek's epigraph somewhat ironically, as I am critical of much of his argument, justifying continued hierarchies based on wealth and property. And yet, having taught *The Constitution of Liberty* for the better part of two decades, the constant, critical engagement with his work suggests that we have much to learn from his assertion that voices of difference and opposition need to be heard and there can be no genuine progression of ideas without dissent. Thus the epigraph, in which he is making a case for the reaffirmation of liberal principles, is entirely appropriate, though deployed here to different purposes than he might have been comfortable with. Friedrich Hayek, *The Constitution of Liberty* (London: Routledge, 1990), 1.

2. Under the leadership of Professor Alissa Trotz of the University of Toronto's Caribbean Studies Program, a remarkable series of events were hosted in October 2008, among them an audiovisual presentation by Shalini Puri, "Operation Urgent Memory: The Grenada Revolution and the U.S. Invasion Twenty-five Years Later"; a lecture by Brian Meeks, "Pan-Caribbean Futures Twenty-five Years after Grenada"; and two cultural presentations reflecting on the Grenada Revolution, one at the University of Toronto and the other at the Jamaican Canadian Association building, featuring the writers Merle Collins, Jacob Ross, and Dionne Brand, among others.

3. See Rupert Roopnaraine, "Resonances of Revolution: Grenada, Suriname, Guyana," paper presented at the colloquium "Remembering the Future: The Legacies of Radical Politics in the Caribbean," Center for Latin American and Caribbean Studies, Pittsburgh University, April 3–4, 2009.

4. "Thirty Years Later: The Regional Legacy of the Grenada Revolution," Caribbean Studies Association Thirty-fourth Annual Conference, Kingston, June 1–5, 2009, 50.

5. See Wendy C. Grenade, *Beyond the Legal Chapter: An Opportunity for Rebirth*, e-mail courtesy the author.

6. See Patsy Lewis, "Grenadian Reflections," *Stabroek News*, www.stabroeknews.com September 14, 2009.

7. Randal Robinson, "Forgiveness Day?" *Stabroek News*, www.stabroeknews.com, September 14, 2009.

8. See Jorge Heine, "The Return of Bernard Coard," *Jamaica Gleaner Online*, http://gleaner-ja.com.

9. Ibid.

10. Ibid.

11. Roopnaraine 2009, 14.

12. Brian Meeks, *Caribbean Revolutions and Revolutionary Theory: An Assessment of Cuba, Nicaragua, and Grenada*, Warwick University Series (London and Basingstoke: Macmillan, 1992), 172.

13. Ibid., 155.

14. See Fidel Castro, *Nothing Can Stop the Course of History: Interview by Jeffrey M. Elliot and Mervyn M. Dymally* (New York: Pathfinder, 1986).

15. See Maurice Bishop, "Maurice Bishop Speaks to U.S. Working People, June 5, 1983," in *Maurice Bishop Speaks: The Grenada Revolution, 1979–1983* (New York: Pathfinder, 1983), 287–312.

16. I owe many thanks to the late Jamaican prime minister Michael Manley, who in his very generous speech at the launch of my 1992 book on Cuba, Nicaragua, and Grenada made the mild critique that he would have wished for more of my personal narrative as a "participant" in the historical record. This paper attempts in part to redress that earlier failure.

17. Robert "Bobby" Clarke, "Statement on Grenada by Robert 'Bobby' Clarke," e-mail document, October 14, 2009.

18. See Castro 1986.

19. See Meeks 1992, 169–70.

20. See Meeks 1992, interview with George Louison, 170.

21. Clarke 2009, 4.

22. Ibid.

23. Ibid.

24. For somewhat different approaches to this period, see Perry Mars, *Ideology and Change: The Transformation of the Caribbean Left* (Wayne State University Press and the Press, University of the West Indies, Barbados, Jamaica, Trinidad and Tobago, 1998); and Brian Meeks, *Radical Caribbean: From Black Power to Abu Bakr* (The Press, University of the West Indies, 1996).

25. The WLL was the pre-party organization that became the Workers Party of Jamaica (WPJ) in 1978.

26. See Departments of State and Defense, *The Grenada Documents: An Overview and Selection* (Washington, DC, 1984); and Paul Seabury and Walter A. McDougall, eds., *The Grenada Papers: The Inside Story of the Grenadian Revolution and the Making of a Totalitarian State—as Told in Captured Documents* (San Francisco: Institute for Contemporary Studies, 1984).

27. See Brian Meeks, "Social Formation and People's Revolution: A Grenadian Study" (Ph.D. thesis, University of the West Indies, 1988).

28. See Meeks 1988, which seeks to understand long term instability as a peculiar feature of the Grenadian "social formation."

29. I borrow this turn of phrase from George Lamming's reflections on the 1983 crisis. See George Lamming, "The Plantation Mongrel," in *Conversations: Essays, Addresses, and Interviews, 1953–1990*, ed. Richard Drayton and Andaiye (London: Karia Press, 1992), 248.

30. This was expressed most vividly in the infamous "Line of March of the Party" speech delivered by Bishop himself (see United States Departments of State and Defense 1984).

31. See Meeks 1988, esp. chap. 3, "The Revolutionary Situation."

32. See Meeks 1992 for a more detailed discussion of the transformation to a vanguard party and some of the resulting political effects.

33. See Meeks 1988, 485–86.

34. For an account of the relationship, see John Walton Cottman, *The Gorrion Tree: Cuba and the Grenada Revolution* (New York: Peter Lang, 1993).

35. For a discussion, see Frederic Pryor, *Revolutionary Grenada: A Study in Political Economy* (New York: Praeger, 1986), 63–64.

36. Dov Zakheim, "The Grenada Operation and Superpower Relations: A Perspective from the Pentagon," in *Soviet/Cuban Strategy in the Third World after Grenada: Toward Prevention of Future Grenadas; A Conference Report*, ed. Jiri Valenta and Herbert J. Ellison (Washington, DC: Kennan Institute for Advanced Russian Studies and the Wilson Center, 1984), 21.

37. "Minutes of Extraordinary Meeting of the Central Committee, NJM, 12–15 October 1983," in United States Departments of State and Defense 1984, 105–1.

38. See Meeks 1992, 177–78.

39. Ibid., 173.

40. See "TAWU Balance of Forces Assessment, August 19, 1983," in Meeks 1988, 460.

41. The primary text, in the absence of easily available histories of Grenada, was the EPICA task force book in celebration of the revolution. See EPICA Task Force, *Grenada: The Peaceful Revolution*, ed. Cathy Sunshine (Washington, DC: EPICA, 1982).

42. See Meeks 1988, 462–63.

43. "Minutes of Emergency Meeting of Central Committee, NJM, 26 August 1983," United States Departments of State and Defense 1984, 111–11.

44. See Gordon Lewis, *Grenada: The Jewel Despoiled* (Baltimore: Johns Hopkins University Press, 1987).

45. See Meeks 1988, 473.

46. Ibid., 485.

47. Ibid., 488.

48. Richard Hart, *The Grenada Revolution: Setting the Record Straight*, Socialist History Society (SHS) Occasional Paper No. 20 (United Kingdom, 2005), 39.

49. Meeks 1988, 493.

50. Meeks 1992, 176.

51. See John "Chalky" Ventour, *October 1983: The Missing Link* (self-published, 1999); and Bernard Coard, *Summary Analysis of the October 1983 Catastrophe in Grenada* (self-published, 2002).

52. Maurice Paterson's self-published book is still the best source about the real extent of Grenadians' involvement in defending their small island despite the political catastrophe

that had occurred in the days before the invasion. It belies the myth of a Cuban resistance and asserts unquestionably the agency of Grenadians acting in defense on their soil. Maurice Patterson, *Big Sky, Little Bullet: A Docu-Novel* (St. George's, Grenada: Maurice Paterson, 1992).

53. See, e.g., Hart 2005, 40–42; Lewis 1983, 53–55.
54. See Coard 2002, 68.
55. Ibid., 62.

References

Bishop, M. 1983. "Maurice Bishop Speaks to U.S. Working People, June 5, 1983." In *Maurice Bishop Speaks: The Grenada Revolution, 1979–1983*, 287–312. New York: Pathfinder Press.
Castro, F. 1986. *Nothing Can Stop the Course of History: Interview by Jeffrey M. Elliot and Mervyn M. Dymally*. New York: Pathfinder.
Clarke, R. 2009. "Statement on Grenada by Robert 'Bobby' Clarke." E-mail, October 14.
Coard, B. 2002. "Summary Analysis of the October 1983 Catastrophe in Grenada." Unpublished manuscript. St. George's, Grenada.
Cottman, J. W. 1993. *The Gorrion Tree: Cuba and the Grenada Revolution*. New York: Peter Lang.
EPICA Task Force. 1982. *Grenada: The Peaceful Revolution*. Ed. Cathy Sunshine. Washington, DC: EPICA.
Grenade, W. C. 2009. "Beyond the Legal Chapter: An Opportunity for Rebirth in Grenada." *Grenada Today*, September 19.
Hart, R. 2005. *The Grenada Revolution: Setting the Record Straight*. Socialist History Society (SHS) Occasional Paper No. 20. United Kingdom.
Hayek, F. 1990. *The Constitution of Liberty*. London: Routledge.
Heine, J. 2009. "The Return of Bernard Coard." *Jamaica Gleaner Online*, September. http://gleaner-ja.com.
Lamming, G. 1992. "The Plantation Mongrel." In *Conversations: Essays, Addresses, and Interviews, 1953–1990*, ed. Richard Drayton and Andaiye. London: Karia Press.
Lewis, G. 1987. *Grenada: The Jewel Despoiled*. Baltimore: Johns Hopkins University Press.
Lewis, P. 2009. "Grenadian Reflections." *Stabroek News*, September 14. http://www.stabroeknews.com.
Mars, P. 1998. *Ideology and Change: The Transformation of the Caribbean Left*. Michigan: Wayne State University Press.
Meeks, B. 1988. "Social Formation and People's Revolution: A Grenadian Study." Ph.D. thesis, University of the West Indies.
———. 1992. *Caribbean Revolutions and Revolutionary Theory: An Assessment of Cuba, Nicaragua, and Grenada*. Warwick University Series. London: Macmillan.
———. 1996. *Radical Caribbean: From Black Power to Abu Bakr*. Barbados, Jamaica, and Trinidad and Tobago: The Press, University of the West Indies.

Patterson, M. *Big Sky, Little Bullet: A Docu-Novel*. St. George's, Grenada: Maurice Paterson, 1992.

Pryor, F. 1986. *Revolutionary Grenada: A Study in Political Economy*. New York: Praeger.

Robinson, R. 2009. "Forgiveness Day?" *Stabroek News*, September 14. http://www.sta broeknews.com.

Roopnaraine, R. 2009. "Resonances of Revolution: Grenada, Suriname, Guyana." Paper presented at the colloquium "Remembering the Future: The Legacies of Radical Politics in the Caribbean." Center for Latin American and Caribbean Studies, University of Pittsburgh, April 3–4.

Seabury, P., and W. A. McDougall, eds. 1984. *The Grenada Papers: The Inside Story of the Grenadian Revolution and the Making of a Totalitarian State—as Told in Captured Documents*. San Francisco: Institute for Contemporary Studies.

United States Departments of State and Defense. 1984. *The Grenada Documents: An Overview and Selection*. Washington, DC: U.S. Defense Intelligence Agency.

Ventour, J. 1999. *October 1983: The Missing Link*. Self-published. St. George's, Grenada.

Zakheim, D. 1984. "The Grenada Operation and Superpower Relations: A Perspective from the Pentagon." In *Soviet/Cuban Strategy in the Third World after Grenada: Toward Prevention of Future Grenadas; A Conference Report*, ed. Jiri Valenta and Herbert J. Ellison. Washington, DC: Kennan Institute for Advanced Russian Studies and the Wilson Center.

6. Remembering October 19: Reconstructing a Conversation with a Young Female NJM Candidate Member about Her Recollections of October 19, 1983

Patsy Lewis

"Remembering October 19" presents a narrative account of the tragic events of October 19 that led to the killing of Grenada's prime minister Maurice Bishop and key members of his cabinet. It seeks to re-create the events of the day through the eyes of a junior member of the New Jewel Movement who had been summoned to Fort Rupert (now Fort George) along with other members of the NJM. The narrative is based on an actual interview with a young woman in her mid-twenties a year after the tragedy. This form of storytelling was chosen to present her interview to protect her identity and also to re-create the mood on Fort Rupert that day. The piece is written from the perspective of the interviewee but shifts in the last paragraph to the perspective of the interviewer, who provides the reader with some insight into her responses to the interview.

Remembering October 19

I went to Fort Rupert in answer to a call that all members of the party should gather at Fort Rupert. Maurice was under house arrest, the people were restless, demanding his release from detention, and schoolchildren were leading demonstrations throughout the streets of St. George's and Grenville, evoking uncomfortable parallels of demonstrations in 1974 against Gairy. There was talk of freeing Maurice from house arrest.

I arrived at the fort. Our purpose there wasn't really clear. We expected to meet with senior members of the party [to be] told how we should address the unrest and clamor for Maurice's release. Our attempts over the last few days, since his house arrest, were demoralizing, to say the least. People who formerly greeted us were openly hostile, virtually chasing us from their doors, closing their ears against anything we had to say: about Maurice's recalcitrance, or the rightness of the party's position in calling for joint leadership and our disappointment with Maurice's duplicity in the matter, and why we felt we could no longer trust him at the head of our revolution. People had laughed with open derision when my boyfriend pointed out Maurice's weakness for women, exhibited in ways that harmed the revolution. And do you remember Hog, who used to be in the Pioneers? Well, his mother chased us away, saying she didn't want to hear anything [from] us and that invasion or no invasion, her son wasn't going to fight for Coard. All she wanted to hear was when we planned to release Maurice and reinstate him as the rightful head of the country.

We were basically milling around the fort, trying to find shade from the midday heat, keeping our ears glued to the radio; Radio Free Grenada, to be exact, listening for developments. Through sketchy details from the radio, fleshed out by news from comrades coming to join us, we learned that the demonstrations and calls for Maurice's release had not abated but had swelled to a massive crowd in the Market Square, demanding his release. Details coming to us from the PRA headquarters at Fort Frederick informed us that the worst had happened: the masses had freed Comrade Bishop. We debated among ourselves the madness that had overcome the masses in refusing to listen to the party leaders, who were, after all, the true leaders of the revolution. A few of us dared ask the inevitable question everyone was shying away from: if Comrade Bishop was prepared to take to the streets and seek to take over the process because of his mass support, how should we deal with him? While we were contemplating this, we heard reports that senior party members who had contacted a cabinet minister, formerly dear to our hearts, but now firmly in Maurice's camp, had rejected their offer of a return to the status quo ante. His retort was something to the effect that "we have the masses on our side now and they would deal with you counters."

We heard a commotion at the bottom of the fort, where the entrance was located. We were located at the top of the fort, some of us in front of the administrative offices, others one level up on the parade square. We had been able to hear the sounds of the demonstrators around the town and Tanteen, as well as the clamor of the crowd restless in the Market Square, but we noted that the sounds appeared to be getting nearer to us. This culminated in a cheering and roaring at the guard post at the entrance to the fort. Before we could figure out what was happening, a jubilant crowd, hostile in its jubilance, poured up the fort. At the head of the [crowd] was Comrade Bishop, supported by members of the crowd, looking at once weak, victorious, and confused. But what really caught my attention and stopped me in my tracks were the placards being held aloft by a few members of the crowd, praising the United States and calling for an end to Communist rule in Grenada.

I saw Major Concord coming toward us. He was armed. To my horror, it became clear that many of the people around him and Maurice were also armed. They were walking toward the soldiers on the fort and demanding that they hand over their rifles. As nothing in their training had prepared them for such a situation, and in the face of Major Concord's insistence that they turn over their weapons and in the absence of alternative instructions, they surrendered their weapons, looking in bewilderment at the people they were sworn to defend, now jeering at them.

Major Concord approached the comrades with a great degree of hostility and menace. Turning his weapon on us all the time, he gathered us together and herded us onto the Parade Square. He castigated us for our betrayal of the "maximum leader" and, pointing his weapons directly at us, told us he was going to "deal" with us. The crowd roared its approval.

It was clear at that point who was in control, and it was not the party. We looked at one another fearfully. I, for one, was scared, in the face of the hostility of the "masses" never before leveled in my direction, and its embodiment in the person of Major Concord. I thought about the two-month-old fetus in my stomach and yearned for life, for motherhood, and all the experiences of life that at twenty-one I was about to be denied. The explosion of rifle fire was followed by the deafening sound of an explosion. I fell flat on my pregnant stomach, my eyes tightly shut, convinced that my death had come. The explosions were followed by the roar of a BTR rapidly ascending the hill. Moments later, still unsure what was happening, but still clearly alive, we saw two soldiers emerge from the tunnel linking the bottom (command) to the parade square. Their faces, as they approached, showed none of the hostility that we had so recently encountered. As with Major Concord, they were also well known to us. They addressed us with "Comrades, you are okay now. You have nothing to fear. We are back in control."

We were sobbing with relief. But I felt another feeling: cold hatred. I had been made to see my life flash before me. I had never contemplated that things would have reached the stage of mere civilians, led by my hitherto beloved leader, for whom, up to that point, I had felt more bewilderment and disappointment, disarming our soldiers and threatening our lives. I had never expected to replace Yankee imperialism and mercenary soldiers, with him, as the enemy. When I saw them leading Maurice, Jackie, Fitzroy, Norris, Bullen, and others I don't care to remember, to the wall ringing the parade square, I felt a deadening coldness. Their time had come to experience what they had planned for us. They were dying instead of me. I may yet see my child born. That is why I felt absolutely no pity when I heard Jacqui, so familiar and well loved to me, pleading for the life of her unborn child. Her pleas unmoved me. The others looked at our soldiers, saying, "Comrades, you really don't mean to kill us, do you?" evoking the meaning of the revolution. Their disbelief that this could really be happening after their own threats to us. They had taken serious business and turned it into child's play. In response, two of the soldiers retrieved Sgt. Mayers's body from the bottom of the fort where he had been shot down by a member of the crowd, and laid it in front of them. The soldier in command said, "This is what you did to our brother. You deserve nothing less. Your judgment will be as short and swift." The rifles barked in unison. The bodies crumpled to the floor. The square, where I had learned drills, a child playing at an adult's game, covered in rivulets of glistening bright blood, swiftly congealing and darkening in the midday sun.

Party comrades were asked to take the bodies away. I did not assist in this. This was done by the men. The women, myself included, cleaned. We used the fire hoses to wash the blood and specks of flesh down: to make the parade square pristine once more, doing this carefully and swiftly, depriving the ever-hovering flies of a meal. We did a good job. We got rid of most of the evidence of what had taken place there that day: that is, except for the memory that clings to the inner recesses of our collective minds and souls like the pungent, nauseating smell of freshly shed blood that the disinfectant poured by the women on Fort Rupert that day could not overcome. And this memory, forever associated with its smell of carnage, emerges at the oddest of times, sometimes fleeting, sometimes overpowering with the grief and sheer bewilderment that it evokes.

She told me this while nursing her three-month-old baby. She told me all of this without a show of emotion, punctuating her flow of memories with a reassuring word to her baby, pausing long enough to rock and kiss him. At that moment, I felt that something had happened in my country's life that had made me alien. I could not imagine the trauma that would have rendered my friend so impervious then, and nearly a year later, to the human tragedy that she had witnessed. I realized then that the story was complex, not to be easily reduced to the stark, unambiguous colors of domino pieces, slapped down on makeshift tables with such resolve, by old and young men outside rum shops from Grenville to St. George's on lazy uncomplicated Friday and Saturday nights.

PART III

Theoretical Critiques of the Grenada Revolution and Lessons for the Future

7. Grenada: Noncapitalist Path and the Derailment of a Social Democratic Revolution

Hilbourne A. Watson

When the Grenada Revolution collapsed in October 1983, a predictable outpouring of reactions erupted from the U.S. state, Commonwealth Caribbean governments, and many trade unionists, media sources, academics, and pundits to the effect that the implosion resulted from a power grab by an authoritarian, antidemocratic, Marxist-Leninist cabal within the New Jewel Movement (NJM) and People's Revolutionary Government (PRG).[1] The dominant theme was and remains that Marxism-Leninism is alien to the democratic institutions that Commonwealth Caribbean societies like Grenada inherited from the British. The *Trinidad and Tobago Express* (Monday, December 14, 2009) claimed that the PRG regime in October 1983 "turned its back on hundreds of years of democratic traditions that had grown up all across the Caribbean." In fact, "democratic traditions" do not have a history of "three hundred years" (ibid.) in the world, including the British West Indies (BWI). From enslavement and indenture, continuing through decolonization and independence, the majority was forced to fight for basic human rights while resisting relentless attempts to commoditize their existence to maintain commodity production for the ends of private capitalist accumulation, which rests on reproducing substantive inequality.

The forms of representative government that resulted from anticolonial struggles were concessions that were extracted from the exploitative and oppressive ruling classes who did as much as possible to ensure that the rights conceded were largely beyond social demand and without social content. Thus they canalized the struggles of oppressed and exploited toilers into footpaths of control to render them compatible with the economic and political interests of the ruling power blocs. Representative government is best understood as a means to an end, as it is impossible to secure freedom from necessity—the operation of the law of value—where the separation of politics from economics is the norm. The high point of representative democracy (Meeks 2000, 170, 171) was social democracy, which the ruling blocs never quite embraced and did not stop until they replaced it with neoliberalism as a project for the restoration of capitalist class power (Harvey 2005).

Authoritarianism is a deeply rooted ruling-class norm that dates back to precapitalist Europe and was preserved in classical liberalism and mercantile (commercial) capitalism (Wood 1995), and it also took firm root in the political institutions and cultural life in Caribbean colonial and postcolonial societies (Bolland 2001). Authoritarianism is covered over in the tracks of liberalism and representative democracy, which treat power as organic rather than a product of the contradictory social relations in capitalist societies. Constitutional and other juridical provisions are built on "despotic power" or "power over society" that girds state power in modern societies (Agnew 2009, 3).

Liberal (capitalist) societies employ decency—repressive tolerance—to smooth out the rough edges of authoritarianism and treat as natural occurrences the separation of economics from politics, the state from civil society, and the individual from society. The persistence of authoritarianism in BWI colonial and postcolonial societies operates through patriarchy, which girds the organization and exercise of state power, party politics, the trade union and working-class movements, the capital–wage labor relation at the point of production, and civil (class) society via religion, family life, and nationalism. Authoritarianism thus effectively conditions the forms of domination, exclusion, and insecurity on which state sovereignty is constructed; however, authoritarianism does not violate the constitutional rules and liberal democratic processes but rather permeates and runs through their arterial system.

I will argue, therefore, that Marxism-Leninism was not the cause of the authoritarianism that featured in the mode of governing that the NJM and PRG[2] instituted; in fact, Marxism-Leninism was of secondary importance in the crisis that overwhelmed the revolutionary experiment in Grenada in 1983. Crisis inheres in the capital relation: under capitalism, the capital–wage labor relation and liberal democratic politics rest on economic compulsion (moment of exploitation) and state domination (moment of coercion) (Wood 1995). Thus all notions of freedom, justice, equality, individual rights, autonomy, and democracy are conditioned by alienation and the juridical right to exploit. Security and order, rather than freedom and justice, are the primary goal of the state under liberal capitalism—both freedom and democracy necessarily form part of a continuous plebiscite in any capitalist society.

The Grenada Revolution unfolded as a significant experiment in radical social democracy; however, it did not become a social revolution with working-class content. Grenada, a very small country of 100,000 people (Jacobs 1979), lacked the means to secure socialism, considering that socialism necessarily rises from foundations of modern capitalism, which means that the prerequisites for securing socialism include modern science and production, skilled and productive labor, industry, finance, and working-class institutions capable of overcoming patriarchy and class and gender inequality for building toward a social revolution. The leaders of the Grenada Revolution created progressive spaces and options to overcome the conditions on which the authoritarian and autocratic regime of Eric Matthew Gairy rested. The NJM adopted certain concepts from Marxism-Leninism and from the Soviet foreign policy theme of the "noncapitalist" approach to national development. The NJM-PRG leaders and cadres drew on Marxism-Leninism during 1983 to explain the Grenada crisis; however, Marxism-Leninism was less important in causal terms because crisis, which inheres in the capital relation, cannot be willed away by rigid interpretations of Marxist-Leninist categories.

In the global context, Grenada during the 1970s and early 1980s faced serious challenges that arose from contradictions associated with the transition from neo-Keynesianism to neoliberalism in international capitalism; however, the NJM-PRG leaders tried to cling to the crumbling edifice of neo-Keynesianism in the face of an aggressive neoliberal capitalism they were not equipped to reverse. The United States viewed the Grenada Revolution as a serpent that had to be decapitated. During colonialism, Grenada functioned as a "grant-in-aid" British colony that depended on British financial subventions to support the colony's annual budget; the preindustrial material culture and productive base of the political economy severely affected Grenada's ability to pursue sustainable domestic and international initiatives; the NJM-PRG encountered setbacks in trying to mobilize international financial and technical resources on a sustainable basis to underwrite the social democratic experiment; the small size and weakness of the working-class base remained an obstacle; Grenada's Commonwealth Caribbean neighbors feared that a successful revolutionary alternative in Grenada might threaten the survival of their regimes; and Cuba's role in the liberation struggles in the Caribbean Basin area was an important Cold War geopolitical factor the regime could not ignore. Substantively, vulnerability and uncertainty stalked the NJM-PRG's revolutionary project.

The NJM-PRG leaders understood from living under Gairy's brutal regime that if democracy was going to become a way of living beyond representative government, they would have to do much more than tinker with representative government to make it "more consistent, meaningful and democratic" (Meeks 2000, 170), because liberal democracy and capitalism form a couplet that severely constrains our ability to realize our full human potential. The PRG turned to Cuba, North Korea, Algeria, Libya, and other sympathetic states and multilateral institutions for loans, grants, and concessional aid to promote and maintain the social democratic experiment while strengthening links with the local capitalists: the noncapitalist path strategy assumed collaboration between capital and the state organized under petit bourgeois leadership.

The Neoliberal International Context

By the early 1970s, the postwar capital accumulation strategy based on neo-Keynesian militarism had run its course. The manifestations of the neo-Keynesian crisis in the Caribbean included the deterioration of primary export prices and rising external indebtedness to which the European Community (EC) responded with the Lomé Convention in 1975 that reinforced the integration of the Africa, Caribbean and Pacific (ACP) countries into the EC political economy. Christopher Layne argues that from "World War II, U.S. strategists . . . conceded that the stability provided by U.S. military engagement abroad is the 'oxygen' without which there could be no economic openness" (C. Layne 2006, 125, 132), on which international capitalism depends. The U.S. state acted as the primary "agent of capital" and constructed "transnational liberalism" to gird the hegemony of its ruling class by strengthening international capitalism and the international migration of its sovereign power (Robinson 2008; Agnew 2005, 2009).

Neoliberalism unfolded with the violent destruction of the social democratic government of Salvador Allende Gossens in Chile in 1973, demonstrating that strengthening representative democracy does not protect a state or society from liberal international violence. Ronald Reagan and Margaret Thatcher brought neoliberalism into the heartland of international capitalism in the early 1980s: during the first decade of neoliberal capitalism, Paul Volker announced that the standard of living of American workers had to decline. The Volker Plan was an important strut for anchoring the Washington Consensus (Holmes 2005, 2–3) on which neoliberalism initially was built. The integration of the People's Republic of China into global capitalism increased the pool of global labor that was put at the disposal of international capital to restructure the international division of labor and the terms of global competitiveness. Revolutionary Grenada clung to a dying neo-Keynesianism in the face of the rising tide of the globalization of high-technology production, which in conjunction with low-wage Asia helped to drive down the global average price of labor power.

Within two years after the NJM-PRG came to power (see E. Layne 2002, 47–83), Ronald Reagan adopted an aggressive strategy and set up the Caribbean Basin Initiative (CBI) as an important strut for anchoring neoliberalism in the Caribbean region. During the early 1980s, the Reagan administration purged the remaining neo-Keynesian influences from the International Monetary Fund (IMF), to bolster neoliberalism, which was designed to restore the class power that capital was forced to cede during the neo-Keynesian moment (Holmes 2005, 4; Harvey 2005). The CBI rested on a three-pronged strategy of extremely limited economic assistance, political subordination, and heavy militarization of the region to provide temporary fixes to the crisis of capitalist accumulation in the United States and abroad.

William Robinson observes: "If neoliberalism was to make the world available to capital it was also necessary to make the world safe for capital" via the production of "more stable modes of political domination and social control. To reestablish . . . capitalist hegemony would require an overhaul of cultural, ideological, and political systems around the world" (Robinson 2008, 273). Militarization, political repression, and an expanded role for the IMF, the World Bank, and the power of the U.S. state via the Federal Reserve, U.S. Department of the Treasury, and Wall Street in the internal affairs of other countries represented elements in the making of a powerful transnational state apparatus to strengthen and expand the rights of capital in neoliberal times (273).

Neoliberalism also emphasized "accumulation by dispossession" via transfers of resources from the public to private sector; shifting a larger portion of the social reproduction burden onto working-class households and communities and away from state and capitalists; broadening the scope of the "informal economy" via austerity programs and imposing structural adjustment programs (SAPs) on certain governments; feminization of labor and deunionization of workers; using outsourcing and subcontracting to depress the average wage; socializing the public debt burden and making it increasingly difficult for workers to make effective demands on the state for social provisions—all ways of strengthening class struggle from above (Robinson 2008, 240–41, 267, 268).

The Making of the 1979–1983 Crisis in Grenada

Bernard Coard highlights the authoritarian tradition in Grenada, arguing that the "armed overthrow" of Gairy in 1979, "by means outside the Constitution," reflected the fact that "Gairy had trampled the Constitution and it was not in force in any case" (Coard 2002, 41; see E. Layne 2002, 91; Singham 1968). Gairy's extraconstitutional rule rested partly on the use of extrajudicial force and violence, electoral fraud, government by fear and fraud, and alienation of private property for his personal accumulation. Jamaica and Guyana granted immediate diplomatic recognition to the NJM-PRG government, and Forbes Burnham sent "military assistance in the form of arms and training officers" (E. Layne 2002, 88). Barbados under Tom Adams recognized the PRG ten days after it took power; however, Adams pleaded with the United States, United Kingdom, Canada, and France to "withhold diplomatic recognition from the new government" to deny the regime international legitimacy (Kellman 2010, 132).

I question the nationalist assertion that the Grenada Revolution marked the "anti-imperialist stage" of the socialist revolution because such a claim relegates the class struggle and exploitation to epiphenomena. The NJM-PRG adopted policies that reinforced the division between politics and economics and separated the national state and society from the global context, implying that without imperialism the path of the revolution would be free of constraints (see Munroe and Rowbotham 1977; Munroe 1983). The imperialism that the NJM-PRG regime had in mind does not equate to the global capitalism of which the Grenada economy remains an integral part. The concept of anti-imperialism rests on a geographically determined false inside-outside dichotomy that loosely conflates empire with hegemony (Agnew 2005) and makes it hard to see that "any particular state necessarily participates in one or several sovereignty regimes that exhibit distinctive combinations of central state authority and territoriality. . . . The emphasis lies in understanding the analytics of power rather than presuming the operations of an undifferentiated territorial sovereignty" (Agnew 2009, 9; see Weber 1995).

I argue that the notion of a "Coard faction," understood as an ultra-left tendency bent on capturing state power to impose its Marxist-Leninist agenda, is misleading, considering that the NJM's Central Committee (CC) minutes for the period of August to October 1983 show that a mere handful of CC members supported Bishop, and the People's Revolutionary Army (PRA) also unanimously opposed Bishop on political grounds. Bishop's key supporters in the CC—George Louison, Fitzroy Bain, and Unison Whiteman among them—often sided with his critics in the party apparatuses. It did not necessarily follow, however, that the overwhelming CC majority did not act in an authoritarian manner in dealing with Bishop's recalcitrance and his disregard for party rules and decisions (Coard 2002).

I will address the main arguments raised earlier, with special attention to the following points: the nature of the capitalist formation in Grenada and the social class structure that developed on and was reproduced through it; the class nature and role of the social transformation strategy, which the NJM leadership dubbed the noncapitalist path; the role of politics and ideology in the relationship between the party, masses, classes, and the state; the unfolding of the crisis and how the party and state leadership responded, bearing in mind that, historically, admixtures of pre- and semi-industrial capitalism and radical populism tend to produce economic and political disaster for the working class; and the role and impact of external forces on the crisis.

The Capitalist Economic and Social Formation in Grenada and the Limits of the Noncapitalist Path Strategy

Richard and Ian Jacobs argue that Grenada's political economy developed as an integral part of the capitalist world economy, from colonial times to independence (1980, 45–71), which contradicts their claim that Grenada met the criteria of the noncapitalist path. In 1979 Grenada's capitalist economic structure remained semi-industrial, with low-technology-based agro-commercial capital dominating the means of production; trade protectionism and the exploitation of market imperfections were typical in production and circulation; the best land was concentrated in the hands of agro-commercial capitalists; the landless rural proletariat exhibited a "dual movement" in which it seemed simultaneously to exhibit peasant and proletarian features (Frucht 1967); fragmentation and extreme parcelization of landholdings were widespread among the small farmers; low labor productivity was tied to the proliferation of primitive techniques of production in agriculture; export production was dominated by primary agricultural commodities, and imports of semifinished and manufactured goods based on capital-intensive techniques put domestic exports at a qualitative disadvantage; and Grenada's structural foreign exchange and balance-of-payments problems were compounded by the lack of a capital market.[3]

Between 1946 and 1951, the agricultural sector was the mainstay of the colony's economy, with a small number of estates accounting for 45.6 percent of total landholdings, or 77,000 acres, and a large number of very small holdings comprising 88.7 percent of all farms. By 1972, the techniques of production available to the small farmers remained rudimentary (Jacobs and Jacobs 1980, 43–48, 143). The small farmers were the mainstay of Grenada's export production, producing around 60 percent of the nutmeg crop, 50 percent of the cocoa, 85 percent of food crops, 30 percent of the bananas, and 93 percent of sugarcane (Ambursley 1983, 196). The growth of tourism contributed to an expansion in construction and real estate; manufacturing remained largely stagnant, and the public sector experienced marginal diversification (193–98).

The dockworkers formed the main organized group within the working class (Ambursley 1983, 199). By 1972 a handful of merchants, hoteliers, and manufacturers were operating in the commercial, tourist, and light manu-facturing sectors (Jacobs and Jacobs 1980, 45–48). The Grenadian proletariat also included an urban working class made up of state employees and oth-ers employed by the private sector mainly in light manufacturing and ser-vices like tourism. Agriculture employed 31 percent of the labor force, and manufacturing and tourism together contributed 33 percent of employment at the end of the 1960s (Jacobs and Jacobs 1980, 50). Until 1974, the "landed aristocracy remained . . . dominant," the state was firmly under the control of the capitalist class, and "non-elected capitalist elements maintained undue influence over the political system." Gairy became a capitalist with member-ship in the Chamber of Commerce and owner of several "self-owned busi-nesses" (46–50). Substantively, Grenada's economic structure was capitalist, which made the claim for the noncapitalist path strategy a convenient move that suited the foreign policy strategy and accumulation requirements of the petite bourgeoisie now in control of the state.

Grenada and the Limits of the Noncapitalist Path Logic and Option

Commonwealth Caribbean scholarship contributed to the debate on the relevance of the noncapitalist theory for the Caribbean (Thomas 1978; Wat-son 1979; Jacobs and Jacobs 1980; Jagan 1980; Ambursley 1983; Munroe and Rowbotham 1977). C. Y. Thomas (1978) offered a critical appraisal of the noncapitalist path doctrine with emphasis on its problematic application to the Caribbean. Jacobs and Jacobs's political and ideological defense of the noncapitalist path strategy as Grenada's route to revolution rests on a weak theoretical and empirical foundation. Cheddi Jagan (1980) and Munroe and Rowbotham (1977) offered opportunistic political support and justification of the noncapitalist path strategy, given the need of their parties for international support for their political programs. The noncapitalist path strategy suggests the need for a period of transition between precapitalism and socialism—a moment said to be neither capitalist nor socialist. Jacobs and Jacobs (1980, 78; Jacobs 1979) insist that the NJM's objectives stated in the 1973 manifesto are extremely similar to the ones outlined by the Soviet scholars Solodovnikov and Bogoslovsky in *Non-capitalist Development: An Historical Outline* (1975). Soviet and other proponents of the noncapitalist path theory attempted to anchor its philosophical premises in the writings of Marx, Engels, and Lenin; however, they mainly arrived at conclusions that are not supported by their analyses.

Jacobs and Jacobs provide an analysis of Grenada's economic reality that does not comport with the historical conditions for which the noncapitalist path theory was designed. The Grenadian capitalist strata supported the NJM strategy primarily because the regime did not threaten capitalist private property, which means that the strategy was built on protecting the right to exploit while drowning the class struggle in ideological torrents about the "masses" and "people." Soviet and other proponents of the noncapitalist path theory imagined an intermediate stage of "socialist orientation" between capitalism and socialism that was expected to lay the foundation for the transition to socialism based on a "long term strategic alliance with the bourgeoisie" (Ambursley and Cohen 1983, 6).

The NJM promised Grenada's capitalists the best of both worlds under the ideological cover of noncapitalist protection and promised to strengthen the economic productive base through infrastructure development, production diversification, and improved access to foreign markets, in addition to projects to protect the capital accumulation base. The capitalist class remained skeptical about the noncapitalist emphasis on the expansion of the state sector, the influence of the "masses" in state policy, and close cooperation with the socialist countries, a concern the NJM sought to allay after capturing state power. The capitalists also benefited from the overthrow of Gairy (Schaap and Schaap 1984) without bloodshed and the right to share state power with the petite bourgeoisie, whose subjective motivation is to join the ranks of the big bourgeoisie by engaging in commodity production and capital accumulation.

The NJM, Working Class, and Revolutionary Strategy

The NJM emerged as a movement of the most disaffected, alienated, and radicalized elements within the ranks of the working-class intelligentsia and petite bourgeoisie. The social origins of the NJM's leaders were predominantly in the professions, the bureaucracy (civil and military), small businesses (merchants and shopkeepers), and medium- and small-scale agriculture. The petit bourgeois orientation of the NJM leadership was reflected in the program of social reform it advanced in its 1973 manifesto and implemented from 1979 to 1983. A series of developments inside and outside Grenada contributed to the radicalization of NJM members. Gairy's running down of the economy, his political victimization and brutal repression of opposition forces, his arbitrary alienation of others' property for his personal accumulation, and his capricious approach to running the government generated contradictions that affected individuals and strata from all classes of the society.

External developments such as the social upheavals that rocked Jamaica in the late 1960s and Trinidad and Tobago in 1970, and the radicalizing influences from the U.S. and Caribbean Black Power movements and other radical black economic empowerment tendencies in the region, helped to radicalize the political consciousness of members of the Grenadian petite bourgeoisie and working class. NJM members founded and participated in organizations like Forum (1970), the Movement for the Advancement of Community Effort (MACE), the Movement for the Assembly of Peoples (MAP), and the Joint Endeavor for Welfare, Education, and Liberation (JEWEL) in 1972. MACE, which identified the need for a mass-based organization to serve as a vehicle for promoting social change, merged with MAP to create JEWEL, which Unison Whiteman founded in rural St. David's parish. JEWEL had as one of its basic objectives the mobilization "of the peasantry and the agro-proletariat in order to undermine Gairy's agro-proletarian base by opposing the contradictions of the Gairy personality, the gap between his words and actions, while . . . providing through the co-operative, an alternative to the programme of patronage that Gairy had been using to ensure support from the underprivileged, underemployed class" (Jacobs and Jacobs 1980, 75, 77). Bernard Coard claims that the Organization for Revolutionary Education and Liberation (OREL) dissolved completely "into NJM years before the March 1979 Revolution" (Coard 2002, 51–52).[4]

JEWEL was effective in mobilizing rural workers and small farmers, including many who had supported Gairy. MAP placed the question of state power on its political agenda with a declaration "to transform the Westminster type state apparatus into one based on more popular control" through "assemblies of the people" (Jacobs and Jacobs 1980, 76). In March 1973, MAP and JEWEL merged as the NJM, espousing an increasingly populist and anti-imperialist agenda, with the acquisition of state power as its political objective. Consistent with its populist outlook, the NJM viewed the rural working class as "peasants" and other groups as "the masses" and "people" rather than as members of social classes. Some NJM leaders were committed to challenging private property; however, their social class origins and objectives "inhibited an unequivocal commitment to scientific socialism" (Jacobs and Jacobs 1980, 82). Maurice Bishop said: "Our party began to develop along Marxist lines in 1974, when we began to study the theory of scientific socialism," which the party also linked to Black Power concepts of black dignity and struggle (Meeks 2000, 161).[5]

According to Jacobs and Jacobs, the NJM strengthened its links with the masses and became "an uncompromising champion of the workers and, for the first time, a reliable institutional link to the organized working class" (1980, 116–17). The NJM 1973 manifesto also drew attention to the political polarization that was developing in Grenadian society.[6] Part of the popular appeal of the NJM came from the insistence that any serious change to Grenada's political impasse had to include a progressive alternative to Gairy.

Politics and Ideology: The NJM, Masses, Classes, and the State

The NJM used the ideological tactic of populism, a tool the petite bourgeoisie routinely employs, to dampen class consciousness and class struggle to broaden and strengthen its popular base. Ernesto Laclau argues that social democratic and radical movements resort to populism "in the presentation of popular domestic interpellation as a synthetic-antagonistic complex with respect to the dominant ideology.... Populism starts at the point where popular democratic elements are presented as an antagonistic option against the ideology of the dominant bloc" (Laclau 1977, 172–73), even as those democratic elements cater to the dominant interests. Populism is routinely employed by classes, fractions, and movements across the left–right political spectrum. The NJM adopted "the ideological complex of which populism is a moment in the articulation of this antagonistic movement within [the] divergent class discourse" (175).

Under its 1973 manifesto, the NJM proposed a new form of government based on "people's assemblies" that would involve the people all the time and assure them of "both their political and their economic rights to ... bring true democracy (under the leadership of) a cross section of society. . . . without regard to favour. . . . It will be made up of representatives of workers and unions, farmers, police, civil servants, nurses, teachers, businessmen, and students. These groups will be consulted in advance and they will choose their own representatives on the government." There were to be four levels of the people's assemblies' structure: village assemblies, parish assemblies, workers' assemblies, and the national assembly (Ambursley 1983, 201). The NJM's notion of a government comprising a cross section of the people rested on four unequally situated classes—the bourgeoisie, petite bourgeoisie, workers, and phantom peasants—with the petite bourgeoisie in control of the state apparatuses. Berch Berberoglu described the state under the PRG as left-wing national state-capitalist under the leadership of "petty bourgeois revolutionary democrats" (Berberoglu 1983, 326, 332). Berberoglu provides an apt description of the Grenadian petit bourgeois forces in power under the NJM-PRG.

The PRG and Capitalist Production Relations: Subsumption of State and Cooperative Sectors under Capitalist Hegemony

The separation of workers from the means of production and the subsumption of labor under capital force members of the working class to sell the only commodity they own—labor power—to have a fighting chance to reproduce themselves at a higher level and improve their standard of living, which requires acquiring and strengthening technical skills, without guarantees. The point here is that the working class is compelled to have its labor power more highly exploited to make progress under capitalism, which also means deepening its subsumption under capital. The PRG exhorted workers to increase their productivity and the nation's productivity by working harder, producing more, and building Grenada (Coard 2002, 21) and to accept wage restraints throughout the economy to guarantee business confidence, good labor relations, and a stable investment climate. The PRG did not appreciate that where the instruments of production belong to capitalists, workers cannot simply increase labor productivity while saddled with low techniques of production. Exhorting the working class to submit to capital amounted to masking the convergence of abstract and concrete labor under the power of private capital, in effect making it more difficult to achieve the social individuality of workers (Blackledge 2012, 11).

From 1979 to 1982, the PRG attempted to increase state revenues by rationalizing the fiscal system by imposing licensing fees on traders and implementing a withholding tax on expatriated profits, with the idea of increasing public-sector recurrent revenues, which increased from EC$53 million (1979) to EC$59 million (1980) and EC$54 million in the first two months of 1981. The "Report on the National Economy" for 1982 and "The Budget Plan for 1983 and Beyond," as presented to the National Conference of Delegates of Mass Organizations, declared: "Because the government is doing so much more work than before, it is also spending a great deal more, and a lot of this money goes to private businesses" (Government of Grenada 1982, 39–40, 42–43).

The PRG promulgated the New Investment Code (NIC) in April 1983 to promote economic growth, with a plan to provide local and foreign capitalists with fiscal incentives. The PRG adamantly opposed any expropriation of private property, declaring that any state acquisition of private property would be based on consultation, negotiation, and adequate compensation to reflect prevailing market value of such properties.

The Marketing and National Importing Board (MNIB), through the state's purchasing of foreign goods, broke the monopoly of the merchants; however, capitalists remained skeptical of PRG promises, exhibiting deep concern over the role of the state in the distributive sector—the traditional domain of the parasitic comprador capitalists. The protests from the capitalists were met by a near capitulation by the PRG. The "Report on the National Economy" mentioned about thirty-two state sector enterprises and projects at various stages of development that received a considerable amount of public investment capital.[7] The PRG raised most of the capital for new public-sector projects from external sources from 1979 to 1983. The airport project at Point Salines was the centerpiece of the PRG's economic expansion program to bolster international tourism, diversify the economy, and enhance foreign exchange earnings, the main beneficiary of which would be the capitalist sector. The airport project consumed 42 percent of the public investment outlays from 1979 to 1983; productive infrastructure in roads and related projects absorbed another 20 percent; other projects accounted for 38 percent. External grants contributed 53 percent; net foreign concessional loans added 18 percent; and institutional sources (IMF) and loans from local banks and insurance companies contributed 27 percent.[8]

Grants and loans from Cuba and Arab sources in 1981 financed the Point Salines airport project. The "Report on the National Economy" (22) shows that of the EC$38.7 million that was spent on the airport project, EC$37.9 million came from those external sources. Grants amounted to EC$27.1 million from the following sources: Algeria ($0.9 million), Syria ($3.2 million), Cuba ($9.2 million in materials and $14.0 million in labor), and Libya, which provided $10.8 million in loans. Less than EC$1 million was raised locally.

In 1980 the PRG created the National Co-operative Development Agency to implement the "idle lands for idle hands" program, for which it allocated EC$1 million to fund the program. Eighteen months later (October 1981), the Ministry of Agriculture, Rural Development, and Cooperatives reported that twelve agricultural co-ops had been set up along with eleven in fishing and handicrafts. Only 146 acres of land and 160 youths were involved (Ambursley 1983, 210). The "Report on the National Economy" mentions that the co-ops were growing slowly because the "youth were more interested in working with government than in joining co-operatives" (31). The co-ops were set up to create low-wage jobs rather than to transform agriculture and were failing because the agro-commercial capitalists monopolized land, small farmers were at their mercy, low productivity remained intractable in agriculture, rural unemployment persisted, and inefficiency, fragmentation, predial larceny, and other issues also impeded progress in the cooperative sector. The petite bourgeoisie ensured that the state and cooperative sectors operated in the shadow of the dominant capitalist sector.

The 1982–1983 Crisis and Incapacitation of the NJM-PRG

Setting the Stage

The NJM-PRG registered impressive accomplishments in less than five years. Unemployment declined from 50 percent under Gairy to 15 percent. The Point Salines International Airport project was near completion by 1983; major returns were anticipated in tourism, modern production was under way in a number of agro-industrial sites, energy production from biogas was in motion, an impressive construction boom was linked to the expansion of commercial activities, and the benefits from the activities of the MNIB and the NCB were in evidence. Income tax was abolished for 30 percent of the lowest-paid workers. The government introduced free public education and provided scholarships for university-bound students. The children of the poorest families received school uniforms and books free of charge; health-care facilities were strengthened, and access was broadened to recipients without direct cost. Cuban doctors and nurses provided medical and related services without charge to recipients. The housing repair and construction program led to improved housing for many persons. Literacy and adult education programs and a teacher in-service training program were implemented. There was near-total unionization of the workforce, and equal pay for women with men became the law. Influential female leaders in the NJM-PRG such as Phyllis Coard and Jacqueline Creft took the initiative to push women's and gender issues to the forefront of the government's social democratic agenda.

The army was to assume responsibility for producing its food crops. Under the new code of People's Laws, the politico-juridical basis of exploitation was declared abolished even as private property in the means of production and property rights were strengthened (Bishop 1982, 148). The state apparatuses were undergoing partial transformation, with politico-juridical structures of "popular power" taking shape via the people's assemblies. The National Conference of Delegates of Mass Organizations on the Economy served as the state's vehicle for monitoring mass expression of popular participation. There was a rapid growth of mass organizations such as the National Women's Organization (NWO), the National Youth Organization, and the trade unions, among others (Bishop 1982, 238, 264). By the summer of 1982, the NJM was being forced to come to terms with hard reality: it could hold to the petit bourgeois line or attempt to build a popular working-class movement from below to advance broad, popular working-class interests (Ambursley 1983, 216). This is the point of departure for addressing the party's position on the role of Leninism in the work of the party.

The debate within the Central Committee (CC) starting in the latter part of 1982 suggested that the petit bourgeois state and the agro-commercial economy had reached their ability to respond to the growing needs of the working class. There was a call to put the NJM on a "Leninist" footing at the (1) "level of organization and discipline; (2) . . . depth in ideological clarity; (3) brilliance in strategy and tactics; (4) and the capacity to exercise Leninist supervision, control and guidance of all areas of work of the party" (Central Committee Minutes, July–October 1983, 9). The CC recognized that Bishop, the avowedly populist leader, had failed to carry out his responsibilities—hence the call for shared responsibilities to improve and strengthen performance standards to deal with the crisis that was engulfing the party, the working class, the mass organizations, the economy, and the state.

The Central Committee and the Crisis

Between October 1982 and October 1983, the CC noted that the NJM was becoming paralyzed and incapacitated.[9] "In the October 1982 plenary meeting which considered . . . comrade Bernard's resignation the Central Committee leveled criticism at itself and criticized the weak functioning of the C.C. and P.B. and the weak chairmanship and leadership of Comrade Maurice Bishop." The CC concluded that the "party stood at the crossroads: two routes are open to the party. The first route is the petit bourgeois route which would . . . try to make Comrade Bernard's resignation the issue. This would only lead to temporary relief, but will surely lead to the deterioration of the party into a social democratic party and hence the degeneration of the revolution." The plenary report identified the "second route" as the "route of Leninist standards and functioning. The route of criticism and collective leadership. . . . The party must be put on a Leninist footing."

The CC convened on August 26, 1983, to discuss further the developing crisis, stressing that the "revolution [was] facing its worst crisis ever and most serious danger in four years" (1). The minutes of the CC stressed that party organizations were "disintegrating," the working class was exhibiting "ideo-logical backwardness and economism," and "ideological infiltration" and "destabilization" had become characteristic of the church's ideological offen-sive. The "militia was almost a thing of the past"; demoralization was growing in the ranks of the PRA; and "conditions for a general upsurge of counterrev-olutionary activity" were maturing (3). The disintegration of the party seemed imminent, and the revolution was given less than a year to survive (4). The CC admitted that it had taken the "Right Opportunist path by hiding from the membership the truth and absolving itself of criticism . . . while pretending all [was] well" (5). The CC misread symptoms of the impending crisis within the party as actual causes of the crisis within the political economy and offered a highly formalistic reading of Lenin, hoping that declaring the party to be on a Leninist footing might end the crisis within the party. The CC was accu-rate in identifying the symptoms of the crisis; however, its prescriptions were unrealistic under Grenada's conditions and the conditions required to build socialism.

The CC criticized Bishop for his reversal of NJM decisions without con-sulting appropriate party organs (Coard 2002, 20–23) and stressed that his strengths in "inspiring the people," "uniting the masses," and holding "high the banner and prestige of the Revolution" were not the "precise qualities . . . required to carry on . . . in these most difficult times and to transform the party into a Leninist one" (9). Thus the CC presented the "Joint Leadership of the Party" proposal to combine "the strengths of Cdes. Maurice and Ber-nard" (10), with Bishop assuming responsibility for propaganda work among the masses, mobilization of the militia, and regional and international work, and Coard taking responsibility for party organization, cadre formation and development, and ideological work, strategy, and tactics (9–10). Bishop would chair the meetings of the CC and Coard the Political Bureau.

The CC's call for renewing joint leadership in 1983 reflected a desperate attempt to address what Coard calls "system overload/system breakdown" problems. Coard argues retrospectively that joint leadership was "the wrong decision . . . in 1983," stressing that because it worked well in the past did not mean it would work well in 1983; he also accused the party of failing to consider that joint leadership meant downgrading, demoralizing, and embar-rassing Bishop, underestimating the reaction of Bishop's core supporters and failing to consider "the reaction of the Cubans to the party's decision on Joint Leadership" (Coard 2002, 26–29; see E. Layne 2002, 82). Coard insists that the Cuban factor was the most decisive because Bishop believed "he could rely on Cuba for military assistance in crushing the party and army of the Gre-nada Revolution," which was "dramatically demonstrated" on the morning of

October 19, 1983, when upon the "seizure of the army's Headquarters at Fort Rupert," Bishop's "first act . . . was to arrange a call to Ambassador Rizo, and ask him to formally request of Fidel Castro Cuban military intervention to crush the NJM and the PRA" (Coard 2002, 31–32).

According to John Ventour, in 1981 the leader of the Cuban military mission in Grenada told Lt. Col. Ewart Layne that the "Cuban battalion would only respond to a request for assistance from the Commander-in-Chief . . . not the P[arty] Leadership, not the PRG; but one man" (Ventour 1999, 11; see Coard 2002, 69–71). At the CC's Extraordinary Meeting held from September 14 to 16, 1983, Bishop made "a plea for individual and collective leadership of the C.C." and pleaded for ways to deepen the "links with the masses" and "a perspective based on Marxist-Leninist criterion to guide the work in the coming period" (13–14). Fitzroy Bain, George Louison, Unison Whiteman, Phyllis Coard, and Selwyn Strachan agreed that Bishop's leadership performance was the main problem facing the CC (16–17). Bishop agreed that "he had several problems over the years especially the style that entails consensus and unity at all costs" (18–19). However, he opposed joint leadership, mindful of its implications for his populist public image and what he subjectively viewed as a power struggle and a lack of confidence that compromised his ability to lead (29). Bishop could hardly repress the syndrome of the charismatic authoritarian personality of the hero, even when CC comrades reminded him that the criticisms were political rather than personal.

Richard Hart, who served as Grenada's attorney general in 1982 and up to the crisis of October 1983, argues that there was "no substantial difference of opinion within the NJM as to the policies to be pursued by the PRG." Hart rejects as "entirely unfounded" assertions made "in the media . . . that there was within the party an ultra-left group favoring . . . instant socialism . . . or that there were those who were opposed to the formal institutionalization of the Revolution and the holding of elections[10] under a new constitution."[11] Coard attended the September 17 Extraordinary Meeting of the CC that Bishop promised to boycott if Coard attended. After reviewing the minutes and being informed of Bishop's opposition to joint leadership, Coard declined to return to the CC and PB and indicated that he had been "seriously affected by the accusation of wanting to undermine the leadership." He said that he had come to the realization that "his ability to influence the process was no longer possible" (44).

The conclusions from the September 22 plenary of the CC indicated that the party had done little work among the working class before the revolution. The NJM had stepped up its work among the workers only after seizing state power in 1979; however, the party would relate to workers as rural villagers and urban dwellers (12), consistent with its populist outlook. Soon after Bishop's return from Eastern Europe via Havana, a rumor began to circulate that the Coards were plotting to kill him (Ventour 1999, 6). Party members interpreted the rumor and Bishop's refusal to uphold the decisions of the CC and the party as a sign of his contempt for the party. In the report on the meeting of the Political Bureau and Central Committee of October 12, 1983, Bishop's stand on joint leadership was again discussed. Bishop was accused of fostering dissent and the possibility of violence and bloodshed, which led fifty-one members attending a party meeting to vote to expel Bishop from the NJM in an act of desperation, while noting that the party would be hard pressed to explain and justify to the masses Bishop's expulsion from the party. Bishop, the new hero, desperate about the implications of his pending marginalization, decided to go over the party's head to the crowd, where he felt secure and confident. The CC accused Bishop of "egoism," "cultism," "one-manism," and authoritarianism (10).

The report on the meeting of the Political Bureau and Central Committee of October 12, 1983, interpreted Bishop's reference to his relationship with "key opinion makers"—the bourgeoisie—as follows: "He [Bishop] spoke of key opinion makers. Maurice Bishop is personally responsible for spreading the rumor as a precondition for mending the Central Committee and chasing the party off the street. . . . This shows that the bourg[eoisie] knows where Maurice Bishop is coming from. They see him as the chosen one to defend the capitalists against the workers" (3). Bishop, having lost legitimacy within the NJM and the PRG, adorned himself with the accoutrements of the hero and turned to the crowd to rally support for a showdown.

The report of October 12 identifies the People's Revolutionary Armed Forces (PRAF) as taking a principled stand to guarantee "the security of the Central Committee Comrades" (9). With Bishop clearly in mind, the CC report says:

> It talks a lot about those who like to maintain their rule based on ignorance. He is vexed that the PRAF knows about cultism, the role of the Central Committee, just as about Gairy. We have lived for 28 years under Gairy's cultism, and we are not prepared to tolerate one single day more. . . . We won't tolerate it even with a Bishop face. . . . If you want to rule with a minority go to South Africa. . . . Based upon these, especially honesty and love for the masses he does not qualify as an applicant. . . . Those who want to turn to guns and bourgeois elements have no right even close to the party. . . . He has to be expelled from the party, dismissed from every state position he holds. . . . This is a hard position and if we can take this decision we can go forward even further. . . . If Maurice Bishop is not

dismissed we would have departed from socialism. . . . Let us not be fooled by those who could make pretty speech and talk revolutionary because Gairy did this in 1951. The only question then is whether he be allowed to operate as a private citizen or arrested and court-martialed for stirring up counter[revolution] against the revo[lution]. (9)

Bishop became increasingly intransigent, especially after his return from Eastern Europe via Havana.[12] The CC decided to inform the Central Committee of the Communist Party of the Soviet Union and the Central Committee of the Communist Party of Cuba of the extent and implications of the crisis. On October 12 the PRAF issued a resolution highlighting the following four points: "unswerving support for the analysis and conclusions of the CC" regarding the decision on joint leadership and putting the party on a Marxist-Leninist path; grave concern over the crisis that was threatening the country and the party; acceptance of the "Leninist principle of democratic centralism," which gave party decisions the force of law; and opposition to "cultism, egoism, individualism and minority rule." The PRAF called on the "CC and the party to expel from the Party's ranks all elements who [did] not submit to uphold and implement in practice the decisions of the Central Committee and party membership." Bishop's charismatic relationship with the masses should have alerted the party leadership and membership that the masses were not looking at their hero through the lens of the CC; his conduct within the party would not necessarily seem egregious to the masses, whose relationship with the party was essentially top-down. It was therefore necessary to think more imaginatively about how the people relate to a charismatic hero figure in the moment of acute crisis, given the impact of Gairyism on popular culture in Grenada.

Coard points out that he and Bishop were advised by security officials to remain in their homes until "passions had cooled and some resolution to the conflict was achieved." Two security considerations were at work—to protect Coard's personal safety and to prevent Bishop from acting to "inflame the situation"—as there was suspicion he might try to contact the Cubans for "military intervention," which was also why security removed the communications system from Bishop's residence. Coard in hindsight interprets Bishop's "house arrest" as the "point of no return" and a sign of "political inexperience, immaturity and naiveté" (Coard 2002, 60, 61; see Meeks 2000, 162). There is no way to justify the decision by Bishop's supporters, "Louison, Whiteman, Radix and others," to go around the "country organizing mass demonstrations," and it was a miscalculation based on political partisanship for the Cubans to provide "dozens of trucks at the airport to bring thousands of demonstrators to the St. George demonstrations," just as it was a sign of poor political judgment for the "dozens of Cuban Spanish teachers in Grenada's schools" to urge "their Grenadian students to join the demonstration" (Coard 2002, 61). Those acts by the Cubans added to the concern and fear among the CC and PB that Havana might have been planning to intervene militarily against the NJM-PRG.

The decision by Radix, Louison, Bain, and Whiteman to encourage Bishop to take the struggle to the streets reflected their reckless individualist impulses and alienation from the masses, who, by their action, were exposed to potential danger. Historically, the bourgeoisie and petite bourgeoisie had been the "classic betrayer of all national movements for true emancipation." The revolution had failed "to break through the bourgeois framework or organically develop its proletarian and socialist character" (Lowy 1981, 191, 146–47), largely because it was not possible to achieve such a breakthrough in Grenada's circumstances, considering that the NJM was a small organization with a much smaller number of overworked cadres that lacked basic resources and the necessary conditions to build socialism in a very small semi-industrial society. Bishop's commitment to provide the working class with social democratic benefits rested on maintaining the division between politics and economics on which capitalist hegemony partly rests and that reinforces necessity and breeds instability. Substantively, Bishop and the NJM leadership in the CC and PB shared authoritarian values and responsibility for the derailment of the social democratic experiment.

The Tragic Period Beginning October 12, 1983

The CC acted to detain Bishop for his refusal to abide by party norms, and the NJM-PRG called for his removal from the party. Coard disagrees with the claim that Bishop's personal ambition took precedence, insisting that Castro's influence and Bishop's hero worship of Castro got the better of him (Coard 2002). Coard's suggestion that Castro's personal influence over Bishop confirms that Bishop was susceptible to hero worship of Castro deserves closer attention; however, it offers only a partial explanation of the complex issues involved. Bishop's fateful decision to go to the military installation at Fort Rupert signaled that he had lost the confidence and support of the PRG, NJM, and PRAF; he also misread the scope of the realistic geopolitical options that were available to the Cubans, in assuming that they could afford to use military intervention to rescue him. He seemed quite naive about the realistic options that were available in the larger U.S.-Caribbean context. Bishop's rash decision to take the struggle to the streets also suggested that he was willing to exploit religious-based anti-Marxist and anticommunist sentimentalism in the population, thereby intensifying opportunities for destabilization (Sunshine and Wheaton 1984; Schaap and Schaap 1984; Coard 2002, 43).

During the crisis, patriarchy was in full display, with the female population, including women who served in the People's Militia and the PRAF, becoming subject to the uncertainties that company crisis. John Ventour claims that women "who were located in Grand Anse—near to Point Salines—and on their own pinned down the U.S. Forces at Point Salines for a couple of days) . . . defending Grenada's Independence and sovereignty" (1999, 17). Coard mentions that the crowd gathered at Fort Rupert, over which "Bishop had little if any control . . . disarmed all soldiers and their officers; holding the latter at gunpoint in the operations room; they stripped female soldiers of their clothes, leaving them in their underwear; beating some of them. . . . No male soldier was treated thus. . . . They armed themselves from the weapons taken from the soldiers, and from opening up the armory" (Coard 2002, 68). Significantly, the crowd targeted armed female military personnel, seeing them as weak and defenseless though armed, exacting patriarchal discipline—putting them in their place, so to speak. The hero's patriarchal move signaled the recklessness that often exposes the female population to unpredictable dangers that surface when force is employed to settle political disputes.

Washington's announcement of Ocean Venture 81 found most of the Commonwealth Caribbean regimes eager to follow instructions, still longing for economic benefits from the CBI (Kellman 2010). The Caribbean regimes readily defined their security within the U.S. "deterritorialized" national security doctrine, which suggested that a perceived threat to U.S. interests was tantamount to a threat to Caribbean regional security, as defined by the United States (see Lamming 1983). Ronald Reagan had deliberately exaggerated the military importance of the Point Salines International Airport, predictably discounting the economic importance of the new airport in Grenada's modernization strategy, considering that Grenada's economic development was of secondary importance to Washington and that capital accumulation rather than economic development is what drives the capitalist process.

Havana's Response to the Grenada Crisis

Fidel Castro told *Newsweek*'s Patricia Sethi, "I made an appeal [to the Coard group] to be broad-minded and generous. What took place in Grenada was that Coard's group was in the majority. This was apparently clean [and] it was legal even according to democratic norms. You have to accept such a situation even if you realize it is a mistake. We could not do more than we did. We are very respectful of the internal affairs of parties and organizations" (Sethi 1984, 8). John Ventour questions Castro's interpretation, accusing the Cubans of trying to influence the domestic policies of the NJM and PRG (1999, 9, 10). Castro also chided the "Grenada revolutionaries" and called for exemplary punishment, fully aware that only the United States had the means to exact such punishment. Castro's assertion about a lack of adequate information seems unconvincing—the minutes of the Extraordinary Meeting of the NJM Central Committee of August 26, 1983, indicate that Cuban comrades in Grenada had expressed strong concerns about the state of the NJM and the level and quality of its work, the state of the youth organizations, the militia, and others (Coard 2002, 1). Around October 12, the NJM Central Committee decided to notify the Central Committee of the Communist Party of Cuba of the nature and extent of the crisis. Coard points out that Julian Rizo, Cuban ambassador to Grenada, "held daily meetings with Louison and Whiteman during this period" of impending crisis (2002, 61).

Cuba's diplomatic and political achievements with Commonwealth Caribbean states and its improved relations with Canada and several European countries, as well as with communist parties in Latin America, were remarkable. Castro's close ties with Michael Manley, Forbes Burnham, and Maurice Bishop forced the weak Marxist parties and movements in the Commonwealth Caribbean and especially the official opposition People's Progressive Party (PPP) under Cheddi Jagan in Guyana to extend "critical support" on "anti-imperialist" grounds to authoritarian ruling parties like Burnham's People's National Congress (PNC). Coard argues that the Cubans "unwittingly undermined and ultimately destroyed Bishop's moral authority within the People's Revolutionary Army, even as they tried to strengthen his hand over . . . the rest of the NJM leaders, in order to make-over Grenada and NJM in their maximum leader image" (Coard 2002, 18–19). Coard seems to discount the fact that Cuba could not afford to sacrifice its foreign policy gains in the region, and the advantages that come with positive state-to-state relations, to use military force in a Commonwealth Caribbean country to protect Bishop, also in the face of an aggressive United States that viewed the Caribbean as its "backyard."

In the October 21, 1983, analysis of Cuba's response to the Grenada crisis, the Revolutionary Military Council (RMC) expressed surprise that it had to learn about Cuba's reaction from the press rather than through the "Cuban Embassy as was the norm" (1)—a signal that Havana did not recognize the RMC as the legitimate power in Grenada. The RMC disagreed with Castro's assertion that personal differences between Bishop and Coard precipitated the crisis, arguing instead that the NJM and the PRAF had united around the CC's decision regarding Bishop (2). The Cubans had clearly sided with Bishop; however, they could not afford the high price of military intervention to protect him.

Bernard Coard's Mea Culpa

According to the *Trinidad and Tobago Express* of Monday, September 14, 2009, Bernard Coard says, in interpreting the causes of the Grenada crisis, "What happened was vengeance. It was a moment of pure vengeance. . . . We were amateurs, we were arrogant and intolerant. And all our mistakes came home to roost." Coard admits to "many errors of commission and omission which contributed to the overwork/overloading of party members through-out the process . . . during the crisis of September–October 1983." He holds other NJM-PRG leaders responsible for major mistakes, listing among the most serious errors of his personal judgment "not going to the airport on October 8 to meet Bishop on his return." He also regrets having failed to over-rule the "caution of security officials" who advised him to remain in his resi-dence for his personal safety. He considers "far worse" his "failure (during the October 8–11 period) to . . . go next door, to Bishop's home, and talk things out with him." He mentions his "failure to propose . . . the abandonment of the Party's decision on Joint Leadership," given what was happening inside and outside of the country. He adds his "failure to foresee the likely consequences of the house arrest of Bishop," which he considers the "single gravest error of the crisis prior to October 19 itself." He also regrets underestimating the role "of Cuba in the crisis—until it was far too late" (Coard 2002, 72–73).

Coard adds the "rumors," "reactions from the population," Bishop's "going with the crowd and seizing Army HQ," the "role played by [the United States] and their regional 'allies,'" the "Party and Army's actions and reactions," and other factors that compounded the uncertainty and instability as events got out of control. He stresses that authoritarianism shaped Grenada's political culture, which was marked by "fratricidal conflict resolution" that produced "a highly dangerous mixture." He acknowledges that authoritarianism was evi-dent in the destabilizing influences "in the political system under the PRG" and the access both sides had to "military means for conflict resolution" that produced the "perfect cocktail for October 19, 1983" (Coard 2002, 73).

Coard's mention of "pure vengeance" suggests that sane minds did not pre-vail to stave off an avoidable disaster; therefore he was no less authoritarian than Bishop, who asserted that he was "just as tough" as his Central Commit-tee adversaries. Tom Adams, leader of the opposition in Barbados in 1970, when the Errol Barrow administration introduced the Public Order Bill to counteract Black Power demands for redress of economic inequality and racism in Barbados, spoke as follows about the authoritarian nature of colonial and postcolonial law and practice:

> Barbadians suffer from having been raised in a Colonial regime. We accept a lower standard of liberty for ourselves than we would if we had been born in England or the United States of America. That is one of the great disadvantages of being a Colonial; you get habits of authoritarianism drilled into you from childhood. The Barbadian Police temper authoritarianism with decency.... The Commissioner of Police ... is trained as a Colonial Policeman ... and he must necessarily have been trained in more authoritarian methods of controlling especially public order than the English Police Forces. ... While the Commissioner of Police in London cannot decide to ban processions and marches and not expect to face the court for it—the Police in Barbados are free from that because the legislation is drawn along orthodox Colonial Office lines, worked out ... since the Jamaican rebellion, and the legislation is drafted in such a way as not to call into question the actions of a civil power.[13]

Adams's extremely insightful observations about authoritarianism in Barbados are equally applicable to other West Indian societies.

The NJM invited Michael Als of the People's Popular Movement (Trinidad and Tobago) to help mediate the 1983 crisis. Als notes that he and Rupert Roopnaraine from the Working People's Alliance (Guyana) were the only Caribbean persons the NJM invited to Grenada to mediate the crisis. WPJ (Jamaica) operatives were active in Grenada at the time. Als mentions that as he was leaving Bishop's residence after the mediation session, Bishop said with confidence, "Boy dem men tough as hell and I just as tough. We go see. They have their model and I have mine."[14] Coard insists that the Cubans overestimated "Bishop's influence within the party, and within the army ... advising him ... to resist the joint leadership decision, and force the party to reverse gears." Coard also dismisses assertions about a "cold-blooded plot by a clique within the CC to kill Bishop" (Coard 2002, 75–76).

Coard was painfully aware that his tactical, strategic, and technocratic skills were not sufficient to raise his stakes over Bishop's in the Grenadian popular imagination, as Bishop's appeal as charismatic hero endeared him to the Grenadian masses. Coard's personal safety depended on being house ridden and immobilized, even when so much was at stake. Populism produces blowback effects, even for those who lack the charm of the hero; charisma has a way of making it difficult to draw distinctions between the hero's positive and destructive behavior.

By Way of a Conclusion: Contesting Elite Antivanguardism and Post-Marxism

Marxist-Leninists did not bring authoritarianism into the NJM or PRG because authoritarianism was rooted in the political soil the NJM inherited and plowed. Critics of Leninism tend to discount the fact that liberalism and authoritarianism are mutually constitutive. Liberalism is not by nature a force for peace or justice, and liberal democracy adeptly masks authoritarianism with repressive tolerance, hiding its deficiencies, such as its lack of social content and its reliance on force and coercion to produce its version of international peace and order.

Largely, the NJM-PRG's strategy to transform Grenada was forged at the inconvenient intersection of a dying neo-Keynesianism and an aggressive neoliberalism, and Grenada's chronic dependence on external assistance in an environment marked by shortages and structural imbalances rendered the fragile revolutionary experiment susceptible to extremes. The NJM failed to build a principled relationship with the small working class, which was too weak to sustain the requirements of socialist transformation in the difficult conditions found in Grenada and the hostile regional and international geopolitical environment.

When the crisis unfolded in 1983, the CC put the question of socialism on the political agenda, arguing for putting the party on a Leninist footing to advance beyond the petit bourgeois moment, which represents the limits of social democracy within liberalism. Critics like Brian Meeks seem comfortable with socialism—social democracy—without Marxism-Leninism and the vanguard party. The CC recognized that the loose populist notion of the Grenada Revolution had run its course. The unity between the PRAF and the NJM around putting the party on a Leninist footing implied that the possibility existed to draw the military arm of the state into the revolutionary process on the side of the working class. The United States used invasion to deepen Grenada's integration into neoliberal capitalism and prevent the transformation of Grenada's military into a vehicle for potential socialist power. The working class cannot hope to come to power and sustain its rule without ending the "division between politics and economics" to bring an end to necessity (operation of the law of value) and deepen the potential of "freedom as real democracy." The CC's mistake was not in insisting on putting the party on Leninist principles; rather, the CC failed to appreciate that even if Leninism could help the NJM reform itself to meet its tasks and challenges, it did not follow that Leninism offered a blueprint for resolving the problems in Grenada's political economy.

Brian Meeks says that the "Leninist vanguard, with all its capacity for the concentration of forces in a mobile, revolutionary situation, is a dangerous

instrument once it is ensconced in power" (2000, 170). It is worth remind-
ing Meeks that, methodologically, we never begin with ideology but rather
begin with the social relations from which ideology arises, considering also
that power is produced through the interplay of contending interests. Marx
and Lenin insisted on the necessity of the dictatorship of the proletariat as a
means to a higher end, mindful that all forms of state power are despotic by
their very constitution. Meeks believes that there are "real openings for pressing democratic reform in the ... national and international focus on representative democracy." He thinks that a "new left might make significant headway
... at the far more practical effort to make representative democracy more
consistent, meaningful and democratic." Meeks imagines that a separation
of powers could improve representative democracy in the Commonwealth
Caribbean by "separating the executive from Parliament in order to reduce
the dictatorial powers of the current party-dominated, prime ministerial
arrangements" (170, 171). The reality is that the Commonwealth Caribbean
democratic model was built on the "division between politics and economics," which puts the right to exploit in charge of mediating the working class's
access to individual rights, equality, freedom, justice, and democracy under
capitalism. For Meeks, winning state power no longer seems to be the priority; rather, it is how to make representative democracy more democratic in a
system where democracy lacks social content.

C. L. R. James's notion that "the vanguard party" was overtaken by "historical events and ... the proletariat could, acting through workers councils,
spontaneously transform society" borders on romantic fancy, considering
that James's model leaves coercive power out of the equation. James was
emphatic: "Thackeray, not Marx, bears the heaviest responsibility for me"
(James 1963, 41). James's eclectic outlook was suffused with notions that
reflect the cultural influence of liberal ideology, especially the influence of
spontaneity. In contrast, Marx connects the existence of classes to phases of
production, the class struggle and the dictatorship of the proletariat with the
"abolition of all classes" in the direction of a "classless society" (Blackledge
2012, 21). The importance of the vanguard party lies in its potential to offer a
way to "raise theory to the level of practice" (18, 21). Beate Jahn argues against
viewing freedom and liberty as a "purely interior reality, which is ... typical
of the idealist mentality [but] as part of already existing societal relations"
(1998, 623), as theory is part of the problem of reality we try to grasp to
change the world.

Lenin's relevance transcends textbook notions of antielitism that anti-
Marxist liberals and post-Marxists and post-Soviet cynics attach to the

vanguard party, all of which feed on the "culture of contentment." If we are serious that the working class has an important role to play in the fight against barbarism, which must include the fight for socialism, we can hardly avoid thinking about the role of the vanguard party as an unavoidable necessity, precisely because the vanguard arises from concrete material, social, and political conditions of fragmentation, atomism, sectionalism, sectarianism, alienation, subsumption, and necessity that the working class is forced to endure under capitalism and representative democracy. The problem with the vanguard party lies not in the party itself; rather, the problem arises when the vanguard fails to become "the organized leadership of real movements from below" (Blackledge 2012, 15).

The global concentration of wealth is scandalous, thanks to the quality of the representative democracy that makes excess and abuse of the working class necessary. Ecocide has become a permanent threat to human existence. In the United States alone, a full 30 percent of employment is contingent and includes workers who lack any form of security or protection from the vagaries of the market, a predicament that intensifies for workers in all countries. As ties between capital and the state deepen to protect capitalist power, workers in all countries find it increasingly difficult to rely on the state for any support, in the face of the neoliberal offensive of "accumulation by dispossession" and the relentless transfer of wealth to the top (Harvey 2005). Exploitation and inequality in capitalist societies stem from the production for private accumulation based on the operation of the law of value—a reality that the vanguard party could not have invented.

The choice between socialism and barbarism turns to a degree on what representative democracy can do to empower the majority, considering that it is a way of governing where necessity obtains rather than a way of living. The challenge is to build alternative education, skills, communications, effective organizing, and community leaders and leadership, deepening social and political work among the working class across gender and other divisions, building at the community level to bring about socialist assemblies of the people, to produce activists armed with strong socialist infrastructures cutting across production and ecology (Albo, Gindin, and Panitch 2010, 118–20), and understanding that what is at issue is a different relationship between humans and nature, for we are a part of nature, not its enemy.

Social democracy was a moment in the twentieth-century working-class struggles in which the working class won limited gains designed to tether them to bourgeois norms. Neoliberalism was designed to erode those gains and set the working class back significantly. There is no definitive path through social democracy to harness representative democracy for the tasks thrown up by neoliberalism. The merit of social democracy today depends on the role it would have to play in the struggle against barbarism to achieve a way of living, which representative democracy, so called, does not represent.

Notes

1. The paper on which this chapter is based was originally presented at the Ninth Annual Caribbean Studies Association Conference, Basseterre, Saint Kitts, West Indies, May 29–June 2, 1984.

2. Hereafter referred to as NJM-PRG because they formed a more or less unitary structure, and for convenience.

3. In 1972 one ton of Grenada nutmeg bought a typical automobile imported into Grenada; in 1982 it required five tons of nutmeg to purchase a similar automobile. The 1982 purchasing power of the Grenada dollar (EC) had declined to one-fifth of the 1972 purchasing power (Bishop 1982, 264).

4. http://www.thegrenadarevolutiononline.com/page2.html (accessed December 21, 2012).

5. http://www.thegrenadarevolutiononline.com/page2.html (accessed December 21, 2012).

6. See appendix, "Manifesto of the New Jewel Movement," in Institute of International Relations 1974 (for details, see Jacobs and Jacobs 1980, 78–79).

7. See "Report on the National Economy" and the "Budget Plan for 1983 and Beyond," presented to the National Conference of Delegates of Mass Organizations, 1982.

8. Ibid.

9. The discussion in this section draws heavily on the available minutes of the Central Committee deliberations from July to October 1983. The CC documents were seized by the United States during the invasion and occupation of Grenada.

10. See Coard 2002 for his interpretation of the role fear played in the NJM's failure to hold elections (8).

11. http://www.thegrenadarevolutiononline.com/page7.html (accessed December 24, 2012).

12. John Ventour says, "When Cletus St. Paul telephoned Ram Folkes from Cuba on the night of October 7, 1983, . . . he told him, 'Ah hear all yuh trying to f——k up the Chief, but blood goin' flow.'"

13. Barbados House of Assembly Debates (Official Report), Third Session, 1966–71, p. 1691.

14. http://www.thegrenadarevolutiononline.com/page7.html (accessed December 24, 2012).

References

Agnew, J. 2005. *Hegemony: The New Shape of Global Power*. Philadelphia: Temple University Press.

———. 2009. *Globalization and Sovereignty*. New York: Rowman and Littlefield.

Albo, G., S. Gindin, and L. Panitch. 2010. *In and Out of Crisis: Global Financial Meltdown and Left Alternatives*. Oakland, CA: PM Press.

Ambursley, F. 1983. "Grenada: The New Jewel Revolution." In *Crisis in the Caribbean*, ed. Fitzroy Ambursley and Robin Cohen. London: Heinemann.

Ambursley, F., and R. Cohen, eds. 1983. *Crisis in the Caribbean*. London: Heinemann.

Amin, S. 1994. *Re-reading the Postwar Period*. New York: Monthly Review Press.

Barbados. 1971. "The House of Assembly Debates (Official Report), Third Session, 1966–1971." Bridgetown, Barbados: Government Printing Department.

Berberoglu, B. 1983. "The Class Nature of the State in Peripheral Social Formations." *Journal of Contemporary Asia* 13 (3): 324–39.

Bishop, M. 1982. *Forward Ever: Three Years of the Grenada Revolution; Speeches of Maurice Bishop*. Sydney, Australia: Pathfinder Press.

Blackledge, P. 2012. "In Perspective: John Holloway." *International Socialism*, no. 136 (October 8). http://www.isj.org.uk.

Bolland, N. 2001. *The Politics of Labour in the British Caribbean: The Social Origins of Authoritarianism and Democracy in the Labour Movement*. Kingston, Jamaica: Ian Randle.

Coard, B. 2002. "Summary Analysis of the October 1983 Catastrophe in Grenada." Unpublished manuscript. St. George's, Grenada.

Castro, F. 1986. *Nothing Can Stop the Course of History: Interview by Jeffrey M. Elliot and Mervyn M. Dymally*. New York: Pathfinder.

Frucht, R. 1967. "A Caribbean Social Type: Neither 'Peasant' nor 'Proletarian.'" *Social and Economic Studies* 16 (3): 295–300.

Goldberg, D. T. 2009. *The Threat of Race: Reflections on Racial Neoliberalism*. Malden, MA: Blackwell.

Government of Grenada. 1982. "Report on the National Economy (1982)." St. George's, Grenada.

Harvey, D. 2005. *A Brief History of Neoliberalism*. New York: Oxford University Press.

Hilton, Rodney, ed. 1978. *The Transition from Feudalism to Capitalism*. London: Verso.

Holmes, B. 2005. "The Scandal of the Word 'Class': A Review of David Harvey, *A Brief History of Neoliberalism*." Interactivist Info Exchange, Collaborative Authorship, Collective Intelligence. http://info.interactivist.net (accessed December 28, 2013).

Institute of International Relations. 1974. "Independence for Grenada: Myth or Reality?" Institute for International Relations, University of the West Indies, St. Augustine, Trinidad and Tobago.

Jacobs, R. 1979. *The Grenada Revolution at Work*. New York: Pathfinder.

Jacobs, R., and I. Jacobs. 1980. *Grenada: The Route to Revolution*. Havana: Casa De Las Americas.

Jagan, C. 1980. "Caribbean Economic Development and Industrialization." Mimeograph. Georgetown, Guyana.

Jahn, B. 1998. "One Step Forward, Two Steps Back: Critical Theory as the Latest Edition of Liberal Idealism." *Millennium Journal of International Studies* 27 (3): 613–41.

James, C. L. R. 1963. *Beyond a Boundary*. London: Hutchinson of London.

Kaufman, M. 1976. *Jamaica under Manley: Dilemmas of Socialism and Democracy*. New York: Monthly Review Press.

Kellman, R. 2010. "A History of Barbados' Foreign Policy: 1966–1998." Ph.D. thesis, University of the West Indies, Department of History, Faculty of Humanities, Cave Hill Campus, Barbados.

Laclau, E. 1977. *Politics and Ideology in Marxist Theory*. London: New Left Books.

Lamming, G. 1983. "Lamming's Challenge to Barbadians." *Caribbean Contact*, December.

Layne, C. 2006. *The Peace of Illusions: American Grand Strategy from 1940 to the Present*. Ithaca: Cornell University Press.

Layne, E. 2002. "The Making of the Grenada Revolution." Unpublished manuscript. St. George's, Grenada.

Lewis, W. A. 1951. *The Industrialization of the British West Indies*. Bridgetown, Barbados: Advocate Printery.

Lowy, M. 1981. *The Politics of Combined and Unequal Development*. London: Verso.

Mandel, E. 1968. *Marxist Economic Theory*. Vol. 1. New York: Monthly Review Press.

Marx, K., and F. Engels. 1845/1976. "The German Ideology." In Marx and Engels, *Collected Works*, vol. 5. London: Lawrence and Wishart. http://www.marxists.org/archive/marx/works/1845/german-ideology.

Mathiason, N. 2012. "The World's Super-Rich Have Stashed $21 Trillion in Offshore Accounts." Bureau of Investigative Journalism, July 26. http://www.thebureauinvestigates.com.

Meeks, B. 2000. *Narratives of Resistance: Jamaica, Trinidad, the Caribbean*. Kingston, Jamaica: University of the West Indies Press.

Munroe, Trevor. 1983. *Grenada: Revolution, Counterrevolution: Talks by Trevor Munroe*. Kingston, Jamaica: Vanguard Books.

Munroe, Trevor, and Don Rowbotham. 1977. *Struggle of the Jamaican People*. London: War on Want (TU).

Robinson, W. I. 2002. "Capitalist Globalization and the Transnationalization of the State." In *Historical Materialism and Globalization*, ed. Mark Rupert and Hazel Smith. London: Routledge.

———. 2008. *Latin America and Global Capitalism*. Baltimore: Johns Hopkins University Press.

Schaap, Ellen, and Bill Schaap. 1984. "U.S. Crushes Caribbean Jewel." *Covert Action Information Bulletin*, no. 20 (Winter).

Searle, Chris. 1983. *Grenada: The Struggle against Destabilization*. London: Writers and Readers Publishing Cooperative Society.

Sethi, P. 1984. "An Interview with Fidel Castro." *Newsweek*, January 9.

Singham, A. W. 1968. *The Hero and the Crowd in a Colonial Polity.* New Haven: Yale University Press.

Sunshine, C., and P. Wheaton. 1984. *Death of a Revolution.* Washington, DC: EPICA.

Thomas, C. Y. 1978. "The Non-capitalist Path as Theory and Practice of Decolonization and Socialist Transformation." *Latin American Perspectives* 5 (2): 10–28.

Trinidad and Tobago Express. 2009. "Bernard Coard's Telling Review." Opinion. September 14.

Ventour, J. A. 1999. "October 1983: The Missing Link." Unpublished manuscript, St. George's Grenada.

Watson, H. A. 1979. "Populism and Popular Movements in the Commonwealth Caribbean." Paper presented at the Latin American Association of Historians (Mexican Chapter) Center for Latin American Studies, National Autonomous University of Mexico, February 13–19.

———. 2012 "Transnational Capitalist Globalization and the Limits of Sovereignty: Security, Order, Violence, and the Caribbean." In *Caribbean Sovereignty, Development, and Democracy in an Age of Globalization*, ed. Linden Lewis, 35–67. London: Routledge.

Weber, C. 1995. *Simulating Sovereignty: Intervention, the State, and Symbolic Exchange.* Cambridge: Cambridge University Press.

Wood, E. M. 1995. *Democracy against Capitalism: Renewing Historical Materialism.* Cambridge: Cambridge University Press.

8. C. L. R. James and the Grenada Revolution: Lessons Learned and Future Possibilities

Tennyson S. D. Joseph

> There is another lesson of history that must never be forgotten, one of the greatest lessons which history teaches. It is this. Know it and never forget it. Any government that is not conscious of the power of the people, is bound to be a bad government. That is to say, it will fool you, cheat you, and if need be, reduce you to hewers of wood and drawers of water, and without mercy keep you in what it considers to be your place. This is the last hill which the people of the West Indies will have to climb. It is the hardest of all. When you climb it you will have arrived at a height from which you will never fall.
>
> —**C. L. R James,** *Party Politics in the West Indies* (1962)

This chapter uses the historical moment of the third decade after the U.S. overthrow of the Grenada Revolution to reexamine its theoretical lessons as the Caribbean region experiences the impact of the post-2008 Great Recession and the associated crisis of global capitalism.

The chapter uses the theoretical concerns of C. L. R. James for such a task, since not only was James one of the leading Marxist theoreticians from the Caribbean, but, by ignoring James, the Grenadian revolutionaries revealed some critical tactical and philosophical weaknesses whose implications need to be grasped as a guide to the future. Moreover, James is relevant to any review of the Grenada experience because of his insistence on post-Stalinist and post-Leninist interpretations of the relationship between party and mass, democratic centralism, socialist democracy, and several other critical features of the nineteenth- to late-twentieth-century revolutionary experience that were important in the rise and fall of the Grenada Revolution.

James's ideas are thus critical to the delineation of a post-Stalinist Marxist socialist alternative. Given the trauma of the Caribbean Left as a result of the overthrow of the Grenada Revolution and the global reversal of communism,

James's perspective, the basis, and, equally importantly, the relative earliness of his pronouncements make his lessons particularly relevant to any analysis of radical alternatives after Grenada. In particular, specific attention will be paid to James's idea of the "mass party" as a distinct alternative to the vanguardist, authoritarian, postcolonial party forms of the Caribbean.

Finally, the chapter uses James's critique of the Grenada Revolution as a basis for a wider assessment of Jamesian thought in itself. In particular, it identifies and discusses some weaknesses in James's critique of the Grenada experience and engages in a wider analysis of the relevance of James's key theoretical and methodological assumptions and approaches to the politics of the early twenty-first century.

Following this introduction, the chapter's second section presents the central assumptions of James's Marxist thought, highlighting in particular the questions that have direct relevance to understanding the denouement of the Grenada Revolution and the construction of a post-Stalinist socialist alternative. The third section applies James's Marxist perspective to the Grenada experience. Finally, the fourth section shifts its gaze to the future, showing the relevance of James in clarifying future revolutionary possibilities. It presents James's mass party as a future alternative and focuses on the realities of the present that explain and justify James's optimism in a post-Stalinist revolutionary future. The final section also critiques James's perspective, placing particular emphasis on his romanticizing of the revolutionary potential of the working class. The chapter assesses the validity of James's optimism against the reality of twenty-first-century radical politics.

Marxism, Postcommunism, and the Theoretical Ideas of C. L. R. James

The State and Socialism

A critical area to understanding the relevance of James to the Grenada Revolution is his perspective on the role of the state in establishing socialism. This question has been the focus of much disagreement within Marxist political theorizing and the source of many errors in actually existing socialism.

It is a central axiom of Marxism that the capitalist state is "nothing but a committee for managing the common affairs of the whole bourgeoisie" (Marx and Engels 1968, 5). From this perspective, the state is seen not as a neutral arbiter among contending interests but as an instrument whose essence lies in safeguarding the interests of the economically dominant class. Despite the apparent agreement on this view, however, one critical area of disagreement

among Marxists has been how to overcome the state in establishing socialist society, and indeed whether the necessity of its overthrow has lost the
urgency it assumed before Marxism's first concrete political victories.

Indeed, one of the early debates among revolutionary intellectuals (the
anarchist-Marxist debate) revolved around the role of the state in a postcapi-
talist order. While the anarchist camp led by Bakunin called for the immediate dissolution of the state, the Marxists advocated the proletarian seizure of
state power as a necessary prelude to its withering away (Engels 1978, 339–40).
Similarly, the Marxist-revisionist debate between Lenin and English revision-
ism (Eduard Bernstein in particular) was also concerned with the question
of state power. It was primarily a debate about the means through which state
power could be seized by the workers, but never fully addressed the question
of the state's existence after the seizure of power (Wallerstein 1984, 51).

Where C. L. R. James enters this debate, it is his absolute disillusionment
with the state as a facilitator of socialism that comes to the fore. It is the
"withering away of the state," rather than the seizure of state power that is
the dominant concern. James insists that a state system that was characterized by the alienation of the majority from decision making, the absence of
avenues for democratic expression, and the existence of standing armies and
paramilitary units standing above society could not be socialist. To James,
socialism would exist only after the bourgeois state, both its structure and
functions, has been replaced by organs of proletarian participation, ownership, and control.

In outlining the differences between Stalinism and his conception of socialism, James (1992, 199) asserts that "the Stalinists seek to establish themselves
in the place of the rival bureaucracy. The Fourth International must not seek
to substitute itself in the place of these, not after, not during nor before the
conquest of power. Theory and practice are governed by the recognition of
the necessity that the bureaucracy as such must be overthrown." James argues
further that, "in their varying degrees, all states today, based upon property
and privilege, are the negation of the complete democracy of the people. It is
this state which is to be destroyed, that is to say, it is this state which is to be
negated by the proletarian revolution" (James 1980b, 79–80).

James's insistence on the "withering away" of the state anticipates the later
perspectives of writers like Immanuel Wallerstein (1984) who have ques-
tioned the viability of socialism as a single-state project, abstracted from its
location in the global economy. James, like Wallerstein, is aware that socialism cannot truly be achieved in one country existing within the confines of a
dominant world capitalist economy (Robinson 1992), and like Toffler (1981),
James argues that socialism cannot be built on a mode of production that
has not qualitatively superseded the industrial-capitalist mode of production.

In *State Capitalism and World Revolution*, James (1986, 38–39) argues that "the whole tendency of the Stalinist theory is to build up theoretical barriers between the Russian economy and the economy of the rest of the world. The task of the revolutionary movement, beginning in theory and . . . reaching to all aspects of political strategy, is to break down this separation." This insistence on dissolving the separation between local and global places James's thought squarely in the modern era of globalization.

In addition, James's criticism of Stalinist socialism was based on his awareness that a socialist state structure would have to be democratically superior to the capitalist state in terms of avenues for direct participation in decision making, and in the abolition of worker alienation, and would have to be constructed on a far more technologically advanced mode of production that dispenses with the division of labor in all spheres of life. Whatever the new state form, it could only be socialist to the extent that workers participated in the decision-making process, particularly at the level of production.

Indeed, James's categorization of the Stalinist bureaucracy as "state capitalism" was based on its effectiveness in exploiting the proletariat along capitalist lines. Thus James writes of the division of labor in the context of state-instituted socialism:

> This is capitalist production, this hierarchy. The special functions are performed "within the conditions of production themselves by special agents in opposition to the direct producers." These functionaries, acting against the proletariat in production, are the enemy. If this is not understood, then workers' control of production is an empty phrase. (James 1992, 191–92)

James's concept of state capitalism therefore rejects the assumption that nationalization of the means of production is synonymous with socialism. From a Jamesian perspective, state ownership by itself does not guarantee worker input in decision making in production and distribution. Nationalization succeeds only in enlarging the scope and power of the state and ensures the creation of "special agents in opposition to the direct producers." To James, therefore, ownership and control should not be undertaken on behalf of workers by an alien and abstract bureaucratic organization, but instead workers should own and control the productive sectors directly through their own organizations (James 1992, 199; 1937, 28; Glaberman 1992, 46–47).

The Party and Socialism

James's rejection of the state form as an instrument of socialist construction led logically to his rejection of the political party—of whatever variety—as a mechanism of working-class empowerment. To James, the contradiction inherent in the political party as an instrument of liberation was twofold.

First, the principle of "representation," which explains the party's existence, is a product of the division of labor of the industrial-capitalist mode of production. Thus the Taylorite separation between management and labor (thinking and being), which socialism needs to overcome, is incorporated into the very structure of the party itself (Toffler 1981, 61). Much of James's critique of the Leninist vanguard party that was central to the Grenada experience was based on that formulation.

In *Notes on Dialectics*, James (1980a) stresses that the separation between the "proletariat as being" and the "proletariat as knowing" that the party symbolizes is no longer necessary and should be done away with. Elsewhere he writes:

> The Bolshevik party of Lenin was the greatest political party the modern world has known.... But even this party in the last analysis was a type of parliament with representatives of the workers divided into debating factions, increasingly removed from the actual conditions of social and particularly proletarian life. Today a party on that model in an advanced country can be nothing else but an instrument of oppression, tyranny and acute failure. (James, Lee, and Chaulieu 1958, 94)

Second, since the political party is concerned with the acquisition of state power, its raison d'être ultimately limits its capacity for social transformation and socialist construction. James had realized that because of the political party's fixation with state power, it was often opposed to spontaneously created worker socialist democracy. Thus, to James, episodes of socialist organization such as the Paris Commune (1871), the Russian soviets (1905 and 1917), and the Hungarian workers' councils (1956) have always been crushed by "revolutionary" governments bent on strengthening state power (Arendt 1963, 250–51; James, Lee, and Chaulieu 1958). Arendt (1963, 252–53) states:

> Each time they appeared they sprang up as the spontaneous organs of the people, not only outside of all revolutionary parties but entirely unexpected by them and their leaders.... They were utterly neglected by statesmen, historians, political theorists and most important, by the revolutionary tradition itself.... They failed to understand to what an extent the council system confronted them with an entirely new form of government, with a new public space for a new freedom which was constituted and organized during the course of the revolution itself.

From this perspective, the existence of such organs of working-class democracy makes the party unnecessary, for they perform all the political functions of the party, and indeed the executive functions of government as well (Lenin 1943, 40–42; Albert and Hahnel 1978, 329). It is for these reasons that in all periods where such councils have existed, they have met with hostility from the party. To Arendt (1963, 260), such conflict is inevitable since, the party, being

> firmly anchored in the tradition of the nation-state . . . [,] conceived of revolution as a means to seize power. . . . What actually happened, however, was a swift disintegration of the old power, the sudden loss of control over the means of violence, and, at the same time, the amazing formation of a new power structure which owed its existence to nothing but the organizational impulses of the people themselves. In other words, when the moment of revolution had come, it turned out that there was no power left to seize, so that revolutionists found themselves before the rather uncomfortable alternative of either putting their own pre-revolutionary "power," that is, the organization of the party apparatus, into the vacated power center of the defunct government, or simply joining the new revolutionary power centers which had sprung up without their help.

For these reasons, James advocated the transcendence of the political party, since the party by its structure and function was a bourgeois and an antiproletarian organization. He argues that "the modern political party, whatever its policy or program, the moment it takes hold of any government, whatever its democratic intentions, becomes a system and a method and an organisation which is opposed to the masses of the people" (James 1966, 28).

James was also aware of a contradiction between the party as government and the party as mass mobilization. While the "government did not give any power to the party" and it is the "party that gave power to the government," the two exist in constant conflict because the government, being placed "in the middle of the battle," needs to make concessions, compromises, and retreats at the expense of the party and the people who form the party (James 1977, 176). The only resolution to this contradiction was through the transcendence of the party and the creation of worker organizations that mirror, in structure and function, the historical examples of the commune, soviets, and workers' councils.

James is therefore adamant that the "theory and practice of the vanguard party, of the one party state, is not . . . the central doctrine of Leninism" (James 1964, 3). Similarly, Miliband (1983, 159) maintains that the "extraordinary fact, given the whole cast of Lenin's mind, is that the political element which otherwise occupies so crucial a place in his thought, the party, receives such scant attention in *The State and Revolution.*" Belle (1994, 100–101) also insists:

> We really miss the central contribution and example of Lenin when we ossify his category and make it a fetish and fail to appreciate that it was his mastery of dialectical negation that preserves Lenin's outstanding historical role in and contribution to the labor movement. . . . For Lenin should be appreciated in the "*Why he introduced the vanguard*" not in the vanguard itself.

Free Creative Activity: Working-Class Organization

It is clear from these reflections that C. L. R. James placed little hope in the political party, both in the seizure of the bourgeois state and in the postseizure construction of socialism. James instead advocated unfettered mass activity as the only guarantee that the bourgeois state would not only be seized but overthrown and replaced by new socialist structures. This element of James's thought has opened him to the criticism of romanticizing the working class and exaggerating the efficacy of their spontaneity. Central to this criticism is the notion that while James privileges the spontaneity of the underclass, he underplays the importance of organization in channeling proletarian politics into definite and predetermined directions, favorable to the advancement of socialism. However, in contrast to the emphasis on "spontaneity," James's identification of proletarian forms of organization such as the soviets and communes suggests his awareness of concrete mechanisms through which proletarian democracy can be realized.

James's awareness of the limitations of single-state-led socialism in the context of a global capitalist system, his rejection of the state and party as genuine revolutionary institutions, his elucidation of the new forms of proletarian democratic alternatives, his concern to resolve the contradiction between the "party as being" and the "party as consciousness," as well as his rejection of bureaucratic Stalinist "state capitalism," were all important lessons for the Grenada Revolution.

C. L. R. James and the Grenada Revolution: The Lessons

Of the several analyses of the demise of the Grenada Revolution, the view that the implosion was caused by the struggle between two mutually opposed ideas of socialism provides the most useful framework for analyzing the events surrounding the disruption of the revolution. Indeed, this identification of a struggle between statist and popular structures of socialist democracy has been applied to previous episodes of revolutionary struggle, long before Grenada. John La Rose (1985, 3) notes:

> Grenada is not the first place in this century, following from the October Revolution in 1917, that revolutionary power has been seized, then could not be consolidated and was lost. The liberating waves of the October Revolution in Russia in 1917 rippled out to other countries and inspired revolutionary uprisings and the formation of soviets in Bavaria, Germany and Hungary in 1919, but power was not held for very long. This power lasted for months, not years as in Grenada.

Such a perspective is the foundation on which C. L. R. James's socialist thought is based, and should form the basis of any Jamesian analysis of the events that occurred in Grenada from the early 1970s to the U.S. invasion in 1983. The validity of this perspective lies in its recognition that during periods of transformation, the struggle operates on two levels: the first waged by a new political elite seeking to replace the old, and the second by the underclass to smash completely the very structures that the new elite aspire to occupy (James 1977; Arendt 1963).

Hence a Jamesian analysis of the Grenada Revolution should begin not in 1979, when the state apparatus was seized by the People's Revolutionary Government (PRG), but in the early 1970s, when a very deliberate process was set in motion aimed at replacing the old state structures by institutions of popular democracy, as was witnessed in the programs and activities of the early anti-Gairy groups such as the Movement for the Advancement of Community Effort (MACE), the Movement for the Assemblies of the People (MAP), and the Joint Endeavour for Welfare and Educational Liberation (JEWEL). This effort found concrete expression in the 1974 independence manifesto of the New Jewel Movement (NJM), which was framed with the assistance of the Jamesian scholar Franklyn Harvey (see Marable 1987, 208). The manifesto stated unequivocally:

> Since politics deals with the making of decisions, and since politics is largely the process which decides who gets what, where, how and when, New Jewel does not consider it to be the function of an "exclusive club." NJM stands solidly behind Peoples' Assemblies as the new form of government that will involve all the people all the time. Through this form, people will be assured of both their political and their economic rights. To us, Peoples' Assemblies will bring in true democracy. (New Jewel Movement 1974, 9)

The manifesto identified the NJM as

> rejecting the party system for many reasons. Firstly, parties divide the people
> into warring camps. Secondly, the system places power into the hands of a small
> ruling clique. That clique victimizes and terrorizes members of the other party.
> Thirdly, the ruling elite seizes control of all avenues of public information, for
> example, the radio station, and use[s] them for its own ends. Finally, and most
> important, it fails to involve the people except for a few seconds once in every five
> years when they make an "X" on a ballot paper. (9)

Evidence of the early moments of the Grenada Revolution as a genuinely
antielitist democratic movement can be found in the political programs of
the main parties in the anti-Gairy struggle. The concrete activity of these
groups adhered to the political programs presented to the 1973 Congress by
the MAP, whose main aim was "the organization of a mass movement to
seize political power" through "the strategy and tactics" of a "mass uprising"
(Sandford 1985, 13). The activities of MACE, MAP, and JEWEL, and later the
NJM, were consciously geared toward an enlargement of democracy in Grenada, the political education of the Grenadian masses through the medium
of the mass meeting, and the involvement of the Grenadian people through
mass demonstrations. Moreover, the proposed establishment of people's
assemblies was a concrete attempt at replacing the existing centralized state
structures with mechanisms of popular democracy (Hodge and Searle 1981,
23–24). That this demand formed a major part of the agenda of the Grenada
Revolution until its eventual demise is perhaps the most significant political
development to have occurred in Grenada, and indeed the entire Caribbean,
during that period.

This populist-democratic outlook characterized the politics of Maurice
Bishop and his followers and marked them out from the state party orientation of Bernard Coard and his supporters (Sandstrom 1988). It is this difference in the perception of socialism, rather than the more popular "personality
differences" or "power hunger" explanations, that accounts for the internal
struggle and the eventual demise of the Grenada Revolution (Sandstrom
1988, 22, 41). As Marable (1987, 250–51) notes:

> What actually distinguished the two factions were their conflicting definitions of
> "socialism," and their profound difference over the relationship between the party
> and the masses.... For Bishop, Radix and the NJM founders, socialism meant the
> self-conscious development and empowerment of workers and farmers. Bernard
> Coard and the NJM cadre closest to him ... tended to view the problems of the

revolution from the tradition of statist socialism: emphasis on individual incentives to promote productivity; the pursuit of central planning and an all-inclusive economic program for society; a hierarchical system of decision making; a firm conviction that all power should reside within the party organization.

It is the dominating influence of such an outlook that is perhaps responsible for Bernard Coard's curt dismissal of C. L. R. James as a "neo-Trotskyist" (Marable 1987, 215). Later, when the Grenadian crisis was coming to a head and the Grenadian masses were becoming increasingly restless over the incarceration of Bishop, Coard was reported to have replied to George Louison's plea that the Grenadian masses would never accept the new situation without a struggle with the following retort:

> The people can march, they can demonstrate, and we won't stop them. But they'll get tired. Gairy let them march and demonstrate almost daily for two months in 1973 and 1974. The same happened in Trinidad in 1970. The masses will get tired and life will return to normal. And we will continue the revolutionary process, on a more Marxist, more Leninist footing. (Quoted in Marable 1987, 260)

It is clear, therefore, that Coard's approach, when juxtaposed against the theoretical prescriptions of C. L. R. James, recalled the "organization versus spontaneity" or the "centralization versus democratization" debates that found expression in the Lenin-Luxemburg disagreement over the vanguard party model or in the later Trotsky-Stalin controversies. What is clear, however, is that Coard's tendency was consistent with that of the statist-oriented "socialist" whose primary aim, as stated earlier, is to occupy the position held by the former controller of state power rather than to smash the bourgeois institutional forms and replace them with new structures more suited to working-class empowerment. The socialism envisaged by such revolutionaries is one that is imposed on a passive people rather than one that seeks and encourages their active participation and support at every stage of the process.

Many factors account for the deliberate transformation of the NJM from a party of mass mobilization to a closed, secret, conspiratorial vanguard party, "limited to the exigency of seizing state power" (Ambursley 1983, 205). The failure of the mass demonstrations and general strikes of 1973–74, following the "Bloody Sunday" beatings of Maurice Bishop, Hudson Austin, and other NJM leaders, to topple the Gairy regime was one of the factors that resulted in a reassessment of the role and strategy of the NJM. Of key importance, too, is that the NJM, although being an important catalyst for the demonstrations of 1973–74, had been left out of the Committee of Twenty-two that had been the formal organizers, deciding when they would end, and excluding the NJM on the grounds that the committee wanted to remain a "non-partisan" body (Sandford 1985, 19). After their exclusion, the leadership of the NJM undertook an analysis that concluded:

> The root cause for the failure of the 1973–74 revolution . . . was the backwardness of the economic structure of Grenada, resulting in a strong petty bourgeoisie and an under-developed, ideologically weak working class. This in turn led to ideological and organizational weakness on the part of the NJM itself: an "ultra-leftist" tendency characterized by over-reliance on spontaneous revolutionary action by the masses themselves. The party had failed to organize and lead the exploited masses, particularly the working class, as an independent force with its own tactics. Consequently, the bourgeoisie had been able to "sell out" the revolution when it grew alarmed at the NJM's mobilization of the masses. (Sandford 1985, 20)

Therefore the transformation of the NJM into a Leninist vanguard party was due to the increasing urgency to topple the Gairy regime and the imperative of seizing state power. The elevation of this aim into an all-consuming priority rendered the old strategies and tactics of the party wholly untenable. Thus the later internal conflict within the NJM, and the subsequent demise of the Grenada Revolution itself, resulted from the conflict between the old populism and the new need to structure the party along "Marxist-Leninist" lines (Sandstrom 1988, 20). The increasing impatience of the Coard faction, which had grown in stature as a consequence of the shift to Leninism, with the "ideological backwardness" of the populist faction, accounts for the party schism and for the subsequent implosion of the revolution. According to Sandford (1985, 197), "The presence of Bishop as a popular leader long after the party had moved beyond him ideologically was an aggravating factor."

This shift to "Leninism" had many consequences for the development of the revolutionary process in Grenada, of which arguably the most disastrous was the alienation of the Grenadian masses from the revolutionary process, and the divorce of the party from the people. Meeks (1993, 151–53) observes:

> This was the central tension on the final lap to insurrection. Each Leninist measure which made the party more capable of taking power, also increased its tendency towards hierarchical decision-making and enhanced the autonomy of the leadership both from ordinary party members and the people. . . . If Leninism was the necessary ingredient for victory then it had to be implemented. Leninism prepared the party for insurrection, but also at the same time it made it more

hierarchical. The populist elements in the Jamesian approach had been thrown out with its tactical weaknesses.

Closely related to this was the shrinking size of the NJM as increasingly more rigid criteria for party membership were implemented, as a result of the party's new conspiratorial outlook, its desire for secrecy, and its need to maintain a Leninist vanguard character. La Rose (1985, 5) observes:

> In a country in which the mass struggle against Gairy had seen demonstrations of 20,000 people in a population of just over 100,000 and massive demonstrations of popular support for the People's Revolutionary Government after March 13th, 1979, there was an entire membership of less than 200 in the New Jewel Movement [by 1983].

The shift in the ideological orientation of the NJM meant that the problems facing the party were blamed on the deviation from strict Leninism. This outlook deepened once the NJM seized political power and was confronted with the responsibilities of government. Meeks (1993, 178) observes:

> At each turning point in the Grenada revolution, the leadership, almost instinctively sought to solve problems and crises from above. In 1982, with Coard's resignation, the answer was to intensify Leninism. In July 1983, with increasing fear of foreign intervention and a demoralised population, this again was the first response. When revolt within the party threatened everything, the leadership at last recognized a deeper crisis, but the first answer was again on course. This inability to escape from a deeply-entrenched cumulative and available ideological context of Leninism and hierarchy and not the chimera of conspiracy was the critical element in the denouement of the revolution.

With such developments, the stage was set for a conflict between the party and state organs and the people of Grenada seeking to maintain the independent development of their organizations (Ambursley 1983, 214–15). The increasing demands of the party to control every aspect of political development in Grenada diminished the importance of popular assemblies (La Rose 1985, 6). It can perhaps be concluded that the Grenada Revolution had come to an end long before October 1983. The events that led to the subsequent U.S. occupation of Grenada were merely a more overt enactment of a performance that had taken place behind the scenes within the thin ranks of the ruling clique of the PRG. The uprising of the Grenadian people to force the release of their leader serves as the most poignant indication of the turn that the revolution had taken.

As Fidel Castro (1983, 6) pointed out, the Revolutionary Military Council (RMC) formed after the slaying of Maurice Bishop was "morally indefensible," since "the party, the government and the army had divorced themselves from the people, [so that] it was also impossible to defend the nation militarily, because a revolutionary war is only feasible and justifiable when united with the people." From a Jamesian perspective, therefore, the attack on the Grenadian people by the People's Revolutionary Army (PRA) was a mere reenactment of events that had unfolded elsewhere in the twentieth century. As Dujmovic (1988, 19) notes, "The PRA was the true defender of the revolution, as in Hungary 1956, Czechoslovakia in 1968, and Poland in 1981, the army fulfilled its duty to save the party."

Given these realities, therefore, and given James's views on popular socialist democracy, which at the time of the Grenada Revolution were being realized, in his view, in the Solidarity movement in Poland, he remained extremely skeptical about the Grenada Revolution. Indeed, James had always searched for his notion of proletarian democracy outside the largely peasant-based, agricultural, neocolonial societies of the Caribbean. In his writings, he comes perilously close to dismissing any possibilities of socialist revolution in the Caribbean, and yet at other times he would concede that the Caribbean, given its history and its mode of incorporation into the global economy, is capable of new forms of political organization that can point to future global revolutionary possibilities. Indeed, this was the underlying message of his famous work *The Black Jacobins* (James 2001), yet it was not forcefully applied to the Caribbean in the period of socialism.

It is therefore closer to the truth to suggest that James had little confidence in the Grenada Revolution, given his suspicion of Stalinist-type communist projects, and his own concerns about the readiness of the Caribbean for an advanced worker-council-based grassroots democracy. In a series of lectures and study circle discussions held by James in Canada in the 1960s and published in 2009, he appeared skeptical about the possibilities of socialist revolution in the Caribbean:

A socialist society to an educated person must be a socialist society. Note something which I am going to tell you. I never in the Caribbean speak about Marxism. Never. I make the analysis etc. I never say Marx. There is no need for me to do that. None whatever. In their eye, Marxism is a communist who is going to shoot everybody. When we are talking, I can go into that, and it does not prevent me from writing as I like about Marxism in an internal party magazine or journal. It does not prevent me from writing an article in the paper. But I do not go to the public saying: "Marx says therefore . . ." I say this, "All these foreign parts, they should go." (Cited in Austin 2009, 182)

This reluctance by James to address the possibilities of Caribbean socialism is seen more frontally in an article titled "C. L. R. James Views Grenada: From Self-Defense to Self-Destruction" (James 1985, 61), in which he presents the emergence of socialism in Grenada as accidental bungling, rather than conscious development:

> The leftists in the middle class (educated people, talking a lot about socialism and the development of the Caribbean nation) now find that they have to do something. And they are not able *to do* anything. So the people move with power, but empirically. In 1979 the people moved, they took power and to Bishop . . . the people said: "well alright, you are talking all the time, here you are Bishop—do something." That is a crude expression of what actually happened. (61)

Clearly in this instance James has great difficulty in addressing the Grenada Revolution in language commensurate with what he would have adopted for a more advanced economy. Elsewhere, in an unpublished analysis of the revolution, he writes of Bishop in similar terms:

> Bishop took power. He came to Trinidad to see me more than once but all Bishop told me was: "CLR I know that as a Marxist I ought to do this and to do that, but there is no industrialism, there is no proletariat, what can we do? It is a peasant country." I used to tell him: "Find something by which you will make the people realize that they have made a revolution and this is what they are getting from it. But don't keep on saying that you cannot do anything because there is no proletariat, there is no large scale industry, we have a lot of peasants and we don't want you to take away the peasants' land." (James, n.d.)

The critical Jamesian lesson that can be learned from the Grenada revolutionary experience is that the movement for socialism cannot be divorced from the movement for democracy. This holds particularly true for the English-speaking Caribbean, where all the major advances in the political development—from the abolition of slavery to decolonization—can be measured in the democratic rights and freedoms and civic, social, and economic empowerment that has accrued to previously disenfranchised people. From the Jamesian perspective, the movement for democracy and the movement for socialism are not mutually exclusive but inextricably intertwined. Socialism cannot be "decreed from above" but must involve the active participation of the people at every stage of the process.

The Mass Party: James's Organizational Prescription

Despite James's apparent ambivalence toward the possibility of socialist trans-formation in the Caribbean, his period of active engagement in the politics of Trinidad and Tobago on the invitation of Eric Williams in the early 1960s, the developments associated with his eventual break with Williams, and his resultant critique of Caribbean democracy (see James [1962] 1984) provide the context for connecting his theoretical insights on post-Stalinist social-ism, the experiences of the Grenada Revolution, and the future possibilities of socialist revolution, both globally and in the Caribbean region. It is this critique of Caribbean democracy that provides the conceptual link between his ideas on socialism in the advanced capitalist countries and its possibilities in the Caribbean. Relatedly, his prescription of the "mass party" was designed to overcome the weaknesses emergent from the separation between party and government, leadership and mass, and intelligentsia from foot soldiers (thinking from being) that he had identified in vanguardist parties both in the advanced countries and in the Caribbean.

Indeed, James's prescriptions in *Party Politics* point away from the view that he was dismissive of the possibilities of Caribbean socialism. Adher-ents of the "Caribbean unreadiness" view often miss the fact that James saw democracy and socialism as being inextricably intertwined. It is the failure to unite James's discussions on democracy with his aspirations for socialism that accounts for the tendency to treat James's critique of Caribbean democracy as confirmation of the political backwardness of the region, and as confirmation of his doubts about socialist transformation in the region. However, once it is understood that James's critique of Eric Williams's Peoples National Move-ment followed the same rationale as his critique of Lenin's Vanguard Party, then his prescriptions in the Caribbean context can be seen as relevant to the construction of a post-Leninist socialist alternative both in the Caribbean and globally.

Central to James's critique of the postcolonial political party in the Carib-bean was the separation between leadership and mass central to Leninism. Much of James's denunciation of Williams's PNM was founded on its failure to transform itself into a genuine democratic party, capable of transcending the colonial social relations. Thus, to James, the keys to independence and socialism were intertwined in the process of democratizing the party, since the political party always reflects the social relations of the society.

The West Indian problem is therefore the absence of the habit of democracy. The party should thus consciously strive to overcome this weakness. Thus, according to James, while "the British have been learning democracy for at least 700 years," and while "sufficient numbers of every class" in Britain "know when and how they gained their democratic rights, how long they had to fight for them, who opposed them and by what means, how long it took for an accommodation to be arrived at, and what advances have been made since the original victory" (James [1962] 1984, 112), he has "never heard or read a single political leader in the West Indies address himself to this question, or bring it seriously to the public. Not one. They babble about independence and democracy as if it were a kind of medicine or pill that they as doctors administered and thereby cured the population of a disease called colonialism" (114).

To James, the solution to this democratic deficit resides in a new political organization, which would overcome all the old weaknesses inherent in the vanguardist types. The problem with the vanguard-driven organizations was not their lack of success in winning political power. To the contrary, "They are all tremendously successful in breaking up the old order; they find dynamic leaders and create new fighting organisations, either military or political" (James [1962] 1984, xix). However, their weakness lies in their incapacity to fundamentally transform their societies, since "all of them have a breaking point." To James, they "can smash the old order but most of them break down completely when they face the job of creating anew" (xix).

James's mass party was designed to facilitate socialist democracy and to ensure a continuous flow of decisions from the bottom upward. Moreover, it was designed to widen the decision-making structure to include every member of the party's rank and file and to break the decision-making monopoly of the party's leadership—or, more accurately, its leader. It was aimed at ensuring participatory democracy and transcending representative politics in the Caribbean, where the party leadership makes all the key decisions and the role of the people is merely to support the predetermined program.

The mass party was intended to overcome the division of labor between the party as "consciousness" and the party as "being," and similarly to dissolve the separation between the party as "government" and the party as "mass mobilization" (James 1977). The tendency that James ([1962] 1984), Fanon ([1967] 1983), and Gittens (1983) have identified in the party as a mechanism to stifle mass initiative and to take decision-making power from the people is a result of the dominance of the "government aspect" stifling and crushing the "mass mobilization" function of the party. James ([1962] 1984, 153) observes that "Williams formed a party . . . but his main concern is not the party but the government. . . . The masses are to be whipped up to give the leaders the authority and power. After that the government will do everything. Modern democracy has gone a long way from that."

Government is always undertaken in the interest of a particular class, and representative government ensures that rule in the interest of the economically dominant class is not compromised by popular involvement (Miliband 1982). This contradiction is compounded in postcolonial societies, since the dominant economic interest that government serves is a nonresident, external interest. Both James ([1962] 1984, 129) and Fanon ([1967] 1983, 119–20), for example, had lamented that the postcolonial middle-class leadership was not a true "ruling" class, since they lacked economic power. Since their politics are limited by their subservience to a metropolitan power, their political organizations exist principally to limit popular power.

The Jamesian mass party, with its emphasis on mass decision making as a mechanism for socialist democracy, is consciously incompatible with capitalist or neocolonial existence. So certain was James that his party model represented a qualitative democratic leap that he was adamant that with such a party, multiparty political competition would be rendered superfluous. According to James (1966, 28–29) in *Perspectives and Proposals*,

> [In] an underdeveloped country, if a political party organises itself properly and has a real program devoted to the mass of the people and the improvement of their situation, it will become a one-party state. But the opposition can take place, but there is no real room in most underdeveloped countries for any opposition to a party which is a genuinely mass party.

C. L. R. James and the Revolutionary Future: Thirty Years after Grenada

These reflections on the Grenada revolutionary experience through a Jamesian perspective provide a basis for examining revolutionary possibilities in the early twenty-first century, three decades after the revolution's demise. An opportunity is also provided for engaging in critical reflections on the utility of the Jamesian perspective itself in the present context of crisis in mature capitalism.

The great value of C. L. R. James's political thought remains his constant discovery of what constitutes the universal of the socialist movement. James always drew a strict line between the *universal*, which is the ultimate end to which the movement is directed—the liberation of humanity from every basis of exploitation and domination—and the *particular*, which is the specific organizational means adopted in realizing the universal. It is this distinction that explains James's revolutionary optimism in future possibilities. Developments that were considered "setbacks" or "defeats" were scoured by James for the faintest indications of new modes of revolutionary expression that could add to the possibilities of freedom and self-liberation (James 1980a).

James's commitment to the universal and his constant reexamination of the particular provide a useful guide for analyzing post-2000 transformations in the global political economy and for applying Marxist analysis to account for such transformations. In his lifetime, his analyses of politico-economic and technological transformations were always grounded in their relevance to the workers' movement. He believed firmly that socialism involved the appropriation and further development of the products of capitalism by the working class in the interest of the working class. From this perspective, the technological advances in capitalism actually provide a concrete material basis for the future construction of socialism. This is why the concept of an "invading socialist society"—a gradual and barely recognized, daily development—was a favorite conception of James's in explaining the arrival of socialism (James, Forest, and Stone 1972).

Hence the much feared "globalization," which has defined Caribbean development post-Grenada, materially facilitates the establishment of a global proletariat, and a global proletarian consciousness that transcends the "socialism in one country" experiments of the twentieth century. It is through globalization that genuine socialist internationalism and Marx's war cry of "Workers of the world unite!" are realized concretely. For example, while the establishment of the capitalist world market has resulted in unprecedented levels of human suffering, it has laid the technological and material basis— the infrastructure—for a future socialist distribution based on human need. Thus, as Wallerstein (1984, 24–25) explains:

> The capitalist development of the world economy itself moves towards the socialisation of the productive forces. There is an organizational (as opposed to political) imperative, in which the full achievement of capitalist relations of production—through its emphasis on the increase of relative surplus value and the maximum efficiency (free flow) of the forces of production—pushes towards a fully planned single productive organizational network in the world economy.

Wallerstein sees the post–Cold War "victory of capitalism" as marking the near culmination point of this process:

The full triumph of capitalist values is a sign, indeed, *the* sign of the crisis of capitalism as a system. Capitalism has never historically operated in the mode its ideology dictates, because it cannot. . . . The universalisation of the law of value is precisely what will make it finally impossible to maintain the "mystical veil" of commodities, what will complete the process of the "destruction of the protecting strata." This will happen because the contradictory processes of the current phase of the capitalist world-economy will have so thoroughly demystified the techniques of domination that they will render them politically untenable. (Wallerstein 1984, 55)

Similarly, George Belle has identified the global movement toward capitalism and neoliberalism as vindication of both Wallerstein and James:

We have seen with our own eyes the rise today indisputably of a global system of world capitalism. Soviet socialism has collapsed and Islam is "under manners." Wallerstein says this world-economy has been there for five hundred years. Buttressing this system as presently formulated are economic integration movements on a continental scale. In these all the same lie . . . one of the contradictions of the new world order. Let us remember James's "Other of Stalinism": "The Other of Stalinism is an international socialist economic order, embracing from the start whole continents." How else should we get there but maybe through the present historical farce of a new world order, with its regional integration movements led by the European Economic Community, the I.M.F. and the World Bank? (Belle 1994, 106)

In the early twenty-first century, it can be asserted that the "mystical veil" has been removed and the "farce" has been exposed. The prolonged nature of the post-2008 crisis suggests that capitalism may now be entering a period of structural collapse, signaling the point at which it is beginning to perish. An indicator of capitalism's loss of ideological legitimacy is that the earlier Fukuyama-like triumphalism post-Gorbachev has long since been replaced by deep anxiety, and pessimism now permeates the very centers of capitalism itself.

A cursory reading of the financial pages provides strong indications that the confluence of crises (the "credit crisis," "oil price crisis," "food crisis," etc.) presents the possibility of deep structural reversal in the continued viability of capitalism as an economic system. The crisis of capitalism, though still in its infancy, is raising comparisons to the experience of the Great Depression (see Blaine and Strott 2008).

In addition, further delegitimizing the ideological self-confidence of capitalism, the years since the collapse of the Grenada Revolution have witnessed significant developmental challenges in the Caribbean, resulting from the adjustment to global market demands, and the dismantling of the sociopolitical relations that had sustained Caribbean economies in the immediate postcolonial period (see Joseph 1997). Despite their adjustments to globalization and neoliberalism, the expected benefits have not materialized. While the global and regional bourgeoisie have enjoyed the political freedom to pursue their objectives largely unobstructed, the Caribbean poor and working class have borne the burden of adjustment and have been called continually to make sacrifices.

However, there are early indications that the current economic challenges of capitalism, particularly through its impact on the middle class, have undermined the hegemonic infallibility of the system and may provide a new moment for the Caribbean Left to reclaim its confidence in the socialist alternative.

The economic crisis by itself does not automatically guarantee a resurgence of the Left, nor does it resolve the historical internal difficulties of socialism. There must be a deep and objective examination of Caribbean Marxism before and beyond the Grenada Revolution. In line with C. L. R. James's warnings, serious consideration must be given to the previous organizational models, tactics, and approaches accepted by the Caribbean Left. A prime area for reconsideration is the specific organizational and tactical mechanisms adopted to defend and advance the interests of the Caribbean working class. A vacuum has been created by the failure of the vanguardist models, and much of Marxism's crisis lies in the hesitation in reformulating new organizational and tactical mechanisms relevant to modern global capitalism. In the words of Kathy McAfee (1991, 244):

> The Stalinist version of the vanguard party and the bureaucratic socialist state have been widely discredited. Yet the socialist ideal that places the needs of people in front of the right of private property is far from dead. The placing of the collective good ahead of individual gain also resonates with the values of many traditional societies. At the same time, the democratic ideal of a society in which ordinary people have a say in the decisions that affect their lives, and civil liberties are honoured, is also very much alive.

This insistence on pursuing the universal, despite the temporary crisis of the particular, informs the Jamesian response (see Joseph 1994). A Caribbean Marxist response to the present crisis of the state and postcolonial development should encourage the development of popular, community, nongovernmental organizations and groups, since they represent the nearest approximation of worker-oriented democratization of Caribbean politics. Such a response also fulfills the Marxist call for the "withering away of the state." However, the "retreat" of the Caribbean state, while opening up immense possibilities for socialism in the medium to long term, makes possible in the short term the further entrenchment of capitalist social and economic relations, a more complete amalgamation into the global capitalist economy, and heightened recolonization of the region (Raghavan 1990).

Certain aspects of the Jamesian prescription require further reexamination several decades after their original formulation and several years after the collapse of the Grenada Revolution itself. Many writers view as problematic James's tendency to romanticize the working class and to view their actions as inherently "correct" responses at every stage of the development of capital. Since James saw the level of development of the revolutionary movement as inextricably linked to the stage of development of capital, he was often uncritical of the politics of the working class. This glorification of the working class is reflected in the Jamesian method that involved the careful recording and reporting of the daily habits and routines (including the nonpolitical ones) of the ordinary working people, in relation to their use of technology, their social relations, and their work (see Boggs 1968). It is this "anthropology" that fosters in James an uncritical trust in the revolutionary instincts of the working class.

It is also this tendency that has led many to misunderstand James's call for "dispensing with the division of labor in all spheres of life." James was not implying that the division of labor was inherently exploitative. Instead he was simply asserting the connection between technology and consciousness. Improved technology and heightened consciousness would obviate the need for an "educated" bureaucratic elite leading the revolution on behalf of backward and uneducated workers.

The most controversial aspect of this approach is his disagreement with Lenin, and indeed Marx, on the question of the revolutionary consciousness of workers. While Lenin had recognized that workers are not automatically revolutionary, and had devoted *What Is to Be Done* to exploring the political implications of this idea (Lenin 1969), James was more optimistic regarding the revolutionary potential of workers. He agreed with Rosa Luxemburg (1961) that the liberation of the working class was the work of the working class itself, and thus relied less on the organized leadership and more on the instinctive spontaneity of workers. To many practical politicians, this downplaying of the need for organization and the consequent reliance on the objective level of consciousness of workers go against real experience.

However, what is often misunderstood in James's confidence in the revolutionary potential of the worker is that it was based on the realization that transformations in the productive bases of the society (which are always ongoing) would create new organizational models and render obsolete the old. James's central argument was that the new conditions of production in the late twentieth century, and the wider societal and political developments associated with these transformations, meant that the worker of the mid- to late twentieth century was a qualitatively different person from the one who had prompted Lenin's specific organizational concerns. In other words, "The extent of human intervention varies, depending on the particular epoch" (quoted in Meeks 1994, 79).

To a large extent, therefore, the critics of James's confidence in the revolutionary potential of the working class, free of deliberate, externally created organizational catalysts, tend to miss the creative manner in which James explains and understands the relationship between technology, organization, consciousness, democratic possibilities, and revolutionary change. The point is not missed by Meeks, who identifies this as one of the hidden lessons of James's masterful treatment of the Haitian Revolution:

> This is the central field of combat. The issue of determination by agency or by productive forces, or more broadly put, the relationship between the two, is not restricted to some arcane debate between historians or political scientists, but extends into the very core notions of democracy and the relevance of Marxism, not just as a tool for analysis, but for human emancipation. (Meeks 1994, 81)

These questions have direct implications for revolutionary politics in the early twenty-first century. Writers familiar with James's Marxist thinking on the relationship between technology, organization, and consciousness have been pointing to the confluence of these factors in twenty-first-century moments as disparate as the political revolts of the Arab Spring, the protests of Occupy Wall Street and the Global Occupy Movement of 2011, and the grassroots organization responsible for the election and reelection of the first African American president of the United States of America, Barack Obama. Horace Campbell, for example, in an analysis of the Obama 2008 campaign, captures not only the nature of twenty-first-century political organization but the foresight of James in grasping the future directions:

> Every volunteer was seen as a potential community organizer, and the task of the network of Team Obama was to get information to potential organizers so that they could go out and do the work, whether there were paid organizers from the

Obama campaign or not. Tech-savvy volunteers were able to break the distinction between the professional and amateur political campaigner. . . . The dynamics of innovation throughout the campaign ensured that national goals were rooted in the capabilities of grassroots efforts and not imposed from the headquarters in Chicago. This was indeed bottom politics, and it was clear in grassroots fundraising. (Campbell 2010, 134–35)

Fully aware of the relevance of James in explaining the politics in capitalism's main center, Campbell, in a section titled "Beyond Vanguardism in the Twenty-first Century," highlights a number of features of contemporary American politics that demonstrate the applicability of James:

The self-organization and self-mobilization of the different social forces that were drawn into the political process in the United States in 2008 during the election campaign raised new directions for the understanding of revolutionary organization. A society cannot realize the potential for revolutionary change without revolutionary organizations. . . . Eugene Debs, one of the founders of the American Socialist Party in the early years of the twentieth century, believed that radical organizations had to have a "broad tent in which all trends within the socialist movement were represented in the same organization, because it would organize more people." (Campbell 2010, 15–16)

Indeed, this development of a broad tent embracing diverse sectors of the radical movement was seen most clearly in the Arab Spring and Occupy Movement revolts that emerged respectively in Arabic and North African states and later North America and Europe, becoming global movements. The significance of these movements from a Jamesian perspective resides in the reality of their self-organization independent of any commanding vanguard. In addition, having occurred in the midst of a deep crisis of capitalism, they have signaled the reawakening of a determined grassroots opposition to capitalism after nearly three decades of neoliberal hegemonic consolidation without sustained resistance. Whereas the Arab Spring has had limited and tenuous democratic victories, the Occupy Wall Street movement, after bursting into life on September 17, 2011, and stretching to capitals across the United States and Europe, lost momentum after about six months. However, despite their short-term expression, these movements' significance can be appreciated in both their impact on the ongoing economic crisis and the future possibilities to which they point (see Campbell 2011).

Conclusion

These, then, are the possibilities of revolution seen through a Jamesian lens roughly three decades after the overthrow of the Grenada Revolution. The battle lines for future struggle are now becoming clear, and the euphoria over the collapse of European communism has subsided significantly (see Midgett 1998) since the region has reaped scant benefit from unipolar global capitalism. Moreover, capitalism's post-2008 crisis is now wreaking havoc with Caribbean postcolonial development options. The Left, which for decades had been forced into retreat, has seen the emergence of Venezuela as a major regional force under the late Hugo Chavez, and that country now offers more progressive development alternatives through the Bolivarian Alternative for the Americas (ALBA). Thirty years after the Grenada Revolution, therefore, some new concrete noncapitalist options are now presenting themselves.

A Jamesian response to the present crisis of Soviet-type Marxism lies in the adoption of new organizational forms that should seek to address the weaknesses created by the division of labor within the party and trade union, the shortcomings of representative politics, and the distortions resulting from the separation of politics and economics. This will involve a struggle between leadership and mass in both political parties and trade unions. The new thrust of Caribbean Marxism should also aim to further the economic and political democratization of Caribbean society.

These concerns, which had been possibilities of the Grenada Revolution, remained unrealized because of the organizational choices that the revolution adopted. Years before the NJM was even conceived, C. L. R. James had been clarifying some of these very critical questions, albeit in the context of the debates within European Marxism. There is little evidence to suggest that the Grenadian revolutionaries paid much attention to James's ideas and work. Today, a younger generation can ill afford to repeat the sins of the past. In reflecting on Grenada, several decades later, the postrevolutionary generation would do well to use the thought of James as a guide to a new revolutionary future.

References

Albert, M., and R. Hahnel. 1978. *Unorthodox Marxism: An Essay on Capitalism, Socialism, and Revolution*. Boston: South End Press.

Ambursley, F. 1983. "Grenada and the New Jewel Revolution." In *Crisis in the Caribbean*, ed. F. B. Ambursley and R. Cohen, 199–222. London: Educational Books.

Arendt, H. 1963. *On Revolution*. London: Faber and Faber.

Austin, D., ed. 2009. *You Don't Play with Revolution: The Montreal Lectures by CLR James*. Oakland: AK Press.

Belle, G. 1994. "The Collapse of the Soviet System: Implications for the Caribbean Left." In *Crossroads of Empire: The Europe-Caribbean Connection, 1492–1992*, ed. A. Cobley, 94–110. Bridgetown: Department of History, University of the West Indies, Cave Hill Campus.

Blaine, C., and E. Strott. 2008. "Stocks Rise after Ugly Month." *Market Dispatches*, June 30. http://articles.moneycentral.msn.com/Investing/Dispatch/080630markets.aspx.

Boggs, J. 1968. *The American Revolution: Pages from a Negro Worker's Notebook*. New York: Modern Reader Paperbacks.

Campbell, H. 2010. *Barack Obama and Twenty-first Century Politics: A Revolutionary Moment in the USA*. London: Pluto Press.

———. 2011. "Africa: G20 Summit; Under the Shadow of the Occupy Wall Street Movement." *Pambazuka News Online*, November 10. http://allafrica.com/stories/prim-table/201111110339.html (accessed November 17, 2011).

Castro, F. 1983. *A Pyrrhic Military Victory and a Profound Moral Defeat*. (Speech delivered in Revolution Square, Havana, November 14.) Havana: Editoria Politica.

Dhondy, F. 2001. *C. L. R. James: Cricket, the Caribbean, and World Revolution*. London: Weidenfeld and Nicolson.

Dujmovic, N. 1988. *The Grenada Documents: Window on Totalitarianism*. Cambridge, MA: Institute of Foreign Policy Analysis.

Engels, F. 1978. *Anti-Duhring: Herr Eugen Duhring's Revolution in Science*. Moscow: Progress Publishers.

Fanon, F. [1967] 1983. *The Wretched of the Earth*. Reprint, with preface by Jean-Paul Sartre. Middlesex: Penguin.

Gittens, T. 1983. "Political Parties, Electoral Politics, and Democracy in Post-colonial Societies: The Demobilisation of Mass Mobilization." *Transition* 7:14–30.

Glaberman, M. 1992. "The Marxism of C. L. R. James." *C. L. R. James Journal* 3 (1): 45–56.

Hodge, M., and C. Searle. 1981. *Is Freedom We Making: The New Democracy in Grenada*. St. George's, Grenada: Government Information Service.

James, C. L. R. n.d. "Unpublished Analysis of the Grenada Revolution." C. L. R. James Archives, fol. 430, box 22. University of the West Indies, St. Augustine, Trinidad and Tobago.

———. 1937. *World Revolution, 1917–1936: The Rise and Fall of the Communist International*. London: Martin Secker and Warburg.

———. 1960. *Modern Politics*. Port-of-Spain: PNM Publishing.

———. [1962] 1984. *Party Politics in the West Indies*. San Juan: Inprint Caribbean.

———. 1964. *Lenin, Trotsky, and the Vanguard Party: A Contemporary View*. Detroit: Facing Reality Publishing.

———. 1966. *Perspectives and Proposals*. Detroit: Facing Reality Publishing.

———. 1977. *Nkrumah and the Ghana Revolution*. London: Allison and Busby

———. 1980a. *Notes on Dialectics: Hegel. Lenin. Marx*. London: Allison and Busby.

———. 1980b. *Spheres of Existence: Selected Writings*. London: Allison and Busby.

———. 1985. "C. L. R. James Views Grenada: 'From Self-Defense to Self-Destruction.'" *Intercontinental Press*, February 4.

———. 1986. *State Capitalism and World Revolution*. (Written in collaboration with Raya Dunayevskaya and Grace Lee, with an introduction by Paul Buhle and preface by Martin Glaberman. Chicago: Charles H. Kerr.

———. 1992. "The Class Struggle." In *The C. L. R. James Reader*, ed. A. Grimshaw, 190–201. Oxford: Blackwell.

———. 2001. *The Black Jacobins: Toussaint L'Ouverture and the San Domingo Revolution*. London: Penguin.

James, C. L. R., F. Forest, and R. Stone. 1972. *The Invading Socialist Society*. Detroit: Bewick Editions.

James, C. L. R., G. Lee, and P. Chaulieu. 1958. *Facing Reality*. Detroit: Bewick Editions.

Joseph, T. S. D. 1994. "The Political Thought of C. L. R. James: Its Utility and Relevance to the Contemporary Anglophone Caribbean; A Contribution to the Rethinking of Marxism." M.Phil. thesis, University of the West Indies, Cave Hill.

———. 1997. "'Old Expectations, New Philosophies': Adjusting State-Society Relations in the Post-colonial Anglophone Caribbean." *Journal of Eastern Caribbean Studies* 22 (4): 31–67.

La Rose, J. 1985. *Lessons of the Grenada Revolution*. London: Race Today Publications.

Lenin, V. I. 1943. *State and Revolution*. New York: International Publishers.

———. 1969. *What Is to Be Done? Burning Questions of Our Movement*. New York: International Publishers.

Luxemburg, R. 1961. *The Russian Revolution and Leninism or Marxism?* Ann Arbor: University of Michigan Press.

Marable, M. 1987. *African and Caribbean Politics: From Kwame Nkrumah to Maurice Bishop*. London: Verso.

Marx, K., and F. Engels. 1968. *The Communist Manifesto*. New York: Monthly Review Press.

McAfee, K. 1991. *Storm Signals: Structural Adjustment and Development in the Caribbean*. London: Zed.

Meeks, B. 1993. *Caribbean Revolutions and Revolutionary Theory: An Assessment of Cuba, Nicaragua, and Grenada*. London: Macmillan.

———. 1994. "Re-reading the Black Jacobins: James, the Dialectic, and the Revolutionary Conjuncture." *Social and Economic Studies* 43 (3): 75–103.

Midgett, D. 1998. "The St. Lucia Labour Party Victory of 1997 and the Decline of the Conservative Movements." *Journal of Eastern Caribbean Studies* 22 (3): 48–63.

Miliband, R. 1982. *Capitalist Democracy in Britain*. London: Oxford University Press.

———. 1983. *Class Power and State Power*. London: Verso.

New Jewel Movement. 1974. *Independence Manifesto*. St. George's, Grenada.

Raghavan, C. 1990. *Recolonisation: GATT, the Uruguay Round, and the Third World*. London: Zed.

Robinson, C. 1992. "C. L. R. James and the World System." *C. L. R. James Journal* 3 (1): 57–73.

Sandford, G. 1985. *The New Jewel Movement: Grenada's Revolution, 1979–1983*. Washington: Foreign Service Institute, U.S. Department of State.

Sandstrom, H. M. 1988. "The Ideology of Grenada's Revolution: Dead End or Model?" In *The Caribbean after Grenada: Revolution, Conflict, and Democracy*, ed. S. B. MacDonald, H. M. Sandstrom, and P. B. Goodwin Jr., 19–54. New York: Praeger.

Toffler, A. 1981. *The Third Wave*. London: Pan.

Wallerstein, I. 1984. *The Politics of the Word-Economy: The States, the Movements, and the Civilizations*. Cambridge: Cambridge University Press.

9. The Challenges for Revolutionary Change in the Caribbean

Horace G. Campbell

In 1980 the Jamaican icon Bob Marley echoed in song, "It takes a revolution to make a solution."[1] This paper arises out of a discussion of the concepts of revolution and revolutionary change in the Caribbean thirty years after the Grenada Revolution. Grenada is an island in the eastern Caribbean that gained international notoriety in 1979 when a small group from the New Jewel Movement (NJM), led by Maurice Bishop, seized power in a bloodless changeover of government. For four years, this small group held state power in this territory of more than one hundred thousand persons.

During this period, the NJM embarked on a number of social reforms relating to universal health care, universal adult education, and the provision of food, shelter, and clothing for the Grenadian peoples. The literature on the Grenada Revolution is extensive, and scholars from all sides of the intellectual divide have written extensively on this revolutionary process (see Henry 1990; Roopnaraine 2010).

Although the political leadership had proclaimed that the reforms were revolutionary, the Grenadian economy was still based on the export of primary commodities and tourism. There were no fundamental breaks with the old colonial production relations. Despite this limitation, the reforms in Grenada were far-reaching enough to garner support from other parts of the Caribbean and especially from the Cuban political leadership.

As self-proclaimed revolutionaries, the Grenadian political leaders were propelled into the midst of the global political cleavages and were being called on to make alliances at the global level. Within four years of this experiment, the Grenada Revolution imploded as a result of internal contradictions.[2] The U.S. military opportunistically seized on this implosion and invaded Grenada in October 1983. While the Grenadian reversal had been based on a one-week military invasion, the counterrevolutionary offensive of the Reagan administration in the Caribbean and Central America was unrelenting, with genocidal atrocities carried out in El Salvador, Guatemala, Honduras, Nicaragua, and other parts of the region. In many ways, it was in the aftermath of the capitalist crisis in September 2008 that new discussions of revolutionary possibilities arose. At the intellectual level there was another assault, one on the very idea of independence in the Caribbean. Using the Cuban Revolution as the foil, the spokespersons and ideologues of radical conservatism had sought to dominate the intellectual spaces in an attempt to silence serious discussions about revolutionary ideas and revolutionary change. Despite the history of revolutionary change in the region, the mantra of Margaret Thatcher, "There is no alternative" (to capitalism), had been reproduced in literature, the arts, and the social sciences. Yet in the spaces of the Caribbean that allowed for such activities, organizations and movements emerged to continue to call for profound transformations or, in the words of Franz Fanon, a "change in society from top to bottom."

One of the outstanding issues in the discussion of revolutionary change in the Caribbean is the place of armed struggles in the transformation of society. The paper that formed the basis for this chapter was presented on the island of San Andres in Colombia at the annual Caribbean Studies Association (CSA) conference in May to June 2008. Colombia is a meeting point of different elements of Caribbean and Latin American history, cultures, and experiences. In this society of Colombia, there are self-proclaimed revolutionaries. One group in particular, called the Revolutionary Armed Forces of Colombia (FARC), has been waging armed struggles in Colombia for over forty years. For a long period in the sixties and seventies, the idea of revolutionary change in the Caribbean was associated with armed military struggles. Gandhi's vision of nonviolent resistance and revolution had been frowned on by radicals in the Caribbean and Latin America (Prasad 2012). Supposedly, this armed struggle was only valid if the revolutionaries declared themselves to be Marxist Leninists in a vanguard party. Shortly after the CSA conference in June 2008, the experiences of armed struggles were brought to international attention when some hostages held by the FARC were "rescued." Hugo Chávez, the president of Venezuela, used the occasion to call on the FARC to suspend armed struggles.

The discussion about the Grenada Revolution and revolutionary change afforded an opportunity to break the silences among Caribbean intellectuals on revolution and revolutionary change. This chapter attempts to grasp the quantum leaps in the consciousness of the Caribbean peoples in relation to self-determination, independence, cooperation, and social transformation. After the Tunisian and Egyptian revolutionary openings in 2011, the African awakening opened new discussions on rebellions and revolutions internationally (Manji and Ekine 2012). In 2011, Peter Hallward, a student of the Haitian Revolution, noted that "Egypt's popular revolution will change the world."[3] Hallward noted the innovative aspects of the revolutionary process in Egypt with the following argument:

> For whatever happens next, Egypt's mobilization will remain a revolution of world-historical significance because its actors have repeatedly demonstrated an extraordinary capacity to defy the bounds of political possibility, and to do this on the basis of their own enthusiasm and commitment. They have arranged mass protests in the absence of any formal organization, and have sustained them in the face of murderous intimidation. In a single, decisive afternoon they overcame Mubarak's riot police and have since held their ground against his informers and thugs. They have resisted all attempts to misrepresent or criminalize their mobilization. They have expanded their ranks to include millions of people from almost every sector of society. They have invented unprecedented forms of mass association and assembly, in which they can debate far-reaching questions about popular sovereignty, class polarization and social justice.[4]

I agree with the view that revolution in one region has implications far beyond its own geographical space. This was the case of the Haitian Revolution of 1804 as it is with the revolutionary process in Egypt today.

In this chapter, I seek to engage new conceptual tools that are being offered in the area of revolutionary thought to link up with the historic revolutionary traditions of the peoples of the Caribbean. The chapter's introduction lays out a new theoretical terrain relating to social transformations and the collateral ideas of people's consciousness and political actions. In this sense, the transformations are linked to the conscious activities of the producers who want a new social order. It is the transformation where the working people "who have eyes and ears" will choose to look back to look forward. Looking back draws on the memories of revolution and counterrevolutionary changes in the Caribbean. This analysis also clarifies the differences between the liberal democratic revolution of the United States and France on one side and the thoroughgoing revolution of the peoples of Haiti on the other. In this looking back, I seek to understand the importance of memory.[5] The use of the memory of revolutionary change for the present purpose of setting in motion a new revolutionary period is very much part of the global political concept. In the simplest definition, memory is "the mental faculty of retaining and recalling past experience."

In this chapter, my task is to draw on the numerous memories of revolution by the different peoples of the Caribbean to make choices for the region's future. Within these memories, I attempt to draw out the emancipatory traditions and to distinguish these traditions from the traditions of enslavement, indentureship, colonialism, and exploitation. From these traditions, we can understand that there are many ways forward for the people in the quest for liberation and independence. These choices have been made clear by the experiments in Haiti, Mexico, Cuba, and Nicaragua, and with the ongoing revolution nested within the Bolivarian Revolution. At the same time, it is important to remember that the region's full independence cannot be realized as long as colonial outposts still exist in Cayenne, Guadeloupe, Martinique, Puerto Rico, the Virgin Islands, and about twenty other spaces.

The discussions on independence and revolution have been deepened by new ideas on revolution and the stark choices being placed before humans in the face of the neoliberal logic that had previously sustained the imperial hegemony of the United States. The global capitalist depression, along with the sharp intervention by the U.S. state to prop up the top 1 percent, brought back questions of the socialization of the means of production within the discussion of transition. These changes at the ideological, political, cultural, and economic levels are ongoing as political leaders have emerged in the Caribbean and Latin America, searching for new forms of economic cooperation. Throughout the world, from Zimbabwe to Nicaragua, from Algeria to Saint Vincent and the Grenadines, the radicals of yesterday have become stumbling blocks to new thinking about revolutionary change. It was C.L. R. James, who in reflecting on the spurts, leaps, and catastrophes associated with revolutionary change in the Caribbean, saw a clear linkage in the search for freedom from Toussaint-Louverture to Fidel Castro.[6] James was noting the impact of enslavement and the colonial economy in stimulating revolutionary thought and action. Tim Hector (2000, 6), one of the leaders of the progressive movements in the Caribbean, said the following in the wake of the demise of the Grenada Revolution:

> The Caribbean people will move again and when they move, they will move to [ensure] democratic control of [their] economics and politics—the highest form of democracy. Then, they will teach and give an impetus to countries many times larger than themselves.

This chapter seeks to engage the questions of democratic participation and revolutionary change when the Caribbean peoples move again.

Self-Organization, Self-Emancipation, and Peoples' Consciousness in Revolution

Thirty years after the implosion of the Grenada Revolution and nearly twenty-five years after the experiments in Nicaragua, new political movements for revolutionary change have sprung up around the world. I have argued elsewhere that we are in a veritable "revolutionary moment," and the uprisings in Brazil, Egypt, Turkey, Bulgaria, Indonesia, and Spain point to restlessness among the ordinary people.[7] In these discussions from Bolivia, Brazil, Ecuador, Venezuela, and other parts of Latin America, an entirely new feature has been brought into the discussion. That is the role of the ideas of the African descendants and the indigenous peoples in shaping the new political cultures that can emerge from the challenges to the old ideas of the inviolability of the market, domination over nature, domination over women, and dominion over other human beings. James Petras has specifically named the Indian and peasant movements in Paraguay, Ecuador, Guatemala, and Brazil as the organizations guiding the new understanding and practices of revolution.[8] In these discussions, it is no longer possible to write and deliberate on revolution as if the indigenous and formerly enslaved are nonpersons. The debate on revolutions involves a fundamental transformation in people's consciousness about the worth of all humans, and feminist consciousness has deepened the understanding that revolutionary ideas must challenge patriarchal and homophobic ideas about society, the state, and politics.

The proposition of this chapter is that we are not reflecting on revolution in the traditional sense of simply seizing state power; we are talking about a fundamental transformation. These are transformations at the level of consciousness, material organization, the manner of political organization, gender relations, the rights of same-gender-loving persons, new conceptions of leadership, and our relation to the planet Earth and the universe. It is the transformation at the level of our relationship to the planet that Vandana Shiva (2005) calls "Earth democracy." These transformations in consciousness are taking place at the same time as the old ideas that legitimated capitalist exploitation have fallen into disarray. It is from within the United States that the need for the socialization of economic relations has been brought back to the center of politics. These economic and financial changes are occurring at the same time as major advances in the realms of science and technology, especially with the convergence of the many revolutionary technologies: biotechnology, robotics, information technologies, nanotechnology, and cognitive technologies. Mobilizing the resources of the state in the service of the people had been dramatized by the experiences of the Cuban society facing the destruction wrought by hurricanes. This mobilization is now more urgent as the evidence of global warming threatens the future of island societies.

In Cuba, advances in biotechnology and stem cell research have been harnessed to promote the health of the population instead of for corporate profits. Where it is possible to discern scientific changes at the material level with the precision of the physical sciences, it is not so possible to discern the same changes in how the people transform themselves and their consciousness. Usually the transformation of a people's consciousness is a slower process, but from time to time, political and social forces converge to a point where, according to Marx, "the revolution comes like a thief in the night" when no one is expecting it. From the moment of the eruptions in Tunisia in January 2011, humanity has now entered a new era of revolutionary change.

The implosion of the accumulation model of U.S. capitalism, along with the deepening inequalities between the superrich and the poor, means that peoples are actively looking for alternatives. In the process, peoples in the Caribbean are reflecting on the past revolutions while at the same time drawing lessons from other revolutionary possibilities. The revolutionary changes in the Caribbean that have been the most important are the Haitian Revolution, the Mexican Revolution, the Cuban Revolution, the Nicaraguan Revolution, the Rastafarian cultural revolution, the Grenada Revolution, and the Bolivarian Revolution.

The Global Capitalist Depression and the Implications of Linear Thinking

The Bolivarian Revolution set the stage for the new rounds of revolutionary changes, where it brings into being all the lessons of the former revolutions, so that revolution has the possibility to spread like wildfire in the next thirty years in the Caribbean. Hugo Chávez had emerged from one section of society that had been discriminated against for centuries. Chávez understood the structural crisis of capital and understood long before the crash in 2008 that plunder and racist oppression were the forms of recovery that would be adopted by the Euro-American capitalist.

The English journalist Richard Gott noted the impact of white racist ideas on the Left and revolutionary thinking in Latin America and the Caribbean. Writing in the *Guardian*, Gott clearly outlined the impact of European "settler colonialism" throughout the world. Settler colonialism is an evocative idea used in discussions about the British Empire to describe how settlers attempted to exterminate indigenous peoples while setting up social relations of extreme exploitation. Such forms of settler colonialism are based on the principles of white supremacy.[9]

One of the important points about the gender and class structure of settler societies is the ways in which one section of the dominated classes internalizes the alleged superiority of Europe and accepts the idea that European workers would lead other nonwhite workers to revolution because Africa is uncivilized, backward, and bereft of ideas. Between these two extremes were some of the mulattoes who accepted the idea that Europe was a space of enlightenment and progress and Africa a zone of disease, hunger, and savagery. Such a deformation in thinking has stifled creativity and original thinking in many parts of the international progressive movement. Throughout the Caribbean, the stratum that called itself mulatto or the brown intelligentsia has been the group most insecure in relation to its subservience to ideas of linearity from Western Europe. This subservience is also manifest in the belief in a linear conception of the world. The chaos and complexity unleashed by plunder, genocidal wars, genocidal economics, genocidal thinking, and the actual genocide of millions were passed off as an unfortunate but necessary stage of progress. Today this kind of thinking cannot grasp the full dimensions of the current capitalist depression.

One variant of this linear thinking was the view that the Caribbean and Latin America had to go through stages of development (from communalism to capitalism and then socialism) similar to Europe. This was legitimized in the language of the need for the "development of the productive forces." By this logic, the eugenic ideas of the need for European guidance are brought into the discourse on liberation and revolution. This defect at the intellectual level is manifested all over the Caribbean but is most pronounced in a society such as the Dominican Republic, where this deformity inspired genocidal thoughts and acts against Haitians in the 1930s. Thus far it is the novelists and nonfiction writers such as Edwidge Danticat who have broken the silence on the genocide of the Haitians in 1937. *The Farming of Bones* remains a work of fiction that reminds the world of the silences relating to the genocidal violence against the Haitian peoples and sharpens the need for revolution in the Caribbean.

The middle classes, usually the brown middle-class leadership, appointed themselves as teachers and leaders of the Caribbean people. In terms of cultural and intellectual stagnation, one can witness the results of the intellectual leadership of this class, especially their hostility to Africa and indigenous knowledge and indigenous peoples. This stratum has acted as a break in the full understanding of the inner cultural and spiritual strengths of the people. In this way, their intellectual orientation acted as a drag on revolutionary action.

Walter Rodney's admonition that the intellectual must root himself and herself in the activity of the masses then becomes a relevant starting point. It was Rodney who reminded the Caribbean intellectual of the importance of historical memory. In writing on the African Revolution, in celebrating C. L. R. James, Rodney said: "A people's consciousness is heightened by knowledge of the dignity and determination of their fore-parents. Indeed, the African worldview regarding ancestors as an integral part of their living community makes it so much easier to identify to a given generation with the struggles of an earlier generation" (Rodney 1986, 34).

How do we use our knowledge of our fore-parents to empower the present generation to move in a new revolutionary direction? This question brings us to the concept that was introduced in the introduction, which is emancipatory politics rooted in the memory of previous revolutions. Serious discussions of the Grenada experiences after 1979 are necessary to draw out the strengths and weaknesses of that short-lived experiment in revolutionary change. This requires tapping into the knowledge and memory of the people who made this revolution possible. This concept of memory is tied to a new paradigm of what we call the unified emancipatory approach to revolution. This new paradigm, which accords proper respect to memory and clear, deliberate thought and action, should liberate humanity from the mechanical competitive and individualistic conception of the European Enlightenment, in short, liberalism. It is only when we move out of the linear worldview of Europe that it will be possible to accelerate the potentialities for new revolutionary changes. It is the binary in which certain European intellectuals reduced humans to material blobs, and the divisions within the Cartesian model of the separation of spirit and matter, man and woman, black and white, mind and body, heterosexual and homosexual—in short, the kind of separation that breaks the links between human beings and the universe. Bruce Lipton (2005) has written about the interconnectedness of all humans and the fractal wisdom that must be mobilized to benefit from this interconnectedness. It is this interconnectedness and unified emancipatory approach that inspires the lyrics of our other liberation fighter, Bob Marley, who exhorts: "Emancipate yourself from mental slavery."

The revolution in the twenty-first century seeks to arise out of democratic traditions and democratic relations between human beings. It is in this sense that the new ideas about interconnectedness of humans seek to transcend ideologies that are exclusivist and vanguardist. In other words, in some revolutions there were revolutionaries who were quick to exclude others based on their beliefs or backgrounds. This was certainly the case in the U.S. revolution of 1776, where the revolutionaries felt that it was possible to fight for freedom from British colonialism and yet continued to enslave African descendants, while also carrying forward genocidal ideas and genocidal practices against the First Nation peoples (see Stannard 1992). A similar fate befell the Mexican revolution of 1910, when the ruling classes sought to align themselves with the liberal democratic traditions of the United States. The rulers who emerged within the dominant political party reversed the struggles for land and freedom that had inspired the massive participation of the indigenous peoples. This limitation in relation to the politics of exclusion has only been compounded in the bloodletting of the Bolshevik revolution. In 1917 there were those who thought that they were correct to believe that whoever held on to state power must be the ones with the correct ideological line. A consequence of this belief is that under Joseph Stalin an orgy of violence was carried out against those who were out of power. This political tradition, rooted in vanguardism and exclusivist ideas, was copied in Grenada, in the Caribbean, with disastrous consequences.

The ideas of Ubuntu, which connects all humans, seek to break with the binary categories that perpetuate division and the politics of exclusion. Ubuntu is a philosophy that is alive in Africa and among indigenous peoples that links humans to one another and to the universe. There is no adequate translation of Ubuntu in the English language, but loosely translated it is about love, sharing, forgiveness, and reconciliation. I have elaborated on these ideas in my book *Barack Obama and Twenty-first Century Politics: A Revolutionary Moment in the USA*. Ubuntu presupposes democratic relations between humans and a spirit of the appreciation of human beings beyond hierarchies based on superiority and inferiority. The promise of entrenching this hierarchy of human beings has been signaled by the pharmaceutical companies and biotech companies who want to patent all life-forms and develop a market in body parts.

In the attempt to move beyond mechanical and hierarchical thinking, some scholars have been theorizing the concept of quantum societies and quantum politics.[10] These theoreticians are seeking to draw on the spiritual energies of human beings to unleash new capabilities for free human beings, that is, human beings who are freed from the complexes of racial, gendered, and sexual hierarchies. Some have already begun to rethink how human beings can unleash their spiritual energies.

How do we achieve that quantum leap in our consciousness, so that the Caribbean tradition of emancipation based on self-determined politics and self-determined activity becomes the reference point for the people and for the new phase of revolution? It is memory to which we must appeal, and not to the activities of those who carried out genocide, enslavement, and indenture. Only then will the new thinking become the reference point away from what is known as "modernity," "progress" and "development."

There had been a circumstance in which a certain branch of Marxism, as a doctrine, turned to the crude determinism of what is called dialectical materialism, which outlines the stages of development of human beings and draws a caste line from a lower to a higher stage of development. It is now urgent to reflect on whether this rigidity contributed to progressive societal and spiritual decay. These stage theories buy into the linearity and homogeneity of Enlightenment theories. This mode of thinking about stages has prevented us from moving into that self-liberating consciousness.

There are numerous historical memories in the Caribbean, but the two most powerful have been the memory of the fight against slavery, indenture, and genocide; and the memory of chaos, wars, genocide, slavery, indenture, and colonialism. The memory of genocide and colonialism is the one that has been celebrated as "modernity." Each of these two memories sets in motion different intellectual energies. To the extent that the first memory references possibilities, it produces a positive input/output cycle, whereas the second memory (which is called progress, technological advancement, and the European civilizing mission) reproduces counterrevolutionary cycles. We now turn to the lessons learned from the first and most profound revolution in the Caribbean, the Haitian Revolution.

Lessons from the Haitian Revolution

The Haitian people were the first to imagine the break with bondage and with European thought. The Haitian Revolution banished slavery, colonialism, and white supremacy in one blow. It was a novelty that shocked the Western world, and the spirit of 1804 still inspires the people of the Caribbean. More clearly, the Haitian Revolution influenced major revolutionary changes in the thinking of the peoples of the Caribbean. It was the society that inspired the struggles for independence and self-determination in Central America and Latin America. In the words of C. L. R James:

> Toussaint L'Ouverture and the Haitian slaves brought into the world more than the abolition of slavery. When Latin Americans saw the small and insignificant Haiti could win and keep independence they began to think that they ought to do the same. Petion, the ruler of Haiti, nursed back to health the sick and defeated Bolivar, gave him money, arms and a printing press to help in the campaign which ended in the freedom of the Five States.[11]

Despite this record, in the main, the scholarship in Latin America remains silent on the linkage between the Haitian Revolution and the role of Simón Bolívar as a liberator. The majesty and pride of the historical struggles have been overshadowed by another history, that of militarism, dictatorship, and brutal repression of the ideas of the majority. This brutal history is documented in Michel-Rolph Trouillot's book *Haiti: State against Nation*. Imperial opposition to the Haitian Revolution, along with the racial and social imbalances within Haiti, led to chronic political instability.[12] Patrick Bellegarde-Smith (2004) used the metaphor of the "breached citadel" to convey the varying forces that continued to work against the realization of the full potentialities of the Haitian peoples.

So what do we understand about the Haitian Revolution today? The Haitian Revolution is a nonevent in the history books on revolution, and this rendering of the Haitian Revolution is manifest in the silences on the importance of the events of 1791 to 1804 (Trouillot 1998). From the scholarship of Carolyn Fick, C. L. R. James, and Michel-Rolph Trouillot, the radical overthrow of slavery in Haiti qualified as a revolution. The Haitian Revolution set itself on the stage of human history, about which James asked: "How is it that this revolution could defeat two major powers of the world?" Ultimately the Haitian Revolution was defeated politically. The internal contradictions of the Haitian Revolution meant that it could not survive in the world within which it was inserted. But it sent a message to people that in the midst of the most oppressive forms of human relations, human beings can make a revolution. James correctly noted: "The transformation of slaves trembling in hundreds before a single white man, into a powerful people able to organize themselves and defeat the most powerful European nations of their day, is one of the great epics of revolutionary struggles and achievement."[13] Haitian revolutionaries such as René Depestre have also underscored the epic nature of the achievements of the Haitian Revolution. Depestre was writing in an effort to understand the reversal of the revolution and the militaristic traditions that emerged from the need to defend the revolution against those who wanted to return the people to slavery. In many respects, the implosion of Grenada in 1983 emanated from the fact that many on the Caribbean left did not fully study the Haitian Revolution.

We have not yet learned one of the fundamental lessons of 1804: that the people through their self-organization and self-mobilization could precipitate revolution. This is because the standard texts on revolution in the Americas exclude Haiti from the revolutionary tradition. Michael West sought to make up for this lacuna in Caribbean historiography by drawing from the song of the popular musician David Rudder "Haiti, I'm Sorry." West maintained: "The slave revolt turned revolution in Saint Domingue was, quite simply, the single most cataclysmic and transfiguring event of its time, the Age of Revolution, a historical verity recklessly omitted from the literature on that era."[14]

Within mainstream academia, Theda Skocpol's *States and Social Revolutions: Social Revolutions in the Modern World* is suggested to students to enable the Western bourgeoisie to monopolize the discourse on revolution. Skocpol is referenced as the authority on political revolutions in France, Russia, and China. Despite the Western view of the Haitian Revolution, I can agree with C. L. R. James and Michael West that we can learn from the Haitians about how these enslaved peoples overcame obstacles to realize self-liberation and defeated the French, British, and Spaniards. The poor people had to fight for liberty, for their very lives. It is this fear of the replay of revolution by the most oppressed that continues to exercise the brains of Western bourgeois scholars.

The Lessons from the Cuban Revolution

According to C. L. R. James, "What took place in French San Domingo in 1792–1804 reappeared in Cuba in 1958." Counterrevolution refers to the opposition to revolution, particularly those who act after a revolution to try to overturn or reverse it, in full or in part. In the case of the militaristic dictatorship since 1804, there has been a continuity in the rise of social forces who sought to return Haiti to the class and racial composition and the principles of white supremacy that existed before the revolution. Returning Haiti to colonialism and slavery was not possible, and the governments of the world grudgingly accepted Haiti's claim to national sovereignty while undermining its efforts toward economic independence. Such was the hostility within and without Haiti that even in the wake of the kind of genocidal violence visited on the Haitian peoples by their own leaders and by Trujillo in the Dominican Republic, there is not the kind of international outcry that would oppose the counterrevolution.

The revolution in Mexico of 1910 to 1920 has been followed by a similar wave of counterrevolutionary ideas and practices. For the peoples of Mexico (who had been robbed of their land by the expansion of the U.S. territory), the forms of governance in the nineteenth century had brought a succession of dictators. The Mexican Revolution sought to end the years of dictatorship, to end the marginalization and exploitation of the indigenous peoples, and to create a platform for land reform. Although the revolution laid the basis for regular elections, the results of the revolution in Mexico would place it within the category of a liberal democratic revolution, similar to the U.S. revolution.

As in the United States, where it required the Civil War to bring about the rights of African Americans, so it is in Mexico, where the landless and the poor have been waging numerous forms of political and social struggles to complete the tasks begun in the revolution of 1910. In the 1990s, the Zapatistas in the Chiapas region took inspiration from this revolution to call for a new struggle against dispossession, exploitation and the politics of exclusion.[15]

The Survival of the Cuban Revolution

The more recent literature on revolution and counterrevolution in Latin America and the Caribbean moves the discussion beyond class struggles to include questions of racism, environmental degradation, culture, gender relations, and the rights of same-gender-loving persons. It is in the case of the successful defense of revolutionary principles in Cuba where the success is more important, because this revolution has survived the hostile onslaughts of the United States for the past fifty years. The literature on the origins, consolidation, and survival of the Cuban revolutionary process is extensive, so I will not revisit this literature here.[16] In "Whither Cuban Socialism? The Changing Political Economy of the Cuban Revolution," Douglas Hamilton (2002) identified six periods in the annals of the consolidation of the Cuban Revolution.

What became clear from the different periods is that it was the popular mobilization of the people of Cuba that prevented the reversal of the revolution, especially after the fall of the Berlin Wall in 1989. The impressive gains in the areas of the delivery of social services such as health care and education have been acknowledged by international organizations such as the United Nations Development Program (UNDP) and the United Nations Children's Fund (UNICEF). These transformations of education and health services have been associated with the kind of popular leadership that can mobilize a society for defensive purposes. It was in the society's defense against natural disasters such as hurricanes where the full importance of the committees for the defense of the revolution emerged. These committees were associated with mass organizations of workers, students, women, cultural workers, writers, and small-scale agricultural workers.

Another aspect of the narrative of the Cuban Revolution has been told by women, who have argued that the revolution is still grappling with the heritage of patriarchy and misogyny. While acknowledging the successes of the revolution and the important benefits it has brought women in relation to reproductive health, these critiques relate the issues of sex and revolution to the new stage of transformation that is necessary to combat all forms of domination and oppression. Within Cuba, there are also people of African descent, who point to the ways in which the policies of the Special Period that strengthened foreign interests in the tourism sector conspire with the new attitudes of privileging whiteness to the detriment of some citizens of African descent. Some of the Cuban writers and activists making these criticisms within the revolution can be distinguished from those who do not distinguish between the successes of the Cuban Revolution and the continued counterrevolutionary project from those who are ensconced in the United States, especially the Cuban community in Florida (see C. Moore 2008). The binaries between certain brands of black nationalism and socialism continue to hold back serious discussion on the future of revolutions in Latin America and the Caribbean, and revolutionaries must be open to challenging all forms of chauvinism, whether from the right or left. Today the Cuban Revolution is confronted with the challenge of how to transform the consciousness of the people beyond the generation of political ideas that emanated from the Cold War period. It is here where we can understand that successful defense of the revolution can bring new challenges. Can the society repair and heal from the traditions of colonialism without confronting Eurocentrism? Revolutionary Cubans are confronted with the same question as Vietnam and China. Vietnam and China have been confronted with whether revolution is based on rapid industrialization and what is called development of the productive forces. Do you develop the industrial productive capacity of the society at the expense of the cultural or social knowledge of the people?

Cuba is confronting this crossroads at a later period than Vietnam and China because it was not able to invest in rapid industrialization in the ways that China has. The consequence of this rapid industrialization in China, however, has been income inequality, ecological destruction, and the intensified exploitation of the producing classes. The Cuban Revolution stands at a crossroads of whether to build on the elements that preserved the revolution—the elements of people's power and the committees for the defense of the revolution—or to go toward a direction of foreign direct investment. If Cuba moves toward the path of the consolidation of people's power, it will have to have a better appreciation of the diversity and the unity of the different peoples in Cuba, especially the African population. How Cuban society deepens its sense of justice and transformation regarding the legacies of African knowledge systems and religious and spiritual forms will help to preserve the nation's independence. At the same time, Cuba will continue to distinguish itself from societies such as the Dominican Republic, Jamaica, and Puerto Rico.

The democratization of race and gender relations is a major challenge that no society can solve by itself. These challenges can only be solved within the wider anti-imperial, antiracist, and antisexist struggles that seek to repair the history of genocide, deformed masculinity, sexism, slavery, and racism. This challenge can only be solved in relationship to the ongoing revolutions in other parts of the Caribbean. Yet despite these challenges, it is possible to agree with Walter Rodney that the Cuban Revolution will be written in the history books as the forerunner of the socialist transformation of the Americas.

The Rastafarian Revolution: From Cultural Resistance to Cultural Transformation

The Rastafarian intervention has been one of the most profound attempts to transform the consciousness of the Caribbean people in the sense that the Rastafarian movement confronted humanity's relationship with the universe, with the spirits, and with matter, as well as how to reorganize society. In its own way, this movement that arose out of the hills of the Jamaican countryside challenged the old forms of agricultural production and the ways of organizing agriculture and organizing the Earth. It is at the plane of Earth democracy where the Rastafarian movement is at one with one of the most profound movements today, the environmental justice movement. Hurricanes and storms in the Caribbean have been the most dramatic reminders of the imminent dangers of global warming.

The Rastafarian philosophy attacked crude consumerism, as well as the idea of white supremacy and black inferiority. Yet it should be acknowledged up front that this movement inherited many of the contradictions that emanated from the ways in which it extended itself to identification with an African monarch. One would, therefore, seek out the wisdom of Amílcar Cabral on how to grasp the dialectic of the positive and the negative in the cultural struggles of a people. Contrary to the sociological and anthropological studies of the Rastafarian movement that labeled the movement millenarian, escapist, and cultist, my study of over thirty years ago, *Rasta and Resistance: From Marcus Garvey to Walter Rodney*, identified the movement as a major force for cultural and political resistance. The study identified the Rastafarian song as a song of deep memory of African independence and autonomy. In more recent times, my work has focused on Bob Marley and the transition from the memory of slavery to the memories of emancipation and freedom. Marley emerged as a Caribbean revolutionary who wailed: "It takes a revolution to make a solution."

Of his many renditions of emancipatory politics and the emancipation of the mind, Bob Marley turned to religious language and images to reach a section of the population that is not usually reached by traditional discourses on revolution. Those who study wave theory and the physics of music are examining the lyrics and vibrations of the music produced by Bob Marley and reggae artists to see how this art form and spiritual message emerged as a revolutionary form. Bob Marley used religious metaphors to stimulate the imagination of the sufferers. In the song "It Takes a Revolution to Make a Solution," he starts out with the need for a memory of truth. Eusi Kwayana, the Caribbean revolutionary, grasped the importance of the Marley intervention and called his contribution one of the landmark achievements of the Caribbean Revolution.

When the Rastafarians and Bob Marley call on us to "emancipate ourselves from mental slavery," they are admonishing the intellectuals and the activists to make a break with the epistemologies that justify and cover up oppression. Because social movements are not static, the dynamism of Rasta culture has been challenged by the mainstream attack on the Rastafarians along with the attempts at co-optation within the system. However, one of the movement's severe weaknesses was the extent to which some of its most conscious elements succumbed to homophobic and patriarchal ideas.

The Lessons from the Nicaraguan Experiment

The other two revolutions that are important to the memory of Caribbean revolution and revolutionaries are the Nicaraguan Revolution of 1978, which brought the Sandinistas to power, and the Grenada Revolution in 1979. Nicaragua, along with Haiti and Cuba, shares a history of U.S. military occupation and brutal dictators. Not only did the United States intervene militarily against General Sandino, but after the first defeat of the popular rebellion, the United States supported the brutal dictatorship of General Anastasio Somoza for over thirty years.

It was the memory of the revolt that the people drew on to launch a new struggle in the seventies that culminated in the removal of Somoza in 1979. The revolutionaries called themselves the Sandinistas and moved to carry forward the reforms that had been initiated in an earlier period. This revolution did not survive because the Reagan administration carried out one of the most sustained counterrevolutionary onslaughts in the Caribbean in the form of support for the counterrevolutionaries, who were called the Contras.

This counterrevolution involved the support for conservative and militarists forces all over Central America and the Caribbean. It was in the counterrevolutionary onslaught that the U.S. government intensified its alliance with those who were involved in the shipment and sale of narcotics so as to finance its war against the Nicaraguan revolution. This counterrevolutionary philosophy inspired brutality and violence, supported armed thugs, and strengthened the drug cartels in Latin America and the Caribbean. Gary Webb, in *Dark Alliance: The CIA, the Contras, and the Crack Cocaine Explosion*, chronicled the web of destruction wreaked by this alliance all across the region, especially the initiation of the crack cocaine epidemic inside the United States by the intelligence services.[17] When the United States is democratized, the full extent of this nested loop of drugs, militarism, counterrevolution, and dictatorship will be revealed. What is important to this analysis is that the Caribbean revolution had attempted to make a break from external covert rule in this global political climate. What is also important about Nicaragua is the reality that, among some revolutionaries, sexist and patriarchal ideas abound, and these ideas stifle revolutionary breakthroughs.

Revolution and Counterrevolution in Grenada

In preparing would-be Caribbean revolutionaries to understand the world revolution, Walter Rodney had written a document on the Russian Revolution titled *Two World Views of the Russian Revolution*. Rodney was warning the freedom fighters that they could not depend on the Russian émigrés or the bourgeois writers for their analysis of the Russian Revolution. Drawing from the historiography of the French Revolution, he pointed to the differences between several interpretations, that is to say, the "liberal" Thiers, the "conservative" Taine, the "social democrat" Jaures, and Marx himself.

Rodney sought to point out that just as there were many differing interpretations of the French Revolution, so there were differences between the Bolshevik analysis, the Trotskyist, the academic Marxist, and the bourgeois interpretations of the Russian Revolution. In many ways, going through these interpretations was a clearing ground for a critical assessment of the problems of building a revolutionary movement and carrying forward the transformation of society. The chapters on the problems of peasant collectivization and issues of industrialization brought to the fore that whatever the context, transformation could not be carried forward with dictatorial tendencies. The Grenadian experiment also brought out another question, the issue of secrecy in handling contradictions among the leaders.

It was in this section of the book that Rodney developed the critique of vanguardism and the party form that celebrated the virtues of democratic centralism, where there was a lot of centralization but no democracy. In conclusion, Rodney sharpened his point regarding the need for an African point of view on the Bolshevik revolution by noting that the African point of view had to be radically different from the bourgeois or the Marxist view, which was distorted by bourgeois lens. In the book's last paragraph, Rodney wrote:

> Ours clearly could not be that of the bourgeois. Is it that of the Soviets? They have their national interests, their great power interests and historiography reflects that—but we are likely to be very close because of the similarity of our present and past with their past in the period under study. Current developments might complicate the issue of taking a stand with the Soviets; but essentially what we need to do is define our own stand first and see where it coincides. Assuming a view springing from some Socialist variant not necessarily Marxist but anti capitalist, assuming a view that is at least radical humanist—then the Soviet Revolution of 1917 and the subsequent construction of socialism emerge as a very positive historical experience from which we ourselves can derive a great deal as we move to confront similar problems.[18]

Rodney was seeking an understanding of the internal dynamics of the contradictions within Bolshevism that could have produced the kind of leader such as Josef Stalin. Here Rodney was developing a critique of the subservience to a certain type of Marxism. It is a brand of Marxism that does not take into consideration the particularities of a people's history. Rodney also sought to specify the aspects of Marxism that were relevant in the contemporary period of revolution.

Revolution in Grenada

The numerous books and articles on the Grenada Revolution serve to remind Caribbean scholars of ways in which the revolution electrified the spirit of the peoples of the Caribbean. The idea that a small island of the size of Grenada, just 133 square miles, could consider itself a force for change on the world stage was itself a manifestation of the boldness and self-assertiveness of the Caribbean peoples. Numerous studies of this experiment have showed what was possible when a government placed itself in the service of the people. Maurice Bishop had been associated with a tendency in the Caribbean known as the "New Beginning," influenced by the ideas of C. L. R James. Thus, in Grenada, Bishop and the NJM sought to embark on a new course that placed the workers, farmers, small traders, and youth at the forefront and organized agrarian reform to benefit small farmers and farmworkers. The NJM rapidly expanded trade union rights, advanced women's equality in the workplace, established literacy programs, and instituted free medical care. These reforms were dubbed as communist by the internal and external opposition in the Caribbean.

Early after the seizure of power, sharp divisions arose within the NJM over questions of the ideas, organization, and leadership and the path being embarked on in Grenada. Shortly after seizing power, one faction of the NJM dictated the line that the party should declare itself as a Marxist-Leninist vanguard party. Here was a small society of nearly one hundred thousand people where the people all knew each other and lived peacefully in communities. Those who called themselves Marxists insisted that the society should embark on a path of Marxism-Leninism with a tight-knit secret vanguard without regard for the history of Grenada. This small group was aligned at the regional level with a group across the Caribbean that was associated with Marxists in Jamaica called the Workers Party of Jamaica.

Bob Marley's song "Revolution" begins with the line "Revelation reveals the truth." Thirty years after the Grenada Revolution, the revelation of truth is urgently needed to move the region out of the grip of the economic and social retrogression that set in after the overthrow of the Grenadian experiment. This truth is needed, insofar as the events and causes of the implosion that led to the arrest and assassination of Maurice Bishop are still clouded by partisan feelings. Rupert Roopnaraine, a witness to the events on the ground in October 1983, has written a compelling account of the challenges facing the leadership and why the secrecy about the differences among the leaders had weakened the revolutionary process. Patsy Lewis has also borne witness to the actual balance of forces. In his book *Grenada: Revolution, Invasion, and Aftermath*, Hugh O'Shaughnessy has provided an in-depth account of the nature of the political struggles within the NJM and the factors that led to the assassination of Maurice Bishop. Tim Hector was scathing in his treatment of the role of Trevor Munroe and Bernard Coard in the destruction of the Grenada Revolution:

> Munroe and the Coardites, following absurd Stalinist texts, abandoned even in the Soviet Union, went for the grandiose state project, rather than the peoples Revolutionary project, housing themselves, and organising themselves to do so. Our Caribbean Nation tendency was shunted aside, and the Munroe-Coard tendency elevated. We had no voice inside Grenada and ACLM-NJM relations once very fraternal, deteriorated beyond belief. (Hector 2000, 6)

Nadia Bishop, the daughter of Maurice Bishop, has entered the discussion on the Caribbean futures by invoking the spirit of Ubuntu, forgiveness and reconciliation.[19]

U.S. Invasion and Counterrevolution

After the assassination of Maurice Bishop on October 19, 1983, the political leaders of Barbados, Dominica, and Jamaica aligned themselves with the political leadership of Ronald Reagan to provide diplomatic and political cover for the U.S. invasion. One of the incomplete lessons of this invasion was the extent to which the political leadership within the Reagan administration had wanted to use the invasion as a provocation to intensify military action against Cuba. As it was, the invasion of Grenada was as traumatic for the Caribbean as the overthrow of the government of Salvador Allende had been for the Chilean people when the United States supported the military overthrow of his government on September 11, 1973. These military interventions, at a time when the United States was arming the Contras and integrating itself with the financial barons of the international narcotics trade, set the stage for counterrevolution not only in the Caribbean but throughout the world. It was the Reagan doctrine of military supremacy, in the context of Grenada, that laid and refined those elements in the military management of the international system by the United States. The essence of this military management has been well documented. In *The Liberal Virus: Permanent War and the Americanization of the World,* Samir Amin has argued that the U.S. project for military domination and crude materialism had its roots in the liberal ideas of Western Europe. Amin pointed to the memory of genocide and the potential for genocide as growing from a mode of economic organization that placed profits before humans. For Samir Amin, the new and more dangerous form of liberalism is related to the particularities of U.S. history. "American society despises equality. . . . Extreme inequality is not only tolerated, it is taken as a symbol of 'success' that liberty promises. But liberty without equality is equal to barbarism" (Amin 2004, 59).

David Harvey deepened the clarification of how neoliberalism was associated with the class project of those in power. Writing on whether we were at the end of the neoliberal project, Harvey claimed: "My interpretation is that it's a class project, masked by a lot of neoliberal rhetoric about individual freedom, liberty, personal responsibility, privatization and the free market. These were means, however, toward the restoration and consolidation of class power, and that neo-liberal project has been fairly successful."[20] The relevant lesson from revolution in the Caribbean is that there must be a complete break with liberal interpretations of the world. The philosophies of Mohandas Gandhi, Martin Luther King Jr., and Nelson Mandela have assisted this break from liberal understandings of human transformations.

I have identified the following features as elements of the restoration and consolidation of class power in the Americas from the period of Reagan up to 2009: (a) resegregation; (b) economic polarization and the dominance of the top 1 percent (this is pure neoliberalism); (c) designer eugenics (eugenics that really reproduce and reinforce white supremacy); (d) armaments culture (wars, the spread of wars, massive intelligence and surveillance apparatuses, development of private military contractors and mercenaries); (e) environmental degradation (pollution and global warming); (f) big pharma (genetically modified food, genetically modified seeds); (g) media disinformation and mind control (psychological and informational warfare); (h) racism; (i) sexism, homophobia, and misogyny; and (j) religious fundamentalism.

These elements constitute the contemporary counterrevolution. Where this counterrevolution was most manifest was in the small Caribbean territories through the level of gun violence, misogyny, and homophobia. In societies such as Guyana, Jamaica, and Trinidad and Tobago, the levels of gun violence and murders have made life utterly miserable for the poor and suffering. Many communities have become no-go areas as criminal enforcers terrorize the people. One of the challenges for revolutionary change today is to recover from this counterrevolutionary violence and murder throughout the Caribbean. This will require reconfiguring communities and reorganizing the priorities of those societies.

Revolution and Democratic Participation

The spread of counterrevolutionary violence thirty years after the Grenada Revolution brought back the burning questions of peace, justice, healing of the people, security, and democratic participation. One of the outstanding criticisms of the Grenada Revolution, even by those who were sympathetic to the revolution, was that the leadership, in their effort to establish vanguardism over the people, forgot the elementary principles of democratic participation. One of the revolution's leaders has elaborated on how this undemocratic tendency reproduced sharp binaries:

> That was a lesson to me; a lesson that our world is not made of exploiters and exploited. A lesson that our world is not made up of oppressors and oppressed, working class and capitalists. Our society is made up of people, of human beings. I came to realize that if one could see beyond the categories and the formula, if one could see beyond the science, reach out beyond the collective descriptions and reach out to the human being, then so much is possible. And I recognize in a

more profound way than ever before, that with all our imperfections, humanity is still God's greatest creation, and shall so be treated. (Layne 1988, 99)[21]

There is no doubt that revolutionaries must oppose and expose exploiters, but the conflict model of human society can no longer serve as the basis for political engagement and democratic participation. Tomorrow's revolution must be undergirded by a conception of democracy that deepens the model of sharing and cooperation that had existed before rapacious capitalism. This is the democracy that C. L. R. James espoused in his writings on the Caribbean revolution. James had already pointed to this kind of democratic participation by distinguishing the democracy of the people's assemblies from that of parliaments. In *The Black Jacobins*, James noted that revolution starts with the self-mobilization of the people, "but phases of a revolution are not decided in parliaments, they are only registered there" (James 1989, 81).

Thus it is necessary to reassert that while representative democratic participation is an important component of revolutionary change, the central aspect of change is not in the contest for positions. Democracy is not simply about voting every five years. This is part of the neoliberal and counterrevolutionary democracy, the democracy where there is no accountability once a person is elected. James (1956) had written extensively about a new democracy where every cook can govern:

> The over-riding idea was to organize the mass of the people not just to vote, but to govern—to govern through organs in village and town. To govern through Councils on Trade and Foreign policy, which would bring business, unions and the people to discuss the initiatives their Parliamentary leaders were pursuing, or to propose new initiatives—to govern by way of over-sight committees in every ministry. That way for sure, government would be of the people. By the people could come later when the people in councils, in their own self-movement, would take back from the State, the remaining power vested in the State. And then proceed to a new and unparalleled democracy which would make even ancient Greek democracy look pallid by comparison.

This is the new revolutionary place that we are in at this moment, in this new century, when popular forms of expression are breaking out as peoples develop new techniques of self-organization and mobilization. This revolutionary process seeks to draw a line of steel between the traditions of revolution and counterrevolution and breaks down the vanguardism and leaderism of the social classes that looked to Europe for guidance and intellectual leadership. It is also now possible to enrich the observations of James by looking not only at Greek democracy (which was limited) but also at the social collectivism of the African village community and the communities of the indigenous peoples of Central America and South America, the cooperative institutions of the indigenous peoples in Latin America, and the Iroquois concept of democracy.

This new basis for democracy is informing the indigenous movements all across Central and South America. The Zapatistas of Mexico, whom James Petras and others see as being the forerunners of the new revolution, are already practicing what they call fractal concepts of self-emancipation, self-organization of how the people can be the basis for new political relations. This self-organization for revolution is very different from self-organization for representative politics. It is a kind of self-organization where the people take themselves from one level of consciousness to the next. At the same time, one of the most profound aspects of the Zapatistas has been the ways in which they have deepened the mobilization of positive cultural values from their history. Another important aspect of this revolutionary approach is the need to build community power so that the power shifts to the people away from the old state machinery of violence and domination. The Zapatistas have also moved to end the romance with armed struggles. One of the leaders the Zapatistas, Subcomandante Marcos, has been clear in his writings that revolutions are first of all ideas and not violence. These ideas were spelled out in the great anthology titled *Our Word Is Our Weapon: Selected Writings*. The militarism of the drug cartels and the counterrevolutionary forces has taught the Zapatistas that armed means should be used only in exceptional circumstances. Ewart Layne came to the same conclusion in his reflection on the Grenada Revolution:

> It is against the background of all of the above that I say to our people, armed struggle, viewed as a preference for solving political problems is politically immature and in my view, morally wrong. It is possible for a people to pursue their aspirations for a better life and to change society, so that there are more opportunities for more and more equitable distribution of society's fruits, through legal and constitutional means. I believe that the experiment now underway next door in Venezuela may well provide strong evidence of this. (1988, 99)

From the Zapatistas to the Bolivarian Revolution

Looking back over the past thirty years, I have attempted to grasp the balance of forces to conceptualize revolutionary change for the next decades.

In Mexico, the Zapatista movement sought to bring back the memory of the 1910 revolution to launch a new protracted struggle for revolutionary change. In this new stage, the Zapatistas have mobilized the new information technologies while moving to strengthen the cultural spaces where the politics of self-emancipation can emerge. This brings the Caribbean face-to-face with the new Bolivarian process that is energizing both the Caribbean and Latin America.[22]

The Bolivarian Revolution is enriched by the main social movements in the Caribbean and Latin America. There are six principal movements: (1) the environmental justice movement; (2) the movements of workers and farmers; (3) the women's movement; (4) the peace and social justice movements, or movement against neoliberalism; (5) the antiracist movement of the former enslaved and indigenous peoples; and (6) the reparations movement.

Hilary Beckles (2013) has contributed to the importance of the movement for reparative justice by pointing out how contemporary questions of health are linked to the outstanding forms of social relationships inherited from the period of slavery. The traditional revolutionary movements in Latin America have been reluctant to confront this past of enslavement. Since the World Conference against Racism (WCAR) in Durban in 2001, peoples of African descent have been forthright in advancing the antiracist struggle, but the traditional Left has continued to look to their relationship with European parties of the Cold War era. It was the arrival of the Venezuelan process that had a major impact on the views of Latin American leaders toward Africa. Hugo Chávez, in his period of political leadership, made a fundamental break with Eurocentric conceptions of transformation.

In Venezuela the leadership that is associated with the Bolivarian Alliance for the Peoples of Our America (ALBA) emboldened a new cadre of political leadership and new social forces that were clearly antiracist. The political leadership in Venezuela was confronted with the reality that they need more than simply financial resources to repair the blight of social exclusion. The physical space of the urban areas of Venezuela bears all the markings of apartheid housing and apartheid engineering, most apparent in the masses of people who are forced to live in poor housing conditions.

After fifteen years of holding power and with an economy flush with revenues from high oil prices, the Bolivarian Revolution in Venezuela has made important proclamations in the direction of radical reforms. Some of these reforms in community *missiones* have provided health care for the poor, but these reforms have not dented the entrenched class and racial inequalities. Some of these measures seek to deepen the social democratic traditions that had existed within Venezuela, but the ideological rigidity of the liberal forces in the bureaucracies acts as a break on the transition in Venezuela. One of the most profound tasks in Venezuela remains the challenges to the oppression of women and the forms of patriarchy that had been buttressed by a culture of *machismo*. It is at the intersection of these struggles where the women's movement throughout the Caribbean is standing up to all forms of oppression. The women's movement opposes rape, violence against women, homophobia, child pornography, and all elements of oppression that emanate from patriarchy. From as far as South Africa to the small islands in the Caribbean, women are calling for opposition to rape and violation.[23]

At the level of gender relations, the new revolutionary movement is challenging the weaknesses of all previous movements, whether in Haiti, Cuba, Grenada, or Nicaragua. From Nicaragua to other parts of Latin America, revolutionary leaders have been accused of sexual abuse and violation of women. While placing a critique of patriarchy and sexist ideas at the center of revolutionary thinking, the progressive women's movement has successfully challenged the labor theory of value and influences our understanding of the centrality of household production. Female labor power was never properly calculated in the economic models of many Marxists. Radical women in Guyana have been some of the leaders of the global women's strike. This is the international movement that is placing the question of care at the center of change. It is on this point of care, as well as the deformed legacies of white racism, where there are such a great challenges as the Caribbean seeks to move out of counterrevolutionary politics.

The women's movement joins the workers' movement, the antiracist movement, and the environmental justice movement to enrich the struggles for change beyond the single-issue struggles that have in the past influenced political mobilization. In particular, the reparations movement is calling for society to "reveal the truth" about genocide and slavery. This revelation calls for a rewriting of textbooks and a retreat of the celebration of racist ideas. The revelation of the truth will be another component of the transformation of the Caribbean.

How can we unleash and tap into the revolutionary possibilities of the millions of citizens of the Caribbean and Latin America who have been left out of the political process? These forces face the strength of global capitalism, and democratic struggles over education and health will open up the contradictions for all other oppressed sections of the population. Reparations and the restructuring of knowledge will become revolutionary in these societies if one follows the logic of dismantling white settler privilege and cultural apartheid.

In Bolivia, Evo Morales is looking for revolutionary ideas of transformation within the history of the Indian cultures. On the question of language,

Morales is opening up questions that the Left has been silent on. The country's new economy would be based in new forms of energy (solar and hydrogen), new forms of health care, and biotechnology, along with new forms of construction and housing. If this task of building the alternative economy is not initiated, the oil economy will strengthen the old oligarchy and white power in education, medicine, transport, communications, and housing and will cripple the advances of the Bolivarian project.

Conclusion

Despite the counterrevolutionary onslaught, the peoples of the Caribbean maintain a spirit of freedom, laughter, and song. These songs of freedom have inspired millions from all parts of the world and have kept the revolutionary optimism that remained in the Caribbean since the Haitian Revolution. Revolutionary optimism is alive in the songs of Bob Marley, who sang that "everything will be all right." It is the same spirit that was communicated by Che Guevara, who believed in the capacity of the working people to effect profound changes. Guevara believed that a better future could be built if one unleashed the power of all the citizens. Guevara, like Bob Marley, believed that love is an explosive force in politics. For this reason, Guevara noted that a true revolutionary is guided by profound feelings of love.

Thirty years after the Grenada Revolution, momentous changes are sweeping the world as the ideas of neoliberalism and unbridled capitalism have collapsed within the United States. As thinkers and activists, we must learn the positive and negative lessons of revolutions and revolutionary change, so that when the Caribbean people move again, they will move decisively. The Caribbean people, when they move, will move so that Che Guevara's idea of a new person becomes a transformed human being—a transformed human being who will have moved away from all the alienation and complexes of capitalism and the European ideation system.

Martin Luther King Jr. anticipated the major technological innovations of the twenty-first century, and he warned that revolutionaries must escape spiritual death: "A true revolution of values will lay hands on the world order."[24] And he says of war:

> This way of settling differences is not just. This business of burning human beings with napalm, of filling our nation's homes with orphans and widows, of injecting poisonous drugs of hate into veins of people normally humane, of sending men home from dark and bloody battlefields physically handicapped and

psychologically deranged, cannot be reconciled with wisdom, justice and love. A nation that continues year after year to spend more money on military defense than on programs of social uplift is approaching spiritual death.[25]

Increasingly it is the struggle against spiritual and social death that drives the new revolutionary period in the Caribbean. In the next thirty years, the Caribbean will be in the forefront of paving the way for new revolutionary breakthroughs. It is a revolution that will sweep humanity, and its sweep will realize the Cuban Revolution's dream of becoming the forerunner of socialist transformation in the Caribbean.

Notes

1. "Revolution" was sung by Bob Marley in 1980. The song can be found on YouTube at http://www.youtube.com/watch?v=Za3Yv38JzcI.

2. The historical record of the differences within the New Jewel Movement continues to be clouded by partisan memories. For two distinct versions of the implosion in Grenada, see the arguments presented at the 2011 Symposium in Jamaica by Patsy Lewis, Claremont Kirton, and Brian Meeks at the UWI Seminar "Grenada Revolution (1979–1983) Grenada: Retrospective on a Revolution," October 25, 2011. For an alternate view of the implosion, see the October 2009 "Statement on Grenada," by Robert "Bobby" Clarke, http://www.norman girvan.info/wp-content/uploads/2009/10/clarke-statement-on-grenada.pdf.

3. Peter Hallward, "Egypt's Popular Revolution Will Change the World," *Guardian UK*, February 9, 2011.

4. Ibid. For a comprehensive analysis of the tremors across North Africa, see Esam Al-Amin, *The Arab Awakening Unveiled: Understanding Transformations and Revolutions in the Middle East* (Washington, DC: American Educational Trust, 2013).

5. According to the *Stanford Encyclopedia of Philosophy*, memory is "a label for a diverse set of cognitive capacities by which humans and perhaps other animals retain information and reconstruct past experiences, usually for present purposes." http://plato.stanford.edu/entries/memory.

6. C. L. R. James, "From Toussaint L'Ouverture to Fidel Castro," in the *C. L. R. James Reader*, ed. Anne Grimshaw (London: Blackwell, 1992).

7. See in particular chap. 1 of *Barack Obama and Twenty-first Century Politics: A Revolutionary Moment in the USA* (London: Pluto Press, 2010).

8. James Petras, "Che Guevara and Contemporary Revolutionary Movements," *Latin American Perspectives* 25, no. 4 (1998). Petras named the Landless Workers Movement in Brazil, the National Peasant Federation in Paraguay, the Zapatista National Liberation Army in Mexico, the Peasant Syndicate and sectors of the mining unions in Bolivia, the National Federation of Indian and Peasant Organizations in Ecuador, the National Indian and Peasant Coordination in Guatemala, the Democratic Peasant Alliance in El Salvador, and the

Revolutionary Force in the Dominican Republic as new forces of revolution in Central and Latin America.

9. Richard Gott, "Latin America Is Preparing to Settle Accounts with Its White Settler Elite," *Guardian*, November 15, 2006, http://www.guardian.co.uk/commentisfree/2006/nov/15/comment.venezuela.

10. For an elaboration of fractal wisdom, see the commentaries of Bruce Lipton on YouTube, http://www.youtube.com/watch?v=9GaB1VMAXPQ. The theoreticians of quantum politics argue the view that a Newtonian worldview is inadequate to explain today's political phenomena. These theorists believe that the laws and findings of quantum physics provide a more appropriate scientific paradigm. See Dana Zohar and Ian Marshal, *The Quantum Society: Mind, Physics, and the New Social Vision* (London: Flamingo Books, 1990).

11. James, "From Toussaint L'Ouverture to Fidel Castro," 310.

12. Ibid., 298.

13. C. L. R. James, preface to the first edition of *The Black Jacobins: Toussaint L'Ouverture and the San Domingo Revolution* (New York: Vintage Books, 1989).

14. See also Michael West, Bill Martin, and Fanon Che Wilkins, *From Toussaint to Tupac: The Black International since the Age of Revolution* (Chapel Hill: University of North Carolina Press, 2009).

15. Robert McCaa, "Missing Millions: The Democratic Cost of the Mexican Revolution," *Mexican Studies* 19, no. 2 (2003).

16. For a coherent bibliography of the challenges of the Cuban Revolution from the point of view of female scholars in Cuba, see Martha Nunez Sarmiento, "Gender Studies in Cuba: Methodological Approaches, 1974–2001," *Gender and Society* 17, no. 1 (February 2003).

17. Gary Webb, *Dark Alliance: The CIA, the Contras, and the Crack Cocaine Explosion* (New York: Seven Stories Press, 1998). For a mainstream rendition of the role of drugs in the Caribbean, see Ivelaw Griffith, *Drugs and Security in the Caribbean: Sovereignty under Siege* (University Park: Pennsylvania State University Press, 1997).

18. Walter Rodney, "Two World Views of the Russian Revolution," unpublished manuscript.

19. Nadia Bishop, "Forgiveness and Reconciliation," January 12, 2008, http://www.belgrafix.com/gtoday/2008news/Jan/Jan12/Nadia-Bishop-speaks-of-forgiveness-and-reconciliation.htm.

20. David Harvey, "Is This Really the End of Neo-liberalism?" *Counterpunch*, March 13–15, 2009, http://www.counterpunch.org/harvey03132009.html.

21. Quoted from an unpublished manuscript, "The Making of the Grenada Revolution," by Ewart Layne, who was one of the "Grenada 17" convicted for the murder of Maurice Bishop and others. Layne was imprisoned for twenty-six years and wrote this manuscript while in prison.

22. For a reading of one of the principal theoreticians of this Latin American process, see Heinz Dieterich, *Socialism of the 21st Century: Economy, Society, and Democracy in the Era of Global Capitalism*. Though the book is in Spanish and German, see the interview of Dieterich on Venezuela analysis, http://www.venezuelanalysis.com/articles.php?artno=1690. See also Michael A Lebowitz, *Build It Now: Socialism for the 21st Century* (New York: Monthly Review Press, 2006).

23. Mmatshilo Motsei, *The Kanga and the Kangaroo Court: Reflections on the Rape Trial of Jacob Zuma* (Johannesburg, South Africa: Jacana Media, 2007).

24. Martin Luther King Jr., "Beyond Vietnam: A Time to Break the Silence," http://www.hartford-hwp.com/archives/45a/058.html.

25. Ibid.

References

Al-Amin, E. 2013. *The Arab Awakening Unveiled: Understanding Transformations and Revolutions in the Middle East*. Washington, DC: American Educational Trust.

Amin, S. 2004. *The Liberal Virus: Permanent War and the Americanization of the World*. New York: Monthly Review Press.

Beckles, H. 2013. *Britain's Black Debt: Reparations for Caribbean and Native Genocide*. Jamaica, Barbados, and Trinidad and Tobago: University of the West Indies Press.

Bellegrarde-Smith, P. 2004. "Haiti: The Breached Citadel." Toronto: Canadian Scholars Press.

Benot, Y. 1988. *La Révolution Française et la fin des colonies: Essai*. Paris: Éditions La Découverte.

Blackburn, R. 1989. *The Overthrow of Colonial Slavery*. London: Verso, 1989.

Brinton, C. 1958. *The Anatomy of Revolution*. New York: Vintage.

Campbell, H. 1987. *Rasta and Resistance: From Marcus Garvey to Walter Rodney*. New Jersey: Africa World Press.

———. 2010. *Barack Obama and Twenty-first Century Politics: A Revolutionary Moment in the USA*. London: Pluto Press.

Danticat, E. 1998. *The Farming of Bones*. New York: Penguin.

Defronzo, J. 1991. *Revolutions and Revolutionary Movements*. Boulder: Westview Press.

Dieterich, H. 2006. "Venezuela: A Serious Alternative for Latin America." Interview by Carsten Schiefer, *Unsere Zeit*, March 14, 2006. http://venezuelanalysis.com/analysis/1656.

Foran, J., ed. 2003. *The Future of Revolutions: Rethinking Radical Change in the Age of Globalization*. New York: Zed.

Goldstone, J. 2003. *Revolutions: Theoretical, Comparative, and Historical Studies*. Belmont, CA: Wadsworth/Thomson Learning.

Gott, R. 2006. "Latin America Is Preparing to Settle Accounts with Its White Settler Elite." *Guardian*, November 14. http://www.guardian.co.uk/commentisfree/2006/nov/15/comment.venezuela (accessed November 15, 2006).

Griffith, I. 1997. *Drugs and Security in the Caribbean: Sovereignty under Siege*. University Park: Pennsylvania State University Press.

Grimshaw, A., ed. 1992. *The C. L. R. James Reader*. London: Blackwell.

Hallward, P. 2011. "Egypt's Popular Revolution Will Change the World." *Guardian UK*, February 9.

Hamilton, D. 2002. "Whither Cuban Socialism: The Changing Political Economy of the Cuban Revolution." *Latin American Perspectives* 29 (3): 18–39.

Hector, T. 2000. "Yesterday and Tomorrow: Beyond Catastrophe and Death." http://www
.candw.ag/~jardinea/ffhtm/ff001027.htm (accessed October 27, 2000).

Henry, P. 1990. "Grenada and the Theory of Perpetual Transformation." *Social and Economic
Studies* 39:151–92.

Hobsbawm, E. 1962. *The Age of Revolution, 1789–1848.* New York: New American Library.

King, M. L. 1967. "Beyond Vietnam." Speech delivered on April 4, 1967. Meeting of the Clergy
and Laity Concerned at Riverside Church. New York City.

James, C. L. R. 1956. "Every Cook Can Govern: A Study of Democracy in Ancient Greece; Its
Meaning for Today." *Correspondence* 2 (12). https://www.marxists.org/archive/james-clr/
works/1956/06/every-cook.htm (accessed October 27, 2000).

———. 1989. *The Black Jacobins: Toussaint L'Ouverture and the San Domingo Revolution.* 2nd
ed. New York: Vintage.

———. 1992. "From Toussaint L'Ouverture to Fidel Castro." In *The C. L. R. James Reader,* ed.
Anne Grimshaw. London: Blackwell.

Layne E. 1988. "The Making of the Grenada Revolution." Unpublished manuscript. St.
George's, Grenada.

Lebowitz, M. A. 2006. *Build It Now: Socialism for the Twenty-first Century.* New York:
Monthly Review Press.

Lipton, B. 2005. *The Biology of Belief: Unleashing the Power of Consciousness, Matter and,
Miracles.* Santa Rosa, CA: Mountain of Love.

Manji, F., and S. Ekine. 2012. *The African Awakening: Emerging Revolutions.* Oxford: Pambazuka Press.

McCaa, R. "Missing Millions: The Democratic Cost of the Mexican Revolution." *Mexican
Studies* 19 (2): 367–400.

Meeks, B. 2001. *Caribbean Revolutions and Revolutionary Theory: An Assessment of Cuba,
Nicaragua, and Grenada.* Jamaica, Barbados, and Trinidad and Tobago: University of the
West Indies Press.

Moore, B. 1966. *Social Origins of Dictatorship and Democracy: Lord and Peasant in the Making of the Modern World.* Boston: Beacon Press.

Moore, C. 2008. *Pichon: Race and Revolution in Castro's Cuba: A Memoir.* Chicago: Lawrence
Hill.

Motsei, M. 2007. *The Kanga and the Kangaroo Court: Reflections on the Rape Trial of Jacob
Zuma.* Johannesburg, South Africa: Jacana Media.

O'Shaughnessy, H. 1984. *Grenada: Revolution, Invasion, and Aftermath.* London: Sphere.

Petras, J. 1998. "Che Guevara and Contemporary Revolutionary Movements." *Latin American
Perspectives* 25 (4): 9–18.

Prasad, D. 2012. *Gandhi and Revolution.* New Delhi: Routledge.

Rodney, W. 1986. "The African Revolution." In *C. L. R. James: His Life and Work,* ed. Paul
Buhle. New York: Allison and Busby.

———. n.d. "Two World Views of the Russian Revolution: Reflections from Africa." Unpublished manuscript.

Roopnaraine, R. 2010. "Resonances of Revolution: Grenada, Suriname, and Guyana." *Interventions: International Journal of Postcolonial Studies* 12 (1).

Sarmiento, M. N. "Gender Studies in Cuba: Methodological Approaches, 1974–2001." *Gender and Society* 17 (1).

Shiva, V. 2005. *Earth Democracy: Justice, Sustainability, and Peace.* Boston: South End Press.

Skocpol, T. 1979. *States and Social Revolutions: Social Revolutions in the Modern World.* Cambridge: Cambridge University Press.

Stannard, D. 1992. *American Holocaust: Columbus and the Conquest of the New World.* New York: Oxford University Press.

Trouillot, M-R. 1988. *Silencing the Past: Power and the Production of History.* Boston: Beacon Press.

———. 1989. *Haiti: State against Nation; The Origins and Legacy of Duvalierism.* New York: Monthly Review Press.

Webb, G. 1999. *Dark Alliance: The CIA, the Contras, and the Crack Cocaine Explosion.* New York: Seven Stories Press.

West, M., M. Bill, and C. W. Fanon. 2009. *From Toussaint to Tupac: The Black International since the Age of Revolution.* Chapel Hill: University of North Carolina Press.

Zohar, D., and I. Marshall. 1990. *The Quantum Society: Mind, Physics, and the New Social Vision.* London: Flamingo.

PART IV

The Caribbean Left, Party Politics, and Political Transitions in Grenada

10. The Grenada Revolution and the Caribbean Left: The Case of the Guyana Working People's Alliance

David Hinds

In the almost three decades since the demise of the Grenada Revolution, there has been a general avoidance of a comprehensive analysis of its relevance to a proper understanding of postcolonial Caribbean politics and society. Insofar as there has been a discourse on Grenada, it has been confined to shouting matches between supporters of the two sides that squared off in the final months of the revolution. While such an exchange is useful, it never gets beyond emotions and self-serving narratives, which by definition are counterproductive. As Gordon K. Lewis (1987, 164) warned, "The left must not allow itself to be bogged down in the sort of useless and nasty speculation that has characterized the rumor mill since October 1983." Some have dismissed the revolution as nothing more than an orgy of violence by a few political hooligans who in the end slaughtered each other. Others have located the revolution in narrow Cold War terms, a narrative that exalts the evil of Marxism and communism.

In the process, the larger significance of the revolution is either marginalized or erased. The revolution is reduced to an event with little significance to those who lived through it or to the construction of Grenadian and Caribbean history. Yet the events in Grenada from March 1979 to October 1983 deserve more scrutiny, not to determine who were the saints and the devils but to engage something that arose from the bowels of the Caribbean society and has since its demise greatly influenced the region's political motion. Again Gordon K. Lewis is on the ball:

It thus became necessary, and is still necessary, for the progressive movement, in the best spirit of democratic self-criticism, without nostalgia or evasive apologetics or scapegoating, to ask and to seek to answer, the crucial questions: what went wrong in the internal dynamics of the revolution, why did things go wrong, and

213

what are the long term implications for the Caribbean revolutionary cause in the future? (1987, 161)

This chapter attempts to engage this thesis. I make three overriding assumptions here. First, I locate the revolution in the larger struggle of the Caribbean for liberation from various forms of subjugation. In that regard, the Grenada Revolution represents the culmination of three centuries of struggle against plantation bondage. Second, I identify the revolution's immediate roots in the postcolonial radicalism that emerged shortly after independence and was exemplified by the Black Power Movement and the left radical movement it spawned in the 1970s. The Grenada Revolution, therefore, is part of what Bouges (2003) and Rupert Lewis (1998) call the black radical tradition and the Caribbean radical tradition respectively. My third assumption flows from the first two: if the Grenada Revolution was Caribbean in origin and nature, then it follows that what transpired in Grenada had consequences for the wider Caribbean.

The chapter looks at the consequences of the Grenada Revolution for politics in Guyana, in particular for the Working People's Alliance (WPA), which shared a similar orientation with the New Jewel Movement (NJM), the party that led the Grenada Revolution. In particular, I look at the impact of the revolution on the WPA. I argue that the events in Grenada were pivotal in galvanizing the party's popular challenge to the Guyana government and that the revolution's demise was equally critical to the WPA's subsequent shift in emphasis from one of popular insurrection from the outside to greater participation in the formal political process. Toward this end, I examine the political stances of the party in the years during and immediately following the end of the revolution. The chapter's first section looks at the circumstances that led to the rise of the Caribbean Left, and the second section traces the rise of the WPA. The third section looks at the relationship between the two parties during the revolution, and the final section examines the stances of the WPA after the end of the revolution.

The Rise of the Caribbean Left

Independence came to the Anglophone Caribbean courtesy of a nationalist movement that represented a broad consensus among the various segments of the colonized peoples. This nationalist fervor would soon unravel as the new postcolonial rulers began to steer independence away from the overriding principles of the independence movement. Rupert Lewis (1998,

xvii) contends that "the moment of independence was also a moment of re-colonization," and Bouges (2003, 126) calls it "the double transformation of colonialism into post-colonialism, then into neo-colonialism." Under the pretext of the Cold War, the United States implemented a coercive foreign policy that exercised the right to forcefully intervene in newly independent countries that showed signs of self-determination. The geographical location of the Caribbean, coupled with the reality of the Cuban Revolution, made the region a prime target of this policy. This imperialism invariably led to an anti-imperialist response that would be pivotal to the radical praxis of the 1970s. The ready capitulation of the independence leadership to this Cold War policy meant that local policies reflected the imperialist logic.

In particular, economic and developmental policies followed the dictates of global capital and its local representatives. Such policies inevitably reinforced the socioeconomic inequities of the colonial order. As was the case during colonialism, the economic order was accompanied by a political order geared toward perpetuating economic inequality and preventing challenges to the status quo. The postcolonial state, despite slight modifications, maintained the essence of the colonial state. In this context, the monoculture export-oriented economy inherited from colonialism was not overly interrupted.

The first decade of independence, therefore, was quickly transformed into a negation of substantive independence whereby the structures of colonialism were aggressively transformed. While the leaders employed a nationalistic rhetoric, their policies reflected anything but nationalism. It is in this context that the issue of race becomes central. The new leadership downplayed race as a central factor in determining the shape and content of the postcolonial order. They opted for a "brown nationalism" that privileged the European cultural order and marginalized African symbols. Moreover, because the majority of the working class was black, the policies that negatively affected the poor had racial consequences.

The betrayal by the ruling class converged with the coming of age of a new generation of Caribbean scholars. Radicalized by the independence movement and exposed to a new kind of education, these scholars were asking questions about the content and direction of independence. They rejected the independence leaders' gradualist approach to change, which invariably catered to the imperatives of the former colonizers, and advocated instead a decisive break with colonialism and the institution of a political economy that reflected the logic of political independence. In short, therefore, the question was whether independence meant a reform of the colonial order or freedom from its clutches.

This standoff proved to be the seed of a new second independence struggle that began with the Black Power Movement, which later gave way to a radical leftist upsurge. If the earlier independence movement was fueled by the need to get rid of colonial rule, this new movement focused on the need to turn the rights won at independence into real freedoms. By the end of the 1960s, race, class, national self-determination, and Caribbean nationalism were intertwined both at the level of governance and at the level of repose to governance. The power of governance was concentrated in the hands of the brown and black middle class. So too was ownership of the means of production, which meant that the working poor were kept as a source of cheap labor and their fears were manipulated for political ends.

It is against this background that the call for true independence by the Black Power activists was grounded. Black Power not only represented a racial response but was also class based and anti-imperialist nationalist. In this regard, the target was simultaneously international and local capitalism, racism, and authoritarian rule. The message of racial pride, uplift and empowerment, local ownership of the economy, and socioeconomic and political democracy resonated with the middle class, youth, and the working poor. The middle classes were largely animated by the need for social justice, while the poor continued their historical struggle against social, racial, and political marginalization. As Kwayana (2004, 1) contends:

> Revolutions become natural and acceptable when the existing state of things discredits itself so massively that the whole society feels in its bones the need for casting aside the established, or establishment parties, both government and opposition. This was not a need that people generally felt. So where possible, they would change one for the other. This would satisfy the need for a change of government rather than a need for change. So the people connected the establishment parties with the established economies and would tolerate them so long as the economy delivered livelihoods and did not threaten collapse of living arrangements on a massive scale. But the left movements still had a place because they connected the ordinary people and radical elites as well with a wider world, new information, and new standards for measuring the good life, new social goals and often dealt with neglected injustices in the society.

The NJM and the WPA were products of this movement, which can be traced to the demonstrations that followed the expulsion of Walter Rodney from Jamaica in 1968. The Rodney Riots were a popular expression mainly by the urban youth of Jamaica against a government that had done little to turn the dreams of independence into freedom. Rodney, then a lecturer at the

University of the West Indies, had exposed this shortcoming of Caribbean independence at two levels. First, he critiqued the new ruling class for not making a fundamental break with colonialism, thereby abandoning the aspirations of the black and poor peoples of the region. Second, by grounding with the masses and teaching them about Africa and African history, he introduced and expanded a new black consciousness among the popular masses about both their identity and their political capacity. His expulsion exposed not only the hostility of the postcolonial state to popular empowerment but its drift toward authoritarianism. The Rodney intervention—Rodney's activities, his expulsion, and the riots—therefore represented the beginnings of clashes between the Caribbean state and the popular masses and radical section of the intelligentsia on the other hand, a clash that would culminate with the Grenada Revolution in 1979.

The Rodney Riots were followed in 1970 by the February Revolution in Trinidad, where Black Power demonstrations brought the government to its knees. The movement inspired a cultural renaissance among the African-descended peoples that was manifested in a flush of African pride and interest in their African heritage. Second, it ignited a new resistance spirit that would serve as the basis for the broad radical movement that pushed the region to revolutionary action. Third, it inspired a new Caribbean nationalism among the masses based on a shared history and the unity of the ethnic groups.

At the political level, the influence of Black Power radicalism engendered a simultaneous rise in autocratic governance. Fearing the spread of radicalism to their countries, most of the governments took a confrontational attitude to the movement. They passed laws aimed at frustrating dissent and in the process trampled on civil liberties such as freedom of the press and freedom of association. Radical leaders were routinely harassed and persecuted and in some cases were assassinated.

While the governments in Guyana, Grenada, and Dominica were the most extreme in this regard, Saint Lucia's prime minister Kenny Anthony observes that the others were not far behind. According to him, the leadership "was intolerant of criticism and, in many instances, did not hesitate to use force to defeat political opponents. Eric Gairy's Grenada and Forbes Burnham's Guyana were only the most extreme examples of these tendencies. The rest of the Caribbean differed from these countries only in quantitative terms" (Anthony 2004, 263). Civil liberties were routinely undermined, draconian laws were introduced, and opposition politicians and other dissenters were routinely harassed, imprisoned, and assassinated. In short, government became unaccountable to its citizens.

The NJM and WPA

These repressive tactics led to a shift in emphasis by the radicals from race to a more class-oriented approach that advocated a revolutionary socialism that stressed popular democratic participation in politics and economics. This authoritarianism pushed the NJM and the WPA in two directions. First, at the political level, they developed relationships with moderate and right-of-center forces in pursuit of broad antidictatorial alliances. Second, they moved toward an embrace of armed insurrection as a last resort. The latter would take the region in a political direction that would inspire both a freedom moment and a tragic upheaval. As Kwayana (2004, 2) observes:

> The radical parties filled their allotted or achieved political space rather well. The New Jewel Movement (Grenada) seemed at one time to be invading the territory of an establishment party. Then it went beyond that space after failing to win at elections, and deeming the regime a rogue government not removable by elections, and a threat to safety, in 1979 overthrew the government by force of arms endorsed by popular demonstration, especially of the youth.

Both the WPA and NJM were in effect alliances of left-wing progressive groups. Two dominant tendencies characterized these alliances: left-wing Black Power and Marxism. The former represented a black nationalism that was grounded in working-class liberation. Hence it incorporated race and class in a synthesis that downplayed the orthodox Marxist formulation of the primacy of class over race. The other tendency reflected a more orthodox Marxism along the lines of the traditional communist movement. Despite these differences, the two tendencies were united in their commitment to decolonization, Caribbean integration, and revolution. Both parties opted to join the Socialist International rather than the international communist movement. The WPA actually described itself as independent Marxist and was most forceful in advocating for democratic rights, which were frowned on by orthodox Marxists as bourgeois democracy but the WPA contended were rights that were fought for and won by the sacrifices of the working people (Rodney 1979).

The early NJM reflected a similar independent tendency that included a movement away from maximum leadership, the minimizing of the importance of traditional elections, decentralization of power, a preference for mass insurrection, and the need to steer clear of the international communist movement. Brian Meeks correctly attributes these positions to the influence of C. L. R James, whose ideological outlook had a large impact on the Caribbean Black Power Left.

The chosen ideological perspective of 1974 was related of course to the specific experiences of individuals, but a cumulative and available ideological context can be identified, with boundaries delineated by Black Nationalism, an indigenous orientation and most notably an absence of Leninism. (Meeks 2001, 146)

Of the Caribbean Left parties, the WPA, the Workers Party of Jamaica (WPJ), and Tim Hector's Antigua Caribbean Liberation Movement (ACLM) enjoyed close ties with the NJM. The NJM's relationship with the WPJ arose largely on account of Bernard Coard, who had been a member of the pre-party WPJ. While the WPJ adopted an orthodox Marxist-Leninist praxis, the ACLM and WPA were more in line with the independent Marxist strand. More than the WPJ, the ACLM, WPA, and NJM reflected the influence of the Black Power Movement. Maurice Bishop and Tim Hector had developed close ties with Eusi Kwayana, whose African Society for Cultural Relations with Independent Africa (ASCRIA) was one of the founding groups of the WPA.

The NJM and the WPA adopted a collective leadership approach, although the NJM was less rigid in this area. While Bernard Coard and Unison Whiteman were recognized as part of the top leadership, Maurice Bishop emerged as the leading force of the NJM. In the case of the WPA, although Walter Rodney emerged as the foremost leader, the party never named him as leader. Eusi Kwayana, Moses Bhagwan, and Clive Thomas, the leaders of the founding groups, along with Rupert Roopnaraine, were all influential leaders. There seems to have been some suspicions of Coard's ambition in the prerevolution period, leading to a sometimes uneasy relation among the factions. This may have been due to the influence of the Organization for Revolutionary Education and Liberation (OREL), of which Coard was regarded as the unofficial leader. The OREL faction reportedly sought to turn the party into a traditional Marxist-Leninist outfit and was also critical of what it termed the petit bourgeois orientation of the NJM's leadership (Marable 1987, 215). The WPA did not experience the same kind of tensions, perhaps because none of its constituent groups was as orthodox as OREL. However, after Rodney's murder and as the party developed a closer relationship with the Grenada Revolution, there developed a muted tension between those who wanted a more disciplined cadre party and others who wanted to avoid what they saw as the pitfalls of the Grenada Revolution.

By the time of the revolution in March 1979, the NJM seemed to have embraced a Leninist form of organization. In particular, it became wedded to the notions of the vanguard party, the maximum leader, and democratic centralism. This change in the NJM's outlook has to be seen in the context of having to first confront a brutal regime and later manage a revolution amid hostility from the West and the Caribbean right wing. From the evidence, it seems that the orthodox Marxist tendency, as represented by the OREL faction, was the major catalyst. While OREL ceased to exist in a formal sense, its former members held to the principles espoused by the group (Marable 1987, 215).

Brian Meeks, a member of the WPJ who worked in Grenada during the revolution, has argued that the earlier "independent" NJM ideological outlook had peaked by 1974. He contends that the failure of the Black Power Movement in Trinidad, the changing world situation, and the early attempts by the NJM to mount a popular insurrection had prompted a search for alternative paths to revolution that transformed "the agenda of available ideas and [placed] Leninist notions at the forefront" (2001, 147).

The Rise of the WPA

The WPA was founded in 1974 as a pressure group and became a political party in 1979. The alliance was originally composed of four pressure groups: the African Society for Cultural Relations with Independent Africa (ASCRIA), Indian People's Revolutionary Associates (IPRA), Ratoon, and the Working People's Vanguard Party (WPVP). The WPVP left the alliance in 1975. ASCRIA was an Africanist or Black Power organization led by Eusi Kwayana, a former leading member of both the PPP and PNC. IPRA, the Indian equivalent of ASCRIA, was led by Moses Bhagwan, a former leader of the PPP's youth section and a leading party member. Ratoon was a leftist radical organization based at the University of Guyana and led by the economist Clive Thomas; and WPVP, another leftist group, was led by former PPP chairman Brindley Benn. The four groups had three things in common. First, they all opposed the government of the day, which was becoming increasingly authoritarian. Second, they shared a commitment to ethnic unity as a prerequisite for political and economic advancement. Third, they shared an ideological affiliation to socialism and anti-imperialism. These shared values made it easier for the formation of the party, although the WPVP would leave the party over disagreement on how to deal with the other ethnic party.

The WPA was bolstered by the addition to its ranks of three activists who would go on to play decisive roles in the party. First, in 1974, just as the WPA was being formed, Walter Rodney, a renowned scholar-revolutionary, returned to the University of Guyana. The government, however, rescinded the appointment on the grounds that Rodney would pose problems for them. This led to a series of protest rallies or open-air meetings organized by ASCRIA. Unexpectedly, attendance at the meetings was the largest since the

1950s, and more importantly, they were multiethnic. Instead of leaving, Rodney stayed in Guyana, joined the WPA, and emerged as its leading spokesperson and the leader of the multiethnic opposition movement.

Three years later, Rupert Roopnaraine, an Indian Guyanese academic, and Andaiye, a former school principal, returned to Guyana from the United States to join the WPA. Both had been friends of Rodney and were responding to his urgings. Roopnaraine became a leading figure in the party who was seen as the Indian equivalent of Rodney. Kwayana would later refer to Roopnaraine and Rodney as symbols of the new politics. Andaiye had left Guyana seven years before amid controversy over her support of the Black Power Movement while serving as principal of one of the country's secondary schools. Her actions were seen as an act of betrayal by some members of the government, since her father was closely associated with the prime minister. Andaiye would serve as the party's international secretary and editor of its newspaper, *Dayclean*.

The impetus for the formation of the WPA came from three sources. First, the repressive nature of the African-based People's National Congress (PNC) government had begun to negatively affect and alienate sections of the African Guyanese community. Second, given the ethnic nature of the major opposition party, the PPP, there were limitations to its ability to mobilize across ethnic lines. Third, the major African interest group, ASCRIA, had publicly withdrawn its support for the PNC. This served to dismantle the African ethnic solidarity that had been the norm for a decade. Fourth, ASCRIA and IPRA had mounted a successful mass multiethnic "land for the landless" campaign that brought together hundreds of Africans and Indians in a common cause—the first since the demise of the nationalist movement in 1955. Rodney (1976, 120) explained the factors that brought together the groups in the WPA:

> These groups came together in response to at least two important pressures. One was a new demand to overcome a racist-oriented politics, to break with the divisiveness of race as a fact of organization, so that both ASCRIA and IPRA collaborated on issues such as the landless squatters, of both Indian and African descent. The question was dealt with in class terms rather than racial terms. Second, as questions of socialism and ideology were being raised, the aim was to provide an organization, which would take the task of political and ideological education more seriously than any other existing political group.

The WPA's birth broke new ground in Guyanese postcolonial politics. First, it was the first time since the split of the original PPP in 1955 that a political group had declared as its major objective the unity of the various ethnic groups, thus challenging one of the main planks of the PNC's survival mechanism. Roopnaraine (1998) observes:

> On the internal front, Burnham said to the Africans, "You know, the alternative to me is these Indian people who are going to create an avalanche and swamp all of us. So I am really your only hope." He said this to the military, he said this to the police force, to the civil service, to the trade union movement. As a result, he had his bases covered. So the PPP was effectually neutralized. It is not that it did not raise up the cry for free and fair elections; they did. They mounted what protest they could have mounted, but it remained very ineffective because first of all they had no particular presence in the capital city, and that is where the seat of government was. But even if the PPP organized the protest in the rural areas—the farmers—this made no particular impact on the political situation, and Burnham could shrug it off. I recall that in 1973 when Dr. Jagan complained about rigging, he told him, "Well, you have neither the capacity nor the will to do anything about it. March if you will."

Second, although the WPA declared itself Marxist, the party eschewed any affiliation with the Moscow-oriented communist parties. In this regard, the charge of communism that was leveled at the PPP with good effect could not be leveled in the same way at the WPA. Roopnaraine (1998) explains: "Burnham had really mastered the art of dealing with the internal opposition, and he did this in a very clever way. On the one hand, he said to the United States, 'The alternative to me is Moscow; these people are communists, what are you really doing.' So he played off the United States, and as a result, he was able to win their support on the external front against the PPP." The emergence of the WPA also had direct implications for the PNC influence in the African-Guyanese community. Rodney, Kwayana, and Thomas were well-known African leaders whose political and moral standing in that community was significant. Crucially, unlike ASCRIA, which never openly rivaled the PNC politically, the WPA made clear that it was a political group opposed to the PNC and dedicated to combating it in the political arena.

Between 1974 and 1979, the WPA concentrated on mobilization and public education rather than projecting itself as a conventional party. In this regard, it avoided an arena in which ethnic sentiments were most inflamed. The advantage of this strategy was that it relied on transformation from the bottom up, which it hoped would in turn affect the broader politics. For the WPA, therefore, changing the political culture was essential to defeating ethnic conflict. The mobilization took the form of open-air public meetings, smaller "bottom house" meetings, and classes in political economy. The party also published a regular news sheet, *Dayclean*, which it used generally to expose government overreach and scandals but also to advance the party's ideas on issues such as race and ethnicity, governance, and the economy. The WPA's message was a combination of antidictatorship and multiracialism. It addressed what it saw as the twin problems of authoritarian rule and ethnic division. It argued that the survival of authoritarian governance was largely the result of ethnic polarization and that its demise would be achieved through ethnic solidarity (Rodney 1976).

The WPA's praxis was greatly influenced by Walter Rodney, whose political thought and practice represented the convergence of several strands of the problems and challenges faced by the formerly enslaved and colonized peoples of Africa and the Americas. In this regard, he interrogated class and race as interrelated phenomena. Given Rodney's trajectory, it is difficult to pin him down to any single perspective. His early academic work examined African history as a departure point for understanding and reclaiming the history and culture of blacks and achieving true liberation. He was concerned with the impact of slavery and colonialism on postcolonial Africa and the diaspora. He used Africa as his site of inquiry, but his conclusions were geared toward empowering Africa and its diaspora. Therein lay the Pan-African context and intent of his work. Further, Rodney was not content with investigating and explaining the African condition in purely racial terms; he was equally concerned with social oppression within the African and diasporic communities. He therefore extended his analysis to include governance and class, particularly in Africa and the Caribbean.

An important aspect of Rodney's praxis was his ability to build alliances without compromising his core beliefs; he was adept at subordinating his core beliefs in the interest of the broader struggle. His alliance and coalition building had two aspects: ideological and ethnic. Although a Marxist and black nationalist, Rodney did not use these as litmus tests for political relationships. That he opposed the PNC regime, which was black dominated, and professed Marxism-Leninism is testimony to his antidogmatism. He was of the view that the regime was using both black nationalism and socialism to mask its antiblack and anti-working-class policies and actions.

Although Rodney accepted the Marxist methodology, he was less wedded to its dogmas. In this regard, he belonged to the tradition of C. L. R. James and Eusi Kwayana, both of whom rejected the Leninist vanguardist dogma. This nondogmatic tendency was central to Rodney's praxis and was partly the source of his and the WPA's alliance approach. Given the PPP's acceptance of Marxist orthodoxy along the lines of the Soviet Union, ideology was a source of tension throughout the relationship between the two parties. Rodney's

Marxism was also consistent with the Caribbean Marxism that emerged in the 1970s, which integrated race, ethnicity, and aspects of liberal democracy.

The NJM had actually gone the furthest with the principle of broad alliances when it contested the 1976 election as part of an alliance with the conservative Grenada National Party (GNP), a strategy the party was likely to continue at the next election that was due, in 1981. In hindsight, the NJM might have been better served by inviting the GNP to be part of the revolutionary government. While individuals from the private sector did serve in the government, they did not represent an autonomous force.

The Guyana Government and the Revolution

The Guyana government played a positive role in the preparations for the NJM's seizure of power and in the period immediately following the events of March 13, 1979. The PNC facilitated the military training in Guyana of some of the NJM cadres. After the success of the revolution on March 13, 1979, the Guyana government also provided the new revolutionary government with various forms of material support. Maurice Bishop would later reveal to WPA leaders how difficult it was to deal with Guyana given this close relationship with the three major parties at the time: the PNC, the People's Progressive Party (PPP), and the WPA. According to Roopnaraine (2010, 18):

> It was always something of a high-wire act for the NJM to maintain and manage fraternal relations with all three of Guyana's (at that time) main parties, two of which were waging a bitter fight against the third. Burnham—it is now well-enough known—had given active support to the NJM in the preparations for the assault on Gairy, even providing training for senior PRA officers in Guyana Defence Force facilities in Guyana.

The NJM's relationship with the PNC is fascinating. Bishop and the early NJM had developed a close relationship with ASCRIA. This relationship was cemented during the period when the two groups, along with others such as the National Joint Action Committee (NJAC) of Trinidad and Tobago and the Antigua Caribbean Liberation Movement (ACLM) of Antigua and Barbuda, served on the Caribbean preparatory committee for the sixth Pan-African conference held in Tanzania. ASCRIA's Kwayana served as secretary of the committee. Bishop, who visited Guyana during the 1970s, appeared as part of the defense team for the much-publicized trial of a PPP activist, Arnold Rampersaud, who was charged for the murder of a policeman at a toll station.

Bishop, then, would have been on the PNC's enemy list, as the Guyana government was known to be hostile to "meddlers" in the country's internal affairs. His close relationship to Kwayana, who had emerged as one of Burnham's most strident critics after the breakdown of a very close relationship, would also have worked against Bishop. Burnham had actually expelled many of the African Americans who had refused to denounce Kwayana.

The relationship between the NJM and the PNC was actually engineered by Cuba, which enjoyed close ties with both parties. After approaching the Cubans for assistance, the NJM was steered to the Guyana government. The Cubans were obviously mindful that any direct aid to the NJM would have been detected by the United States. The suggested Guyana connection presented serious problems for the NJM, which was split on the issue. Bishop and a few others strongly opposed it on the grounds that the PNC government was as authoritarian as the Grenadian government and the consequences for their relationship with the WPA. They were, however, overruled, and Bishop was sent on the mission to Guyana.[1] While in Guyana, he briefed one of the WPA leaders on the mission. The WPA, for its part, treated the information with the utmost secrecy; it was confined to a very small group, and there was no discussion of the issue within the party.[2]

Burnham reportedly agreed to the scheme without much hesitation. Well known for his Machiavellian political moves, he would have seen the opportunity to neutralize the relationship between his local political opponents, namely, the WPA and the Caribbean radical Left. A similar tactic had been successful regarding the PPP's relationship with the regional and international communist movement. Burnham's announcement that the PNC had become Marxist-Leninist and his implementation of socialist policies such as nationalizing the economy and education had ingratiated him to the communist world, which had hitherto been the main sponsor of the PPP. In any case, sections of the Caribbean Left were impressed with the PNC's progressive anti-imperialist and nonaligned foreign policy, including its support for the African liberation struggle.

Relationship of the WPA and NJM, 1979–1983

The WPA would thus not have been surprised when the NJM seized power on March 13, 1979. Although formal contact between the two parties was almost nonexistent, the WPA would have had a sense of the preparation. Based on recent revelations by WPA coleader Rupert Roopnaraine, the WPA itself was engaged in what he referred to as "preparation for an armed insurrection on the state."[3] According to Roopnaraine, the WPA was accumulating weapons from sources including the Guyana army.

The WPA's first statement in 1979 called it the "year of the turn." It called on Guyanese to find new ways to confront the dictatorial government (*Dayclean*, January 1979). The statement turned out to be prophetic for the WPA, the NJM, and the Anglophone Caribbean as a whole. Apart from the Grenada Revolution, there were other popular insurrections that either led to change of government or seriously challenged the incumbents. In Dominica, the authoritarian Patrick John government was ousted by popular insurrection led by left-wing forces. In nearby Saint Lucia, left-wing activists led by George Odlum spearheaded the electoral victory of the Saint Lucia Labor Party (SLP) over the incumbent United Workers Party (UWP). The Suriname government was overthrown by left-leaning military officers in February 1980, and there was a serious electoral challenge to the Milton Cato–led Labor government in Saint Vincent and the Grenadines.

In Guyana, the WPA led a spirited challenge, popularly known as the Civil Rebellion, to the PNC government. Beginning in July 1979, the party inspired a series of massive street demonstrations and industrial strikes, which brought thousands of people to the streets in protest against the authoritarianism of the government. In the process, Walter Rodney emerged as the leading antidictatorial figure. He was crucial to the WPA's mass mobilization of Guyanese across ethnic lines, a feat that had only been accomplished twenty-six years before around the country's first election under adult suffrage.[4]

Roopnaraine (2010) reveals that the Civil Rebellion was clearly inspired by the success of the Grenada Revolution.[5] One of the slogans introduced by the WPA in the weeks after March 13 referred directly to Grenada: "The Shah Gone! Gairy Gone! Who Next?" Rodney captured the WPA's attitude to the revolution when he told cheering crowds that the best assistance the WPA and Guyanese could give to the Grenada Revolution was to make their own revolution. It is obvious, then, that the WPA viewed the Grenada Revolution as an example to emulate.

The party issued a statement that drew the following lessons from Grenada for Guyana:

> Within hours, a dictatorship which once looked like it could not be touched can be overthrown; when dictators use their power against the people, power has to be seized and taken back by any means necessary; the violence and thuggery of the tyrant cannot prevail against the armed people; the leadership of the revolution is entrusted to those in the frontline of the resistance who become the special targets of the regime and pay a high price at the hands of its forces; a regional

and international public opinion must be mobilized to expose the crimes of the dictator; the task is to build an alliance of all forces opposed to dictatorship and corruption. (Cited in Roopnaraine 2010, 17)

Despite the enthusiasm for the revolution in the WPA, the Grenadian government and the WPA had no close relations during the first two years of the revolution. The WPA was locked in its own struggle against the Burnham dictatorship, and the PRG was fighting to protect the revolution from challenges inside Grenada, from hostile Caribbean governments, and from the U.S. government. The close relationship between the PNC and the NJM would also have made it awkward for the NJM to relate more closely with the WPA. This awkwardness was reflected at the time of Walter Rodney's assassination when the representative to Rodney's funeral was pressured by the PNC to deny that the Grenadian government had claimed that Rodney was assassinated. Bishop had to reiterate the earlier statement that called the murder an assassination. As Roopnaraine (2010, 18) reports about a conversation with Bishop:

> Maurice spoke more somberly about Walter's assassination and the necessary harshness of the NJM statement in June 1980, and of Burnham's displeasure. In fact, Maurice had to repeat the statement that Walter Rodney had been assassinated after the PRG minister who came to the funeral was pressured into denying it.

A third factor may have influenced the distant relationship between the WPA and the NJM during the period in question: the general uneasiness among sections of the orthodox Caribbean Left who considered the WPA not orthodox enough. It is now established that the WPJ, which was somewhat uneasy with the WPA, had enormous influence on the Grenada Revolution. In addition, the OREL faction, which held tremendous sway on the ideological direction of the NJM, preferred closer relations with Guyana's PPP rather than with the WPA.

The WPA's attitude to leadership, in particular its repudiation of one-man leadership and preference instead for a rotating or collective form of leadership, was seen as unorthodox. Ironically the NJM's movement in that direction would be the catalyst for the events of October 1983. As Kwayana (2004, 3) puts it:

> The essential difference between the WPA and other left radical parties was that the WPA has never had a maximum leader. This implies that it anticipates other

approaches in this supremely human project of the overthrow of oppression, especially of the working people, oppression of women and oppression of subject nations.

The WPA also eschewed vanguardism, a central plank of left orthodoxy. The party preferred the strategy of broad alliances without any ideological litmus test. This approach, which the NJM embraced before 1979, was a bone of contention between the WPA and its main ally, the PPP, in the antidictatorial movement in Guyana. Third, although subscribing to the theory and practice of revolution, the WPA, unlike other parties of the Caribbean Left, viewed liberal democratic norms such as free and fair elections, rule of law, and freedom of expression and association as vital to the revolutionary processes. In other words, the WPA viewed those freedoms not as "bourgeois rights" but as "people's rights" that were won by the sacrifices of the working people. While this thesis was most articulated by Clive Thomas, it was also deeply held by other major leaders such as Rodney, Kwayana, and Moses Bhagwan. Finally, others on the Caribbean left were uncomfortable with the WPA's "populism," in particular as it related to Walter Rodney. As Roopnaraine (2010, 19) observes:

> It must be admitted that the WPA was regarded as somewhat heretical in the congregation of orthodoxy that gathered in St George's for the party building workshops. As an independent Marxist party, we had not only long set our face against vanguardism—Guyana was already suffering from two established vanguard parties, Jagan's PPP and Burnham's PNC but had compounded the heresy by institutionalizing co-leadership as a counterexample to the one-manism of the dictator we were fighting.

Rupert Lewis confirms this in relation to the WPJ:

> Well, I know a little about the inner-party discussions on how Walter should be treated. That was a special matter at the 1978 Congress preparatory committee. Because we all knew that Walter would receive a big reception and Walter was not allowed to speak. In fact I know the person who carried that line against Walter. There was an event, a party event, [where] discussions took place in which Walter was seen in a light not too far different from Beckford. And the WPA at a certain point (with its notions of collective leadership) was seen more as a non-Leninist party. Of course the WPA went on a Leninist thing at a certain stage after Grenada, '79. But I would say that the evidence is that Walter would obviously not be seen in the same way as G-Beck, but pretty close to Beckford in relationship to this notion of petit bourgeois revolutionary because I do remember serious

discussion as to how Walter should be treated. Walter could have upstaged Trevor had he been allowed to speak. The second area where Walter and the WPJ had differences was, of course, the Grenada Revolution and the issue of the different attitudes toward freedom of press, and the possibility of elections. Because, coming out of the Guyanese situation, Rodney felt that the role of the New Jewel Movement [NJM] should be to recognize some of the elements of democracy within Grenada, to show in what way it was different, and to strive for a more open revolution rather than one that was reinforcing the strength of the NJM. In other words, it should have a timetable for elections, and it should have some degree of freedom of the press. (R. Lewis 2001, 151–52)

Because of the WPA's ideological orientation, the developments in the early years of the revolution placed the party in a dilemma. While it viewed the revolution as a significant blow for Caribbean freedom that should be encouraged and nurtured, it was uncomfortable with some of the human-rights violations such as the harassment of political opponents and the muzzling of the nongovernment media, including closing down the *Torchlight* newspaper. The party also felt that the delay in holding elections was a costly mistake. Finally, the WPA was uneasy about the cadre party formation that had been adopted by the NJM. While it felt that in the case of armed insurrection it had its merits, it also isolated the party from the popular masses and limits popular discussion.[6] Despite these misgivings, the WPA did not publicly criticize the revolution. It felt that such public criticism would play into the hands of the enemies of the revolution, which in the WPA's estimation was making tremendous strides in transforming the Grenadian society and political economy. Even Walter Rodney, who was known for his fierce independence of thought and action, did not speak out publicly, although he was highly critical in private. The problem for the WPA was that it was fighting for those very rights that the Grenada revolution was trampling on.[7]

The WPA instead concentrated on urging defense of the revolution against imperialist threat, in particular from the United States. In the days after the revolution, for example, when some Caribbean governments hesitated to recognize the revolutionary government, the WPA urged immediate recognition. In a cable to the governments, the party warned that the delay was tantamount to "sabotage" and "foreign intervention."[8]

Relations between the two parties changed in 1981 after a visit to Grenada by WPA executives Rupert Roopnaraine and Andaiye. That initial visit led to an extremely close relationship over the next two years of the revolution. WPA leaders and activists were frequent visitors to Grenada for seminars and other political meetings. Some leaders actually attended executive meetings of the NJM, which was normal practice for close allies such as the WPJ and the ACLM. According to Roopnaraine (2010, 19):

> Our relations with the NJM deepened, including the establishment of systems of communication and mutual assistance. WPA sent delegations to Grenada to participate along with representatives of other Caribbean parties in the political education classes on Marxist-Leninist party building facilitated by the NJM and led by Trevor Munroe, then General Secretary of the Workers Party of Jamaica.

The immediate impact of this close relationship on the WPA was reflected in the party's movement in a Leninist direction, in particular as it related to internal party organization. The party adopted the cadre party formation, which had begun to develop since Rodney's assassination in June 1980. This was a source of some debate in the WPA, as some activists were uncomfortable with the secrecy it encouraged. Another development in the WPA was increased emphasis on political education, which occurred at two levels. First, there were the political education classes, which included the political history of Guyana and the Caribbean and some introduction to Marxism. Second, there were the more advanced classes for the first- and second-level leaderships, which exposed them more fully to Marxism-Leninism. Although these classes had taken place in some form before 1981, they increased with the closer relationship with the NJM.

These developments were accompanied by some degree of factionalization inside the WPA between those who were closer to the NJM, on the one hand, and others who did not visit Grenada often. The differences, however, had less to do with Grenada and more to do with the general direction of the party, which had to considerably alter its approach after Rodney's assassination. There was also some disagreement over the question of elections in Grenada, with some leaders more outspoken than others. Clive Thomas was the most extreme in this regard and did publicly express his views in his capacity as a leading academic, an action that displeased the PRG.[9] Eusi Kwayana was equally adamant that the PRG should hold elections, but did not publicly express his views. Instead he wrote privately to Bishop, outlining his views on the issue.[10]

Members of the WPA attended the celebrations in Grenada to mark the fourth anniversary of the revolution and were impressed with its progress in the areas of the economy and education:

> The Working People's Alliance hails the fourth anniversary of the Grenada revolution and salutes the Grenadian people, the People's Revolutionary Government

and the New Jewel Movement for holding high the banner of Caribbean sovereignty and national independence. . . . After only four years of revolution the shat-
tered economy inherited from the dictatorship has been repaired and set firmly
on the path of reconstruction. In the midst of the most severe crisis of world capitalism which is bringing havoc and devastation to the dependent economics of
the developing countries, the Grenadian economy is growing and the producers of
wealth are benefiting from its growth. Even the World Bank has not been able to
evade the evidence that the Grenadian economy is in an enviable state of health.
In this the year of political and academic education, the revolution has resolutely
and for all time turned its back on the ignorance and superstition of Gairyism and
has set out to mobilize the working people to cast off the bonds of mental slavery
and to become the subject of their history. (WPA press statement, March 13, 1983)

The Events of October 1983

Despite the parties' close relationship, the WPA had no idea of the problems in
the NJM's leadership. Thus the WPA was confused when the matter publicly
erupted. The immediate response was to send a cable to the NJM, expressing
hope that the two sides could resolve the differences in a fraternal manner
and not deliver the revolution to its enemies:

Political Bureau in session conveys to NJM our confidence that revolution will
seize space within principles apparently in dispute in interest mainly of working
people's morale in this hour of reactionary counter-vigilance in region, and will
establish revolutionary composition of issues to permit continued examination.
Respectfully and fraternally request circulation of this message. (*Dayclean*, October 22, 1983)

The party then accepted an invitation by the NJM to mediate the difference. Toward this end, Roopnaraine was dispatched to Grenada with instructions from the WPA to first speak with Bishop. The WPA leadership and
membership went into permanent session as they monitored the developments in Grenada. According to Roopnaraine, he was not allowed to meet
with Bishop, nor did he play any role in the attempts at mediation. His contact
was contained to a member of the Coard faction, who furnished him with
the minutes of the Central Committee's meeting.[11] In the meantime, the WPA
issued a statement based on the limited information it received. The statement wrongly concluded that the crisis did not result from a power struggle
in the NJM:

Was there a coup in Grenada? No. The People's Revolutionary Government remains the government of Grenada. What is the issue? It appears to be about the form of collective leadership in the party. The New Jewel Movement has long been committed to collective leadership. At one point there was joint leadership of Maurice Bishop and Unison Whiteman. The disagreement arose over the implementation of decisions taken by the whole central committee. It is not a power struggle between Bishop and Coard. (*Open Word*, October 17, 1983)

Some WPA members pointed to the close relationship between Coard and Bishop to buttress the party's position. However, others who knew Bishop well doubted that he would renege on a decision without some profound reason. Roopnaraine's presence in Grenada did not help, as he did not have access to both sides. This would later lead to accusations, denied by Roopnaraine, that he sided with the Coard faction.[12]

The murder of Bishop and other NJM leaders shocked the WPA, which issued a strong condemnatory statement. It concluded that whatever the differences, murder was unacceptable:

The Working People's Alliance finds the killing of Prime Minister Maurice Bishop and others, and the explanations given by the Revolutionary Military Council, totally unacceptable. The party is sickened by the killings and can find no justification or explanation to excuse those who were responsible for this act. Because the WPA has had long, close and fraternal relations with the NJM, we believe that it is our duty to say very plainly that the events of October 19 dishonor the name of the New Jewel Movement and cover with shame those associated with the act. The WPA is awaiting the return of our two members in Grenada before a full analysis of the present stage and the party's future attitude can be attempted. We do not intend to shirk our responsibility to understand and discuss with the Guyanese and the rest of the Caribbean people at the earliest possible opportunity. Along with other responsible Caribbean parties and organizations, we must come to know and share with the people in our region what it is in our political culture that could lead to such an ugly explosion which even to close friends was unexpected. (*Dayclean*, October 22, 1983)

The party took the matter to the streets in the form of a public meeting where the speakers discussed both the positives and negatives of the revolution and its relationship to the Guyanese struggle. The speakers also warned of the threat of invasion, which they opined would be a backward step. The WPA also organized a traditional Guyanese wake in Buxton in memory of Bishop and his comrades. According to the party's organ, *Dayclean*:

Last Thursday night, the nine-night, a wake in the memory of brother Maurice Bishop was held in Buxton. Villagers of all age groups took part. There were prayers, hymns and African death or wake songs. Using the "nancy" form, a game played at wakes, a brother told of the part played by the NJM and brother Bishop in the Grenada struggle. They condemned his killing saluted the Grenadian masses on their resistance against the U.S. invaders. (*Dayclean*, October 22, 1983)

After the invasion was launched, the WPA accepted an invitation by the PPP to join a picket of the U.S. embassy. The party also mounted an all-night vigil in Georgetown to protest the invasion. Other activities in Guyana included a church service organized by the Catholic and Anglican churches. The party also paid tribute to Bishop, whom it described as a young and creative statesman:

Despite his reported errors, Maurice Bishop's contribution as a young and creative statesman to the popularization of the ideas of Caribbean dignity and independence, Caribbean renewal and unity, his historic work in linking the struggles of the oppressed of the Caribbean and Latin America, his infectious and genuine revolutionary love are a lasting enlargement of the political culture of our times in this region. (*Dayclean*, October 22, 1983)

Roopnaraine, who was stuck in Grenada, offered his services to the Revolutionary Military Council (RMC) to help defend the country against the invasion, an action that drew strong criticism from the anti-Coard supporters in the region. The WPA issued a wide-ranging statement that contended, among other things, that the party "had no rules to deal with the emergency when it arose and that terrible errors were committed by everyone involved"; "Maurice and the others were not killed in crossfire after the soldiers were killed. They were arrested and then killed"; and "whatever the difficult ties the NJM or the army found themselves in, the execution of Maurice Bishop and others is not excusable." There was not a "conspiracy theory"; the leaders who invited the United States to invade were "guilty of high treason and murder against the Caribbean nation"; attempts to "frame the Cuban people and government [were] vulgar"; Maurice Bishop "was a shield protecting Grenada and the entire Caribbean"; and the events in Grenada "raise a question that all serious parties have to face: whether or not differences which develop inside the party should be put for public discussion before they get out of hand" (Roopnaraine 2010, 28–29).

The WPA's statement was one of the clearest to come from the Caribbean Left. Except for the conclusion that mistakes were made by all involved, it clearly took the position that the anti-Bishop faction must take ultimate responsibility for what happened. The statement, therefore, was not ambivalent about Bishop's execution or his executioners. It did not allow its opposition to get in the way of its assessment of what happened. Thus one may conclude that despite being perplexed with the outcome of the revolution, the WPA came out with as clear a sense of the immediate future as could be mustered in the circumstances. The party recommended that Bishop's banner of the Caribbean as a zone of peace should be taken up by all peace-loving people, especially in Guyana's own circumstances, where the country was still locked in a bitter struggle against the PNC dictatorship. Like all the parties of the Left, the WPA condemned the U.S. invasion that followed the murder of Bishop and his comrades. As news of the advancing U.S. invasion forces emerged, the party issued the following statement:

> The news of 2,000 Marines and 17 U.S. warships advancing on Grenada under the pretext for saving U.S. nationals has alarmed the entire Caribbean. No one who is distressed that so much blood had been shed already, can fail to raise their voices against an outside intervention that can only lead to the shedding of more blood and the suffering of greater numbers. Although we do not accept the killings or the explanations given by the authorities, WPA joins all those who have raised their strong voices against the armed intervention of Grenada. It is reported that non-Barbadian troops are already visible in Barbados. The most backward governments in the region are calling for a joint U.S./Caricom operation which will be under U.S. Command. WPA wishes to remind the people that all examples of landings of this kind have turned out to be major disasters for the population. (*Dayclean*, October 22, 1983)

Unlike other parties of the Left, then, the WPA did not have the luxury of long, gradual introspection. The invasion of Grenada had presented Burnham with the first opportunity since Rodney's murder to redeem himself with the progressive community. His opposition to the invasion and the fact that he alerted the RMC to its imminence set him apart from all his CARICOM colleagues, except the Trinidadian leader. Not for the first time, the WPA had to counter this positive image of Burnham. The party lauded his stance and supported his call for an international fact-finding mission for Grenada but also called for a similar mission to Guyana.

> In the heat of the Caricom meetings over Grenada after the execution of Maurice Bishop and others, Burnham opposed intervention. He did not oppose

intervention in Anguilla by Barbados some years ago. However, this time, he agreed with progressive opinion in the region and with most of the world that there should be no intervention in Grenada. Then he made a call for a very good thing, a fact-finding mission from outside to go into Grenada to investigate what happened. He made another good point. In opposing those who called in Reagan and the U.S. Marines, he said they were acting illegally. This is the same Burnham who is against the idea of observers coming to look at the situation in Guyana because it is a sovereign and independent state. It is the same Burnham who says to people who complain against his abuses of the law in Guyana, "I am not interested in technicalities." Now he has gone on record as being in favour of things being done legally and of a fact-finding mission (observers) in another sovereign and independent state. This is why WPA sent a cable to the Commonwealth Summit in New Delhi saying we support fact-finding missions for both Grenada and Guyana. (*Dayclean*, November 2, 1983)

The PNC countered by charging the WPA with passing information to the CIA through its members in Grenada. The WPA challenged the PNC to name the WPA members it had in mind, a challenge to which the PNC did not respond. The Grenadian debacle had actually interrupted a major offensive by the WPA against food shortages, which had developed into a mass movement reminiscent of the Civil Rebellion of 1979. Starting with a one-day strike by bauxite workers at Linden, the protest grew to include a general strike in the industry, solidarity strikes by sugar workers, and two days of "rest" organized by the WPA. The government hit back by firing striking bauxite workers, which served to prolong the confrontation. This clash between the government and the WPA represented the first major confrontation since Rodney's murder. The WPA had not lost its capacity to mobilize on a large scale. The government's reaction also showed that it still saw the WPA as a major threat.

Given the ongoing battle with the PNC, the WPA moved quickly to announce some major alterations. First, it declared that armed insurrection was no longer on the table. Although the party had begun a retreat from that position after Rodney's murder, it had not completely abandoned it. Second, the party concluded that it was aspiring not to build a Leninist party but to build one that was "most suited to meet the needs of the struggle against dictatorship." The party also announced that it would make the struggle for free and fair elections the center of its activities. The WPA soon declared that it was a Rodneyite party committed to democratization and concluded that should the PNC commit itself to free and fair elections, it was prepared to work with it. Roopnaraine (2010, 20) sums up the WPA's shift: "At its members' conference of April 1984, the WPA formally abandoned the Leninist form of organization, dismantled the clandestine security units, and opted for the electoral path and the building of a mass party." Some critics, such as the PPP, viewed the WPA's declaration that it was now a Rodneyite party as an abandonment of Rodney's ideals and of Marxism. But Kwayana defended the party's position:

> Based on practice in Guyana, Rodney's thought firmly emancipated workers, women's and youth groups and other self-organized groups from party control. On general questions Rodney held that people who had not made revolution had no moral ground for criticizing a revolution made by others. He took no part in the conflict between the USSR and China. Rodneyite doctrine is grounded in self-emancipation of each oppressed group acting together or apart. It did not ideologically dismiss classes, but sought to democratize them, assigning them responsibility for their own spheres for the benefit of the whole society, depriving the predatory classes of power and creating a climate of genuine respect, justice and new rights to the working people, giving them the possibility of pursuing its own emancipation. At the same time he was reeducating the academic and new professionals that their destiny lay with the working people. (Kwayana 2004, 8)

The WPA also concluded that building socialism in Guyana was not possible at that juncture. Speaking at a conference organized by the Critchlow Labor College, Eusi Kwayana reiterated the WPA's position that the PNC's claim to be building a socialist society was not borne out by the actual experience. He argued that the PNC had instead created a form of state capitalism accompanied by an authoritarian state, and recommended as a solution a democratic republic that guaranteed civil liberties and free and fair elections, eschewed ethnic domination, respected the sovereignty of the people and trade union rights, and defended the national independence of the Caribbean (Kwayana 1984, 9).

The WPA also responded to an article by a well-known conservative lawyer, David De Caries, in the *Catholic Standard*, in which he called on the WPA to clearly state its ideological position in relation to Marxism-Leninism. The WPA replied by saying that it was struggling not for the dictatorship of any class but for a democratic society. The party did not view this position as an abandonment of the working class, as it had always stayed clear of "ideological rigidity" despite its Marxist outlook. It argued that the antidictatorial struggle and the reconstruction of the country demanded ideological flexibility (*Catholic Standard*, February 21, 1984).

Conclusion

The demise of the Grenada Revolution threw the Caribbean Left into disarray. The revolution had become the hope for fundamental transformation in the Anglophone Caribbean. It was a popular revolution whose effects reached far beyond the shores of Grenada. No party of the regional Left was more affected than the WPA, not only because of the close relations between the NJM and the WPA, but also because of the startling similarities in the regimes both confronted. Not since the murder of Rodney three years earlier had the WPA been so tested. In the end, the party made some sweeping adjustments to its praxis.

One lesson we may draw from this examination of the WPA's relationship with the NJM and the Grenada Revolution is that revolutions by their very nature are universal and have effects beyond their places of execution. The smallness of Caribbean society and its members' shared identity meant that a revolution in one island could not be contained there. Just as the Haitian Revolution inspired slave uprisings in the United States and other parts of the diaspora, so the Grenada Revolution served as a point of reference for the entire region that could not be ignored. The Grenada Revolution, then, represented the highest form of regional integration: it served as the meeting point for the Caribbean Left, but it also galvanized a unity among the ruling class, who were understandably terrified by a living alternative to their form of governance.

The impact of the revolution on Guyanese politics in general was unmistakable. That the NJM had to navigate between the country's three major parties points to this reality. The impetus the revolution gave to the Civil Rebellion of 1979 was not lost. The WPA could see the possibility of success from the NJM's example and pursued it with renewed purpose. But the revolution also presented the WPA with difficulties. What might have happened had the WPA publicly criticized the shortcomings of the revolution? Could it have made a difference? One can never know the answers to these questions, but it is clear that the lack of public criticism did not help the NJM and the revolution.

Unlike other left parties, the WPA ultimately survived the death of the revolution. This was due largely to the party's shift in tactics. Because it located itself in the concrete needs of the struggle in Guyana, in particular the need to return the country to democratic norms, and because of its insistence on alliances, the WPA was able to remain relevant to the political process. Its subsequent decline arose out of the internal dynamics of Guyanese ethnic politics, where the return of democratic norms was accompanied by a return to ethnic polarization. The key point here is that the WPA did not allow itself to be overly paralyzed by the situation. The left parties were obviously torn by what had happened. In a fight between comrades, it was difficult to come to grips with the fact that one side may be guilty. Perhaps because they had warned about the dangers of a closed party, the WPA was not overcome by a sense of guilt. That explained why the statements following the events of October 1983 were not ambivalent. As they argued, ultimately murder could not be justified. Without demonizing the accused, the statements signaled that for the WPA there was a limit to political reasoning and logic.

Another lesson to be drawn is that closed political parties are diametrically opposed to the notion of democratic leadership. The NJM and other parties of the Left did not sufficiently distinguish between secrecy as a function of security and as a function of limiting debate and discourse on public issues. The revolution was treated as the property of the party rather than of the people who would ultimately be its defenders and nurturers. While the WPA in its practice strove to make the distinction, it did not sufficiently make this a central tenet in its relationship with the NJM. In this regard, Tim Hector and the ACLM, which publicly spoke out on some of the excesses of the revolution, were the most principled. Under the circumstances, one would not be out of place to label the WPA and other fraternal parties, some more direct than others, as enablers of some of the negative tendencies in the revolution.

Some observers have contended that the death of the revolution brought into the open the limitations of armed insurrection as a path to power. While that may be true, I think, more importantly, it exposed the limitations of managing a revolution in the face of inevitable hostility. In light of a reinvigorated U.S. imperialism, as represented by Reaganism, the pressure on the Grenada Revolution was inevitable. Thus the need for the broadest possible shield. The lesson is that any fundamental transformation by necessity required a broad national alliance, which by definition is diametrically opposed to vanguardism. Roopnaraine (2010, 25) is therefore correct when he asserts:

> The experience of Grenada has delegitimized vanguardism and instructs that it is more imperative than ever to build alliances across differences. We must learn the strength of otherness and difference and, above all, we must guard against the fatal arrogance of righteousness. We must focus on what we agree on and work persistently and with integrity on differences that are primary contradictions.

Leadership is vital to all political processes, particularly one whose objective is to revolutionize the state and society. The problem with the Caribbean

Left on this score was the contradiction between its desire to transform the political culture while holding dearly to one of the most discredited aspects of the culture. The one-man leadership model seemed to be too seductive. For the NJM, Bishop became problematic. On the one hand, the party wanted his charisma to sell the revolution to the masses, to be its face. But they were not prepared to deal with the logic of that thrust. Over time, the maximum leader becomes the sovereign. The WPA's Clive Thomas captures perhaps the largest lesson of Grenada:

> After Grenada, no social project carried out in the name of the masses of the Caribbean peoples, whether by government or opposition, will receive widespread support from the popular forces and their organizations if it does not clearly embrace political democracy in its norms of political conduct. (Thomas 1984, 12)

Notes

1. This information was gathered from a private interview with a then-high-ranking member of the PNC.

2. Private interview with a leading member of the WPA, October 31, 2010.

3. Roopnaraine first made this revelation in a documentary on Walter Rodney, *W.A.R. Stories*, produced by the Guyanese filmmaker Clairmont Chung and was released in March 2010.

4. For a full account of the Civil Rebellion, see Eusi Kwayana, *Walter Rodney* (WPA, 1981).

5. Rupert Roopnaraine, "Resonances of Revolution: Grenada, Suriname, Guyana," *Interventions* 12, no. 1 (March 2010): 11–34.

6. Ibid.

7. Private interview with Eusi Kwayana, November 7, 2010.

8. Roopnaraine, "Resonances of Revolution."

9. Private interview with leading WPA member, October 31, 2010.

10. Kwayana interview.

11. Roopnaraine, "Resonances of Revolution."

12. Ibid.

References

Bouges, A. 2003. *Black Heretics, Black Prophets: Radical Political Intellectuals*. New York: Routledge.

Catholic Standard. 1984. "WPA Does Not Stand for the Dictatorship of Any Class." February 18.

Dayclean. 1983a. "No Invasion, No Cover Up." October 22.

——. 1983b. "WPA Supports Fact Finding Mission in Grenada and Guyana." November 2.

Joseph, T., and D. Jules, eds. 2004. *At the Rainbow's Edge: Collected Speeches by Kenny D. Anthony, 1996–2002*. Kingston, Jamaica: Ian Randle.

Kwayana, E. 1984. "Forward to a Democratic Republic." Georgetown: Working People's Alliance.

——. 2004. "The Caribbean Left's Legacy: Sara Abrahams Interviews Eusi Kwayana." *Against the Current*, September–October.

Lewis, G. K. 1987. *Grenada: The Jewel Despoiled*. Baltimore: Johns Hopkins University Press.

Lewis, R. 1998. *Walter Rodney's Intellectual and Political Thought*. Detroit: Wayne State University Press.

——. 2001. "The Dialectic of Defeat: An Interview with Rupert Lewis." *Small Axe* 5 (2): 85–177.

Marable, M. 1987. *African and Caribbean Politics from Kwame Nkrumah to Maurice Bishop*. London: Verso.

Meeks, B. 2001. *Caribbean Revolutions and Revolutionary Theory: An Assessment of Cuba, Nicaragua, and Grenada*. Mona, Jamaica: UWI Press.

Open Word. 1983. "Editorial." October 19.

Rodney, W. 1976. "Guyana's Socialism: An Interview with Colin Prescod." *Race and Class* 18 (2): 109–28.

——. 1979. *People's Power No Dictator*. Georgetown: Working People's Alliance.

Roopnaraine, R. 1998. Interview with CaribNation TV. Washington, DC, November 14.

——. 2010. "Resonances of Revolution: Grenada, Suriname, Guyana." *Interventions* 12 (1): 11–34.

Thomas, C. 1984. "Hard Lessons for Intellectuals." *Caribbean Contact*, September, 12.

11. Exploring Transitions in Party Politics in Grenada, 1984–2013

Wendy C. Grenade

The Grenada Revolution, its demise, and the subsequent U.S. invasion attracted a flurry of scholarly attention in the immediate aftermath of the October 1983 events (Boodhoo 1984; Payne, Sutton, and Thorndike 1984; Pastor 1986; Lewis 1987). With the passage of time, other scholars turned their gaze on the Grenada Revolution: as part of a wider assessment of Caribbean revolutions and revolutionary theory (Meeks 2001); to renew the project of making sense of Grenada's past and present (Scott 2007); to analyze memory and the mixed legacies of radical politics in the Caribbean (Puri 2010).

However, there is a dearth in the literature on Grenada's rebuilding process after the U.S. invasion and the twists and turns of party politics in post-revolutionary Grenada. Gary Williams (2007) seeks to address this gap but provides only a cursory treatment in the epilogue to *U.S.-Grenada Relations: Revolution and Intervention in the Backyard*. He observes, "In a small island society some wounds are too deep to heal. However, with 33 percent of the population under 15 years old, and approximately half under 30 years old, the revolutionary era and the intervention are fast becoming a foreign country for many Grenadians" (177). However, there are fundamental lessons to be learned from the 1979–83 experience. Therefore the purpose of this chapter is to build on earlier works (Emmanuel 1978, 1983, 1992; Emmanuel, Brathwaite, and Barriteau 1986; Ryan 1999; Barrow-Giles and Joseph 2006; Grenade 2013, 2010) to contribute to the annals of Grenadian political history.

The chapter maps the contours of party politics in Grenada three decades after the implosion of the Grenada Revolution and the U.S. invasion of Grenada. Following this introduction, section 2 discusses four broad phases of party politics in Grenada from 1984 to 2013: phase 1, externally imposed coalition and splintering (1984–89); phase 2, technocratic governance in an unstable multiparty system (1990–95); phase 3, electoral dominance of the New

National Party (NNP) (1995–2003) and realignment to the two-party system (2003–8); and phase 4, intraparty conflict and splintering of the National Democratic Congress (NDC) (2008–13). The final section provides conclusions and lessons.

Phase 1: Externally Imposed Coalition and Subsequent Splintering (1984–1989)

The events of October 1983 marked a critical juncture in Grenada. Consequently, in the immediate postinvasion period, there was an urgency to break with the past and establish an externally imposed political architecture. As is the case with many other postcolonial developing states, external domination is not new. However, the self-destruction of the Grenada Revolution set the stage for external forces to invade and subsequently control the construction of a postinvasion party political architecture. This was consistent with the U.S. foreign policy to rid the world of communism and spread the ideas of democracy and free markets. As Lewis commented: "No empire in history conquers a new territory and then evacuates. It sets up a machinery of governance to guarantee its continuing control of the newly conquered province. So, in Grenada, Americans moved in with typical American efficiency to ensure the dividends of their new conquest-investment" (Lewis 1987, 180). Therefore the U.S. and Caribbean governments that had participated in the invasion spearheaded the creation of an Advisory Council (AC).[1] One of the AC's major objectives was to dismantle the People's Revolutionary Government's (PRG's) state-run enterprises through privatization and closures and to remove any and all vestiges of socialism (Martin 2007, 1). The principal responsibility of the AC was to ensure the return to parliamentary democracy through arrangements for general elections.

The reopening of the electoral system saw the rebirth of traditional political parties, the formation of new ones, and political mobilization.[2] The U.S. and Caribbean governments that were part of the invasion successfully pursued an amalgamation of centrist parties, "whose leaders on their own efforts had been unable to coalesce" (Emmanuel, Brathwaite, and Barriteau 1986, 83–84). On August 26, 1984, three Caribbean prime ministers (James Mitchell of Saint Vincent and the Grenadines, the late John Compton of Saint Lucia, and the late Tom Adams of Barbados) orchestrated the Union Island Accord, which created the New National Party (NNP). The NNP was a coalition of three parties: the Grenada National Party (GNP) of Herbert Blaize,[3] the Grenada Democratic Movement (GDM) led by Francis Alexis,[4] and George Brizan's National Democratic Party (NDP).[5]

In his autobiography, James Mitchell recounted that they had to resolve three issues: an anti-Gairy alliance, its leadership, and the name of the party. He reported that Blaize's former experience as a chief minister and his age, inter alia, allowed the younger men to concede him leadership. Importantly, Blaize's emergence as leader was sanctioned by the United States. According to Mitchell, creation of a single party proved more bothersome, and they settled for NNP and agreed on the metaphoric symbol of a house as a hopeful image for Grenada's reconstruction (J. Mitchell 2006, 202; cited in Grenade 2013, 169). The NNP, led by Herbert Blaize, won fourteen of the fifteen parliamentary seats in the 1984 general elections. Voter turnout was relatively high at 85.3 percent.

The Blaize administration depended heavily on the U.S. government for economic advice and financial assistance. As Noguera points out, "During his last term in office [Blaize] was influenced by U.S. economic advisors and relied quite heavily upon their advice in devising economic policies. As a result of this influence, the policies of the NNP government heavily favoured the interests of the business sector and the wealthy, while the needs of the lower class were treated as less of a priority" (Noguera 1997, 224). Thus the traditional GNP policy agenda converged with U.S. interests.

However, when the Cold War ended, the United States turned its attention away from Grenada and the Caribbean. Payne observes:

> By the end of the 1980s the U.S. had, to a significant degree, again withdrawn its particular political interest from the region. The Caribbean was no longer "a circle of crisis" or a "sea of splashing dominoes," the colourful phrases widely used by the U.S. State Department personnel in the mid-to-late 1970s. Other priorities emerged—in Eastern Europe, the Middle East and elsewhere—with the result that the Caribbean was downgraded. The USA in fact considered that its job in the Caribbean had been well done. (Payne 1998, 211)

In essence, "What started out as a marriage made in heaven [had] begun to look more like a one-night stand" (Gary Krist, cited in Noguera 1997, 5). Since the Cold War and the communist threat had ended, Grenada was no longer of strategic interest to the United States. In fact, by the end of the 1980s, there was no longer an East-West ideological divide. Instead the new wave of globalization had intensified, and the neoliberal doctrine was entrenched in the global political economy (see Klak 1998; Thomas 2001; Ramsaran 2002; Barrow-Giles and Marshall 2003; Benn and Hall 2003). Consequently many developing countries, such as Grenada, adopted neoliberal principles and underwent structural adjustment programs (SAPs). In Grenada, a strictly market-oriented approach was adopted. This was in stark contrast to the 1979–83 period, when the PRG embarked on a series of social and economic reforms as part of a centrally planned development strategy (Emmanuel 1983; Brierley 1985). The thrust of the Blaize-led NNP's reform strategy was outlined in the 1986 budget address:

> This Budget is easier to prepare than the last one, as it was fashioned within the framework of a clearly defined development strategy, aimed at transforming the economy from a controlled and narrowly based one to a free enterprise, market oriented one. (Government of Grenada 1986, 14)

The urgency to completely break from the past and reorient Grenada's economy had consequences for the Blaize administration. Mervyn Williams notes that from 1984 to 1990,

> developments in the public sector were the major cause of concern. The central government recorded huge current account deficits following the 1986 Tax Reform Programme. This Reform Programme repealed the personal income tax, the company tax, various taxes on imports, export duty, telecommunications surcharge and the hotel occupancy tax. These taxes were replaced by a business levy, a value added tax, a modified land value tax and a gasoline tax. Reflecting the administrative difficulties of administering the new tax system, tax revenue declined. Despite the fall in recurrent revenue, recurrent expenditure continued to rise. Thus, public savings [were] negligible and domestic savings remained depressed. (M. Williams 2003, 47)

The problem in the public sector was compounded when the government of Grenada (GOG) reduced its activities in some of the state-owned enterprises, causing the public sector to contract. In 1986 the central government implemented a fiscal reform program to boost private-sector growth (M. Williams 2003). By 1987 the GOG embarked on a public-sector reform program designed to reduce the public service by 25 percent or by 1,800 positions. The program was subsequently suspended by the GOG, and instead 450 to 500 positions were eliminated. According to the World Bank (1990), the program was counterproductive, since qualified and highly mobile civil servants left the service on account of the low salaries paid.

The government's neoliberal economic policies created conflict within the NNP coalition government. Brizan (2010) recalled that he and Francis Alexis strongly disagreed with the government's decision to retrench workers. He recounted that as an economist, he advised Blaize that retrenchment was wrong and suggested a different approach. Brizan explained that Blaize did not listen and went ahead with the retrenchment program. It was at that point that Brizan, Alexis, and Tillman Thomas left the NNP and formed the National Democratic Congress (NDC).[6]

In 1989 the NNP further splintered when Keith Mitchell defeated Blaize in the NNP's annual convention and became the political leader of the NNP while Blaize remained as prime minister (Mackoon 1989). According to the *Los Angeles Times* (1989), Mitchell regularly criticized Blaize for making major decisions without consulting his cabinet. Blaize's final year was marked by the threat of a no-confidence motion and defections from his government, which reduced the NNP majority to nine against an opposition of six. With growing friction within the party, Blaize prorogued the parliament, withdrew from the NNP, and, with a group of members loyal to him, launched the National Party (TNP). At TNP's first convention on December 17, 1989, Blaize was officially elected as the party's political leader. He died two days later, and his long-standing deputy, Ben Jones, was appointed political leader of TNP and prime minister (see Grenade 2013). Therefore the first phase of Grenada's transition was characterized by an externally imposed coalition arrangement among strange bedfellows, which splintered within three years.

Phase 2: Technocratic Governance in an Unstable Multiparty System (1990–1995)

One of the consequences of the disintegration of the NNP coalition was the ushering in of an unstable multiparty system. Five parties contested the 1990 general elections: the newly formed NDC, under the leadership of Nicholas Brathwaite;[7] the NNP, now led by Keith Mitchell; TNP, under the leadership of Ben Jones after Blaize's death in 1989;[8] Gairy's GULP; and the Maurice Bishop Patriotic Movement (MBPM), led by Terrence Marryshow.[9] The voter turnout stood at 68.4 percent, which was a relative decline compared to the 1984 rate of 85.3 percent.

The 1990 general elections were held within this multiparty system, and none of the political parties won a clear majority. The newly formed NDC amassed 34.57 percent of the popular vote and gained seven parliamentary seats. The GULP gained 28.13 percent and four seats. The NNP and TNP received 17.52 percent and 17.36 percent of the votes cast respectively; each won two parliamentary seats. The MBPM again performed poorly, obtaining only 2.37 percent of the popular vote and failing to capture any parliamentary seats. The NDC led a coalition government with support from GULP members of Parliament (MPs) and TNP.

Economic issues continued to dominate the policy agenda, and the NDC government adopted a technocratic approach to governance. The new administration assumed office in March 1990 in the context of chronic current account deficits. Will observes:

> Severe economic dislocations in Grenada pose a constant threat of derailing not only the NDC government but even the pursuit of democracy itself. Such dislocations are compounded by the island's limited resource base, continuing market weaknesses within [the Caribbean Community] CARICOM, increased societal divisions, youth migration stemming from the unfavourable status of employment in Grenada, and by Grenada's serious debt and cash flow problems—one of several legacies of the 1984–89 Blaize administration. (Will 1991, 52)

As Grenada's economy took a downward turn, the government faced the prospect of going to the International Monetary Fund (IMF). George Brizan summed the situation up:

> In 1990 I was Minister of Finance and Grenada had lost its credit worthiness from the IMF and there were many who said that Grenada should go to the IMF and sign up to an IMF SAP. Being a teacher of economics I understood what an IMF SAP was. And I said I would never put Grenada into an IMF structural fund—never. But I also recognized that Grenada needed a SAP. So I told the IMF that we would design our own programme and the IMF said "well, you will fail because no other country has done this before." I said "all we want is your blessings." They said "you have it, we wish you luck." Two and a half years later they wrote back saying that "the government must be congratulated, the home-grown SAP has succeeded and Grenada's credit worthiness has been restored and enhanced." (Brizan 2004, 8)

As a consequence of the self-imposed SAP, Grenada regained its creditworthiness from the IMF. However, this came at a high political cost to the NDC. The NDC-led coalition was fragile, and the party experienced intraparty wrangling. Joan Purcell, writing as an NDC insider, admits:

> While we stayed together for the full duration of our term in office, we never became a team. We never learnt to fight gracefully and constructively. We were in the main an un-cohesive and uncooperative group of people attempting to work together, with a sincere wish to see betterment for the country but with widely varying values, views and approaches for getting this done. We never succeeded at developing a true consensus or community. . . . This promising group of people became unglued. (Purcell 2007, 142)

Grenada continued to be an "island of conflict" (Brizan 1998), although conflict was relatively benign in the postrevolutionary period, compared to the political violence that existed before and during the revolution. A major issue during this phase was the trial and appeal of the so-called Grenada 17.[10] Of the eighteen prisoners convicted for the murder of Maurice Bishop and others,[11] one was acquitted, three were found guilty of manslaughter and sentenced to imprisonment for a total of 121 years, and fourteen were sentenced to die by hanging. This was a sensitive legal and political issue that divided Grenadian society and challenged political leaders in the postrevolutionary era. The Grenada Constitution makes provision for mercy to be extended to prisoners on death row (Grenada 1973, secs. 72, 73, 74). Yet there was a general sentiment that granting mercy to the prisoners could jeopardize political capital and further divide Grenadian society. During this period, a decision was taken to commute death sentences of the fourteen to life imprisonment.

The decision was controversial but did not create any disruptions in Grenadian society. However, the NDC party was defeated in the 1995 general elections. Its defeat could be attributed in part to its stringent economic policies and internal wrangling within the leadership of the party and government. This phase of the transition was characterized by the fragility of coalition arrangements and the tension between prudent economic management and political astuteness. As was the case with the PRG, the NDC may have gotten the economics "right," but intraparty conflict led to its electoral defeat. The NDC party wandered in the political wilderness from 1995 to 2008.

Phase 3: Electoral Dominance of the NNP and Realignment to the Two-Party System (1995–2008)

A prominent feature of Grenada's political landscape was the thirteen-year reign of Keith Mitchell (1995–2008). In a multiparty environment, five major parties contested the 1995 general elections: the NDC, NNP, TNP, GULP, and MBPM. Voter turnout stood at 61.7 percent, slightly lower than the 1990 rate of 68.4 percent. The NNP gained 32.37 percent of the popular vote and eight seats; the NDC received 30.59 percent and only retained five seats; Gairy's GULP obtained 26.55 percent and two seats. The TNP received 6.46 percent of the popular vote, and the MBPM 1.59 percent; both parties did not secure any parliamentary seats.

Alliance building, co-optation, and populism defined the early phase of Mitchell's reign. After the 1995 general elections, the Mitchell-led NNP formed the government and entered into a strategic partnership with Gairy's

GULP and, as a consequence, received the support of two GULP MPs "to secure a more effective majority" (Ryan 1999, 97). Tangible evidence was the appointment of Gairy's daughter Frances Marcelle Gairy as high commissioner to Britain and the naming of Gairy as the Father of Independence, which appealed to GULP supporters.

Mitchell balanced neoliberal principles, technocratic leadership, and populism to consolidate the NNP. He satisfied the business class by adopting market-oriented economic and fiscal policies. In the 2000 budget speech, the minister of finance confirmed:

> This Administration remains committed to the principle of small government and a more efficient Public Service. Consequently public sector reform remains a high priority for Government. It is the principal strategy to curb increases in recurrent expenditure. The freeze on hiring in the Public Service will remain in force and we will continue to reduce the size of the Public Service, where appropriate. (Government of Grenada 1999, 19–20)

This chapter does not allow sufficient scope to probe the NNP administration's neoliberal agenda. However, it is necessary to note that Mitchell promoted a private-sector-led growth strategy and created the infrastructural support to attract foreign investment. Yet despite Mitchell's accommodation of the business class, he presented himself as a champion of the poor, using populism to ground himself with the working class. In a Gairy-like manner, Mitchell used clientelism to gain the loyalty of his supporters. In fact, one of the ironies of postrevolutionary Grenada is that the initial NNP coalition was orchestrated to prevent the NJM and Gairy from regaining political power in Grenada. However, as a close observer of Grenadian politics, I can attest that the NNP was able to capitalize on Gairy's support, and the party was consolidated after Gairy's death in 1997.

Issues of governance and benign authoritarianism came to the fore during this phase. Mitchell was accused of being "corrupt, dictatorial and egomaniac" (cited in Ryan 1999, 97).[12] As a consequence of the initial firing of one MP and the resignation of two others, the NNP/GULP coalition collapsed in late 1998. This phase was also characterized by party infighting within opposition ranks. The NDC, in particular, was in disarray and splintered. Purcell reflected:

> Notwithstanding our defeat in the June 1995 general elections the lessons appeared to be lost on us. The culture within the party continued to deteriorate. We continued in a state of competitiveness and anti-community, or more

accurately pseudo-community; pretended unity that was recognized for what it was by all but a few among us. By mid 1997 things were at an all time low in the party. The negative energy was corrosive, the disintegration pervasive and the anti-change position defensive. (Purcell 2007, 237)

Opposition forces were ill prepared for the snap elections held in January 1999 before the constitutionally appointed date. The electorate became even more divided and apathetic, and voter turnout was relatively low at 56.54 percent. Within this context, the NNP gained all fifteen seats in the 1999 general elections with 62.2 percent of the popular vote. The NDC received 24.9 percent, the GULP/UL amassed only 11.6 percent,[13] and the MBPM made its usual poor showing with 0.62 percent. The results of the 1999 elections brought to the fore the distortions of the first-past-the-post system (FPTP). Additionally, the overwhelming victory of the NNP meant the absence of parliamentary opposition in a Westminster-style parliamentary democracy that assumes such an opposition.

Importantly, the ghost of the revolution continued to haunt this period. When asked whether Grenada had recovered from the 1983 trauma, Mitchell responded:

Well, I would not say entirely so. I think there is still a lot of bitterness, there is still a lot of hurt and pain, there are still a lot of unknowns, and there is still a lot of unwillingness to forgive. I think that is certainly prevailing at this time. I think in some ways we have recovered, but I certainly believe it is going to be difficult for any political leader or any leader of this country to ever impose any system of military rule in Grenada again. (K. Mitchell 2000, 6)

In 2001 the Mitchell administration appointed a Truth and Reconciliation Commission (TRC) to "inquire into certain political events" that had occurred in Grenada between January 1976 and December 1991. The TRC's mandate included an investigation of the events leading up to Gairy's overthrow, the political conduct of the PRG, and the events leading up to the demise of the revolution on October 19, 1983. The TRC was to concern itself with "the lingering question of the disposal of the remains of those who lost their lives at the fort that day" (Scott 2007, vii). The TRC reported that

during its extensive and intensive inquiry, it unearthed little more knowledge of the truth of facts and events pertaining to the periods under inquiry, than that which was already known.... The Grenadian government, while duly constituting the commission and providing it with its terms of reference, had very little interest in seeing to it that it was able to carry out the full and serious investigation that was—and is—warranted. (Truth and Reconciliation Commission, 1:12; cited in Scott 2007, vii)

The TRC maintained that "throughout much of its work, the Commission suffered from several setbacks occasioned by the administration; inadequate logistical accommodation; and some unwilling and uncooperative official personnel" (vii). Although the TRC was commissioned, Grenadians were still divided.

Realignment to the Two-Party System (2003–2008)

During this phase, former members of the Grenadian Left were visibly assimilated into the leadership of mainstream political parties. In the immediate aftermath of the 1983 crisis, former revolutionaries were divided,[14] and many of the revolutionary leaders were either imprisoned or had migrated. Despite its claim to promote Maurice Bishop's legacy, the Maurice Bishop Patriotic Movement (MBPM) was unable to achieve electoral success. This can be explained by the fact that the Grenadian electorate was disenchanted with the Grenadian Left and scarred by the implosion of the Grenada Revolution.

Before the 2003 general elections, former revolutionaries (who were perceived to be sympathetic to the Grenada 17) had retreated from public life. This changed in the 2003 general elections, when the electoral contest was primarily between the incumbent NNP and a new-look NDC, whose leadership consisted of former second-tier revolutionaries. The elections were held on October 19, 2003, which marked twenty years (to the day) of the traumatic events in 1983. This was a strategic maneuver against the revolutionary elements of the NDC.

The 2003 campaign was vicious. It was dubbed "the politics of hatred" by a leading NGO representative (Ferguson 2003). The fury was pitched against the revolutionary faction of the NDC. It was argued that the "ghost of the revolution" was haunting Grenada's politics (Johnson 2003). The NNP party was extremely critical of the former revolutionaries, who assumed leading and visible roles in the NDC. According to *Grenada Today* on October 17, 2003:

Mitchell stated that although he has been preaching reconciliation, forgiveness and peace, it would be folly for Grenadians to take the same men who have destroyed the country, hurt our children, our mothers and fathers . . . and put them in charge of this country again. . . . If we Grenadians do that, I will say to everyone "you mad or what."

The 2003 general elections were held against the backdrop of a number of visible achievements by the NNP administration. In its seven and a half years in office, the NNP undertook a number of development projects. However, major campaign issues again surrounded allegations of corruption against the Mitchell administration and high public debt. The campaign was also marked by confrontations between government and leading sectors such as the medical and legal professions, as well as some labor unions. Key trade union leaders appeared on opposition platforms, seeking in their view to prevent the NNP from regaining power and enacting antiworker legislation. *Caribupdate* provided an apt summary:

> The thing the NNP government has done best in the past four years is find ways to, many times unnecessarily so, appear to be at war with significant sections of society; an arrogance grown out of its amazing 1999 victory. Many outsiders who have not followed Grenadian politics closely cannot understand how a government that has done so much and only four and a half years ago won all the seats in a general election, can be fighting for its survival. An administration that had instituted face-to-face, made for television community meetings, missed the point that the best public relations is human relations.[15]

After having won all fifteen parliamentary seats in the 1999 general elections, the NNP thus almost suffered electoral defeat in 2003. The NDC received 44.1 percent of the popular vote and gained seven parliamentary seats, while the incumbent NNP received 46.6 percent and only managed to hold on to eight seats. Why was the NNP not able to transfer its incumbent advantage with such visible achievements to greater political capital? Why such a strong showing by the NDC? As I have observed elsewhere:

> "Softer" issues such as integrity, accountability and transparency were high on the electoral agenda. Although the Mitchell administration scored relatively high in terms of infrastructural development, it was found wanting on questions of governance. For instance, some of the NDC campaign promises were not roads or electricity—Grenadians had those—but some of the campaign pledges included constitutional reform, electoral reform, an integrity commission, an ombudsman and parliamentary oversight committees. An examination of the campaign promises made by the NDC and the election results suggest that

"softer" electoral issues are becoming more important to the electorate as the polity, economy and society evolve. (Grenade 2004, 17)

What is salient is that former revolutionaries were integrated into mainstream political parties. A number of factors can account for the reemergence and acceptance of remnants of the Grenadian Left: the collapse of the Soviet Union and the reconfiguration of global politics beyond the East-West divide; the preoccupation of the United States with Iraq and the war on terror; the professional remake of the former revolutionaries; the high-handedness of Mitchell; and the sheer passage of time. The revolutionaries may have learned the "supreme lesson of Grenada" that "socialism must go hand in hand with democracy" (Rupert Lewis, cited in Ryan 1999, 93).

During this phase, Grenada suffered the onslaught of Hurricanes Ivan and Emily in 2004 and 2005 respectively (see Agency for Reconstruction and Development 2004; Organisation of Eastern Caribbean States 2004). This crisis had political implications. As parliamentary opposition, the NDC called for a government of national unity to manage the crisis. The proposal recommended that the fifteen elected members of Parliament form part of the government with the opposition leader as deputy prime minister (*BBC Caribbean*, September 24, 2004; National Democratic Congress 2004). However, Prime Minister Mitchell rejected the NDC's proposal, indicating that the cabinet is a special element of the government and a government must be made up of "like-minded" people (Leroy Noel, *Caribbean Net News*, 2004). By 2007, the Mitchell administration had managed to successfully spearhead the recovery (see IMF 2007).

Despite the ravages of two hurricanes, there was again tangible evidence of progress under the leadership of the NNP administration: a new port facility, a new national stadium, a much-improved road network, a refurbished market, and several other capital projects were implemented. However, there were concerns about Grenada's high public debt (the debt-GDP ratio spiraled from 56.25 in 2000 to 103.77 in 2007 [Eastern Caribbean Central Bank 2008]) and allegations of corruption. Perhaps more than any other prime minister in Grenada's recent history, Mitchell was repeatedly accused of corruption in public office. His administration was also accused of unsavory relationships with global capital interests. However, a one-man commission of inquiry reported that no evidence had been produced to incriminate him.[16]

This phase was characterized by political stability, visible signs of infrastructural development, and relative economic growth despite the ravages of two hurricanes. This period also brought to the fore some of the challenges that confront small states in the twenty-first century: vulnerability to natural disasters; the tension between sovereignty, policy autonomy, and dependency; high public debt; and threats to governance, such as allegations of corruption.

On July 8, 2008, the NDC defeated the NNP in closely contested elections. The 2008 general elections were contested against the backdrop of a so-called "wind of change" that was blowing through the Caribbean (see Grenade 2008).[17] The large question was: should Mitchell and the NNP be returned to power for a fourth consecutive term? The NNP's campaign strategy was twofold: it reminded the electorate of the progress it had achieved in thirteen years, and maligned the revolutionary faction within the NDC. The NDC's campaign strategy highlighted the excesses of the NNP and promised good governance, transparency, and accountability.

As was the case in 1984, voter turnout was relatively high at 79.48 percent. The NDC received 50.85 percent of the total votes cast (28,998 voters), and the NNP received 47.68 percent (27,188 voters). However, the distribution of parliamentary seats did not reflect a close contest. Given the distortions of the FPTP system, the NDC obtained eleven of the fifteen parliamentary seats, while the NNP held on to four seats. Although the NNP was defeated electorally, there was still widespread support for the party and its leader. Based on the popular vote, the electorate was almost evenly divided.

Phase 4: NDC's Internal Wrangling and Splintering (2008–2013)

Similar to the period from 1990 to 1995, this phase was characterized by intra-party conflict and splintering. After its electoral victory, the NDC administration took two bold initiatives. On May 30, 2009 (Maurice Bishop's birthday), the Point Salines International Airport was renamed the Maurice Bishop International Airport (MBIA). In his official address to mark the airport's renaming, Prime Minister Thomas justified his administration's decision by stating:

> Ideally, I would have loved to have all Grenadians unanimously support this action. However, to those who hold different views, I wish to remind you that whether we like it or not the revolution forms a significant part of our history. . . . You may not believe like I did with many of the things that were done, but the facts cannot change conveniently. Maurice Bishop was a Prime Minister of Grenada, and his government moved to make this project a reality. . . . Many of us suffered innocently during the period of the revolution. . . . I must remind you that I was incarcerated by the revolution for what I believed in, was the defence and the preservation of human rights. . . . I am of the same belief today and will

do the same if the occasion arises. Equally, I have forgiven and embraced those who incarcerated me. It is my view that if I could, you can too. (Thomas 2009, 3)

After this event, on September 5, 2009, Bernard Coard and the remaining six of the Grenada 14 were granted early release from Richmond Hill Prison.[18] Their early release marked a significant juncture in Grenada's political landscape. This was an opportunity for reflection on what some might consider to be a miscarriage of justice. From my perspective, the legal chapter was over, and Grenadians were given an opportunity to put to rest the ghost of the revolution, which may have closed a significant phase in Grenada's postrevolutionary politics.

During this phase, a combination of external and internal issues plagued the NDC. First, in September 2008 a severe financial and economic crisis rippled through the global economy with a domino effect throughout the world. In the global South, the crisis exacerbated development challenges. Given Grenada's overdependency on tourism and foreign direct investment and remittances, the Grenadian economy experienced a severe downturn. Grenada continued to experience high public-sector debt of almost 100 percent of GDP. In 2007 real GDP growth was 6.3 percent. By 2012 it had declined to 1.5 percent (see Kari Grenade's account in chap. 3 of this volume).

In addition to the economic downturn, the NDC was characterized by self-destructive tendencies, similar to those that engulfed the previous NDC administration (1990–95): weak leadership; "good" governance void of political skill; extremely poor public relations (a technocratic government that was disconnected from its own party and out of touch with the realities of the Grenadian people); and, perhaps most self-destructively, unmanaged conflict within the leadership of the party and government. Again the NDC splintered. One of the manifestations of the split in the NDC was a series of resignations and dismissals.[19]

Faced with a minority government, in September 2012, Prime Minister Thomas prorogued Parliament to avert a second no-confidence motion against him. Thomas's political behavior was reminiscent of the prorogation of Parliament in 1989, when Prime Minister Blaize faced a similar fate. Again, benign authoritarianism persisted. While Thomas's prorogation of Parliament did not violate the Constitution, it brought to the fore the contradictions of democracy. That is, for political expediency, Tillman Thomas used the power of the office of prime minister to, in effect, silence the voices of the people through their elected representatives in the Parliament. The irony is that, in the process, Thomas claimed he was promoting his "good governance" agenda.

Table 11.1				
General Election Results, Grenada, 1984–2013				
Year	Party*	No. of seats	Popular votes (%)	Voter turnout (%)
				85.3
1984	NNP	14	58.6	
	GULP	1	35.9	
	MBPM	0	4.8	
				67.8
1990	NDC	7	34.4	
	GULP	4	28.0	
	TNP	2	17.5	
	NNP	2	17.4	
	MBPM	0	2.3	
				61.2
1995	NNP	8	32.3	
	NDC	5	30.5	
	GULP	2	26.5	
	TNP	0	6.4	
				56.3
1999	NNP	15	62.4	
	NDC	0	25.0	
	GULP/UL	0	11.7	
	MBPM	0	0.6	
				57.4
2003	NNP	8	47.7	
	NDC	7	45.3	
	GULP	0	4.7	
	PLM	0	1.9	
				79.5
2008	NDC	11	50.9	
	NNP	4	47.7	
	ULP	0	0.8	
	Independents	0	0.0	
				88.6
2013	NNP	15	58.5	
	NDC	0	40.6	
	NUF	0		
	Other**	0	0.1	

*The Parties:

GULP: Grenada United Labor Party

GULP/UL: Grenada United Labor Party/United Labor

MBPM: Maurice Bishop Patriotic Movement

NDC: National Democratic Congress

NUF: National United Front

NNP: New National Party

PLM: People's Labor Movement

TNP: The National Party

ULP: United Labor Party

**In 2013 a number of smaller parties contested the general elections.

While the NDC grappled with its internal challenges, the NNP presented itself as a united team and government in waiting. In essence, the infighting in the NDC favored the opposition NNP. For Keith Mitchell (2011), the main strengths of the NNP included a clear vision, a perception of unity within the party, and undiluted leadership.

Given Grenada's grave economic outlook, in particular an unemployment rate of over 30 percent, economic issues were central to the 2013 electoral campaign. Two main political parties contested the 2013 elections: the incumbent NDC and the opposition NNP, along with a number of smaller parties and independent candidates. The NNP again won all fifteen parliamentary seats, amassing 32,205 votes, which represented 58.49 percent of votes cast. The NDC obtained 22,377 votes, or 40.6 percent of the votes cast. Voter turnout stood relatively high at 88.58 percent. The NNP continued its electoral dominance after a break from 2008 to 2012. Table 11.1 illustrates the electoral performance of the NNP since its formation in 1984.

Finally, the NDC's electoral defeat brings to the fore the cyclical nature of Grenadian politics. Thirty years after the implosion of the Grenada Revolution, former revolutionaries were assimilated into mainstream political parties. Several of them were particularly visible in the leadership of the NDC. Factions within the NDC, unmanaged conflict in the leadership, and the subsequent split in the party are reminiscent of the past. One of the lessons of the implosion of the Grenada Revolution was the need for dialogue, negotiation, and compromise to reconcile intraparty conflict. However, internal wrangling in the NDC (1990–95, 2008–13) suggests that the leadership of the NDC has not learned some of the crucial lessons from the implosion of the Grenada Revolution. The tension between the state and the party remains unresolved. It is imperative, therefore, that Grenada's political history be analyzed and documented to capture the interplay of forces that shape the political landscape.

Conclusion

One of the consequences of the demise of the Grenada Revolution and the U.S. invasion in 1983 was the formation of a new political party architecture to break with the past and rid Grenada of the vestiges of the revolution and the Gairy regime that preceded it. The new architecture was intended to transcend authoritarianism, intraparty conflict, and political violence to turn Grenada into a showcase for democracy and free enterprise. Within the last three decades, Grenada has transitioned to formal democracy. There are functioning state institutions, and Grenadians enjoy constitutional rights and civil liberties. Seven general elections were held from 1984 to 2013, the military was disbanded, and constitutional rights were restored. Yet despite the trappings of democracy, there is an unsettled "settling" to the two-party system.

Several conclusions can be drawn from the case. First, coalition arrangements, particularly among disparate forces, were a central feature of politics in Grenada from 1984 to 2013. This is not new. The NJM and GNP entered into an alliance in 1976 to oust the Gairy regime. In the postrevolutionary era, political accommodations took various expressions: externally imposed preelection arrangements, postelection strategic alliances, opposition broad tents, and the assimilation of elements of the Grenadian Left into mainstream political parties. What they all had in common was the desire to fight against a common political enemy for control of the state. None of those alliances were grounded in any mass movement. They were all elite accommodations among the political class. Consequently they were all fragile, leading to fragmentation, crisscrossing of political elites among political parties, polarization, and political volatility.

Second, intraparty conflict continued to bedevil political life in Grenada. While internal wrangling is not new, the case brought to the fore some old questions that warrant fresh scrutiny: What type of political leadership for the twenty-first century? Whither the notion of the maximum leader? What should be the relationship between state, government, and party? What should be the role of government in the economy? If the right to dissent is essential in a thriving democracy, how should dissent within the cabinet be managed? Can the traditional principles of Westminster parliamentary democracy hold given changing societal realities and the newly emerging professional political class? Do personality politics matter? Some of these issues led to intraparty conflict in the PRG/NJM in 1983, the NNP in 1984–89 and 1998, and the NDC in 1990–95 and 2008–13. There are no right answers to these questions. Each society evolves and finds solutions out of its concrete circumstances. What seems to be clear is the urgency for mechanisms for peaceful conflict resolution.

Additionally, intra-elite struggles have persistently alienated people from the process of governance. As a participant in the process, I have observed that although voter turnout is relatively high, Grenada is seriously polarized. Voter volatility may reflect dissatisfaction with governance and a "voting out" syndrome. The case brings to the fore the distortions of the FPTP system and Westminster-style parliamentary democracy. During the period of the Grenada Revolution, Grenadians were denied the right to vote in parliamentary elections, but the majority of them were engaged in their governance through parish and zonal councils and other forms of participatory democracy (the PRG's authoritarian style notwithstanding). A glaring irony of the last thirty years is that the restoration of electoral democracy rolled back many of the gains of participatory democracy made during the revolutionary era.

Lessons

We can draw several lessons from the Grenada case. First, political party formation must be organic, since externally imposed arrangements are not easily sustained. Additionally, political coalitions among disparate forces are complex. The dominant actor in the coalition usually seeks to impose his or her identity and decision-making style to shape the nature of the coalition. This in turn can lead to intraparty conflict, splintering, and breakdown. Ironically, the coalition itself can throw up new factions and contradictions. This can create a vicious cycle of coalition formation, fragmentation, and realignment. The Grenada case suggests that political accommodations require political astuteness, compromise, trust, avenues for open dialogue, and mechanisms for mediation. But more so, there is need to transcend the politics of enmity that saturate political life, and to be mindful of the broader struggle.

Second, since political parties are often an amalgamation of forces, intraparty squabbling is constant. What is clear is that people must be at the center of any type of democracy. A close analysis of politics in postrevolutionary Grenada suggests that the struggle for control of the state by the political class can promote electoral democracy at the expense of genuine substantive democracy. The case suggests the need for a democratic ethos that finds creative mechanisms for ordinary people to be involved in their governance.

Finally, despite occasional political volatility, the ghost of the revolution, and the burden of history, Grenada is a stable, well-functioning society. A major lesson is that the collective resilient spirit of a people can shine through the greatest adversity.

Notes

1. The Advisory Council was established on November 15, 1983, as an interim/caretaker government following the U.S.-led invasion. Its primary objectives were to restore public services and economic institutions and to prepare for parliamentary elections. The nine-member council was made up of technocrats and chaired by Nicholas Brathwaite. It possessed legislative and executive powers (for further details, see Martin 2007, 1).

2. The Grenada United Labour Party and Grenada National Party were resuscitated, led by Eric Gairy and Herbert Blaize respectively. Four new parties were also formed under the leadership of new political figures: the Grenada Democratic Movement (GDM) of Francis Alexis; George Brizan's National Democratic Party (NDP); the Maurice Bishop Patriotic Movement (MBPM), led by Kenrick Radix, a former member of the PRG, who was associated with the Bishop faction of the defunct revolution; and two smaller parties: Winston Whyte's Christian Democratic Labour Party (CDLP) (which was generally associated with former detainees of the PRG) and the Grenada Federated Labour Party (GFLP).

3. Herbert Blaize (1918–89) was the political leader of the Grenada National Party (GNP) (1956–84) and the New National Party (TNP) (1989). He served as chief minister (1960–61 and 1962–67) and prime minister (1984–89). In 1976 Blaize participated in the People's Alliance with the NJM. Blaize and the GNP represented the interests of the minority planter class.

4. Francis Alexis (1947–) is a constitutional lawyer who returned from his position as senior lecturer in the Faculty of Law at the University of the West Indies, Cave Hill Campus, Barbados, to contest the 1984 general elections. He served as a member of Parliament and attorney general from 1984 to 1987 and again from 1990 to 1995.

5. George Brizan (1943–2012) was an educator and historian and served as a member of Grenada's executive and legislature from 1984 to 1987 and again from 1990 to 1995 and as Grenada's prime minister from February to June 1995.

6. Tillman Thomas (1947–) was incarcerated by the PRG from July 1981 to October 1983. He was an MP and member of cabinet in the original NNP. Along with George Brizan and Francis Alexis, Thomas resigned from the Blaize-led NNP in 1987 and formed the NDC. He was prime minister of Grenada from 2008 to 2013.

7. Nicholas Brathwaite (1925–) chaired the Advisory Council in the aftermath of the implosion of the revolution. In 1989 he was elected chairman of the NDC, and after the March 1990 general elections, he represented Carriacou and Petite Martinique and served as prime minister from March 1990 to February 1995, when he voluntarily demitted the office of prime minister. Brathwaite had previously resigned as political leader of the NDC in July 1994.

8. Ben Jones (1924–2005) "was a lawyer and prominent Grenadian politician who served as deputy Prime Minister (1984–89) and Prime Minister (December 1989–March 1990). He first contested elections in 1967 as a candidate for the GNP but was not successful until 1984 when he was elected as a member of the NNP. A long-time friend of Blaize, Jones became Prime Minister and leader of the newly formed TNP" (Martin 2007, 128).

9. Terrence Marryshow is a medical doctor and the grandson of Theophilus Albert Marryshow (1887–1958), who was the first Grenadian political leader to achieve Caribbean-wide acclaim and remains Grenada's most revered national hero (Martin 2007, 157).

10. The Grenada 17 and Grenada 14 comprised military, political, and civilian personnel who were convicted for the murder of Maurice Bishop, some members of his cabinet, and others on October 19, 1983.

11. The other persons executed along with prime minister Maurice Bishop on October 19, 1983, were Fitzroy Bain, Norris Bain, Evelyn Bullen, Jacqueline Creft, Keith Hayling, Evelyn Maitland, and Unison Whiteman.

12. See *Miami Herald*, January 20, 1999.

13. Eric Gairy died in August 1997. The 1999 elections were the first general elections since his death. As one calypsonian intimated, the GULP died with its political leader, Eric Gairy.

14. The implosion of the Grenada Revolution in October 1983 was linked to a split between Maurice Bishop and his deputy Bernard Coard (see Coard's account in this volume). Given the vicious execution of Maurice Bishop and several of his colleagues, the Coard faction was maligned for several years.

15. *Caribupdate*, November 9, 2003.

16. The Barbadian Jurist Sir Richard Cheltenham carried out an investigation into allegations of corruption made against Prime Minister Mitchell and found no incriminating evidence against him.

17. Incumbents were defeated in general elections in the following Caribbean countries from 2006 to 2010: Saint Lucia (December 11, 2006); the Commonwealth of the Bahamas (May 2, 2007); Jamaica (September 3, 2007); Barbados (January 15, 2008); Belize (February 7, 2008); Grenada (July 8, 2008); Trinidad and Tobago (May 24, 2010); and Suriname (May 25, 2010).

18. In 2007 the Privy Council ordered the resentencing of Coard and the others convicted of the murder of Maurice Bishop. At the 2007 sentencing hearing, three of the prisoners were released, while Coard and the remainder were sentenced to forty years, including the time already served. The court ordered that the sentences were to be reviewed within two years. They were due to be released in 2010. After the Privy Council's ruling, several of the prisoners were released on grounds of ill health. On September 5, 2009, the seven remaining prisoners were all released from prison. From what I have observed personally, they have reassimilated into Grenadian and Caribbean society.

19. In November 2010, Michael Church, the MP for St. John, resigned from the cabinet. By January 2012, Joseph Gilbert, the former minister of works, was fired from the Thomas cabinet. From April to September 2012, three other cabinet ministers resigned: Peter David, minister of tourism and MP for the Town of St. George; Karl Hood, foreign minister and MP for St. George's South East; and Glynis Roberts, minister of labor and MP for St. George South.

References

Agency for Reconstruction and Development. 2004. *Report on the Reconstruction and Development Programme*. St. George's, Grenada: Government Printing Office.

Barrow-Giles, C., and T. Joseph. 2006. *General Elections and Voting in the English-Speaking Caribbean, 1992–2005*. Kingston, Jamaica: Ian Randle.

Barrow-Giles, C., and D. Marshall, eds. 2003. *Living at the Borderlines: Issues in Caribbean Sovereignty and Development*. Kingston, Jamaica: Ian Randle.

BBC Caribbean. 2004. "Opposition Wants Cabinet Roles." BBC Caribbean.com, September 24. http://www.bbc.co.uk/caribbean/news/story/2004/09/040924_grenada-opposition .shtml.

Benn, D., and K. Hall, eds. 2003. *Governance in the Age of Globalization: Caribbean Perspectives*. Kingston: Ian Randle.

Boodhoo, K. 1984. *Grenada: The Birth and Death of a Revolution*. Miami: Latin American and Caribbean Center, Florida International University.

Brierley, J. S. 1985. "A Review of Development Strategies and Programmes of the People's Revolutionary Government in Grenada, 1979–83." *Geographical Journal* 151 (1): 40–54.

Brizan, G. I. 1998. *Grenada: Island of Conflict*. London: Macmillan.

———. 2004. Interview by author. St. George's, Grenada. July 24.

———. 2010. Interview by author. St. George's Grenada. February 6.

Eastern Caribbean Central Bank. 2008. Economic Statistics [data file]. Basseterre, Saint Kitts and Nevis.

Emmanuel, P. A. M. 1978. *Crown Colony Politics in Grenada, 1917–1951*. Barbados: Institute of Social and Economic Research.

———. 1983. "Revolutionary Theory and Political Reality in the Eastern Caribbean." *Journal of Inter-American Studies and World Affairs* 25 (2): 193–227.

———. 1992. "Elections and Party Systems in the Commonwealth Caribbean, 1944–1991." Bridgetown: Caribbean Development Research Services.

Emmanuel, P. A. M., F. Brathwaite, and E. Barriteau, eds. 1986. *Political Change and Public Opinion in Grenada, 1979–1984*. Institute of Social and Economic Research (Eastern Caribbean), University of the West Indies, Cave Hill, Barbados.

Ferguson, S. 2003. "The Politics of Hatred." *Grenada Today*, October 10.

Government of Grenada. 1986. *Ministry of Finance Budget Speech*. St. George's: Government Printing Office, February 25.

———. 1999. Ministry of Finance. Budget Speech. St. George's: Government Printing Office, December 10.

———. 2013. Parliamentary Elections Office electoral statistics spreadsheet. St. George's, Grenada. Microsoft Excel document in possession of author.

Grenada. 1973. "Grenada Constitution Order 1973." St. George's: Government Printing Office.

Grenada Today. 2003. "Election Date to Be Given on Sunday." October 17.

Grenade, W. C. 2004. "The Challenges to Democratization in the Anglophone Caribbean: An Analysis of the 2003 Elections in Grenada." Paper presented at the 29th Annual Caribbean Studies Association Conference, Saint Kitts and Nevis, May 31–June 5.

———. 2008. "Incumbents under Challenge." *Guyana Caribbean Politics*, January 29. http://www.guyanacaribbeanpolitics.com.

———, ed. 2010. Special issue, *Journal of Eastern Caribbean Studies* 35 (3–4).

———. 2013. "Party Politics and Governance in Grenada: An Analysis of the New National Party (1984–2012)." *Round Table: The Commonwealth Journal of International Affairs* 102 (2): 167–76.

International Monetary Fund. 2007. "Statement by IMF Staff at the Conclusion of the 2007 Article IV Consultation Discussions with Grenada." Press Release No. 07/162, July 16.

Johnson, A. 2003. "The Ghost of Maurice Bishop: Grenadian Leader Haunts Election Process 20 Years after His Murder." *Trinidad Express*, October 2003.

Klak, T. 1998. *Globalization and Neoliberalism: The Caribbean Context*. New York: Rowman and Littlefield.

Lewis, G. K. 1987. *Grenada: The Jewel Despoiled*. Baltimore: John Hopkins University Press.

Los Angeles Times. 1989. "The World: Party Oust Grenada Chief." January 22. http://articles. latimes.com/1989-01-22/news/mn-1357_1_centrist-party (accessed June 23, 2012).

Mackoon, L. 1989. "Political Turmoil Shaking Grenada." South-North News Service. *Sun Sentinel.com*, February 19. http://articles.sun-sentinel.com/1989-02-19/news/8901100039_1_gairy-grenada-grenadians (accessed June 23, 2012).

Martin, J. A. 2007. *A–Z of Grenada Heritage*. Oxford: Macmillan.

Meeks, B. 2001. *Caribbean Revolutions and Revolutionary Theory: An Assessment of Cuba, Nicaragua, and Grenada*. Mona, Jamaica: University of the West Indies Press.

Miami Herald. 1999. "Grenada's Premier Promises to Clean Up Corruption Image." January 20. http://www.latinamericanstudies.org/caribbean/image.htm.

Mitchell, J. 2006. *Beyond the Islands: An Autobiography*. Oxford: Macmillan Education.

Mitchell, K. 2000. Prime Minister of Grenada. Interview by David Hinds, CaribNation Television. St. George's, Grenada, November.

———. 2011. Leader of the Opposition, Grenada. Interview by author. St. George's, Grenada, January 8.

National Democratic Congress. 2004. "The Present Situation in Grenada and the Way Forward." Statement by the National Democratic Congress (NDC). St. George's, Grenada, September 20.

Noel, L. 2004. "Grenada's PM Rejects National Unity Government." *Caribbean Net News*. http://www.caribbeannetnews.com (accessed September 27, 2004).

Noguera, P. A. 1997. *The Imperatives of Power: Political Change and the Social Basis of Regime Support in Grenada, 1951–1991*. New York: Peter Lang.

Organisation of Eastern Caribbean States. 2004. "Grenada: Macro-socio-economic Assessment of the Damages Caused by Hurricane Ivan, 7th September, 2004." Saint Lucia: Organisation of Eastern Caribbean States.

Pastor, R. 1986. "Does the United States Push Revolutions to Cuba? The Case of Grenada." *Journal of Interamerican Studies and World Affairs* 28 (1): 1–34.

Payne, A. 1998. "The New Politics of 'Caribbean America.'" *Third World Quarterly* 10 (2): 205–18.

Payne, A., P. Sutton, and T. Thorndike. 1984. *Grenada: Revolution and Invasion*. London: Croom Helm.

Purcell, J. 2007. *Memoirs of a Woman in Politics: Spiritual Struggles*. St. George's, Grenada.

Puri, S. 2010. "Legacies Left." *Interventions: International Journal of Postcolonial Studies* 12 (1): 1–10.

Ramsaran, R., ed. 2002. *Caribbean Survival and the Global Challenge*. Boulder: Lynne Rienner; Kingston, Jamaica: Ian Randle.

Ryan, S. 1999. *Winner Takes All: The Westminster Experience in the Caribbean*. St. Augustine, Trinidad and Tobago: UWI Press.

Scott, D. 2007. "Preface: The Silence People Keeping." *Small Axe* 11 (22): v–x.

Thomas, C. Y. 2001. "On Restructuring the Political Economy of the Caribbean." In *New Caribbean Thought*, ed. Brian Meeks and Folke Lindahl, 498–520. Kingston, Jamaica: University of the West Indies Press.

Thomas, T. 2009. "Prime Minister's Address on the Occasion of the Renaming of Pt. Salines International Airport." St. George's, Grenada, May 30. http://www.gov.gd/egov/docs/speeches_statements/pm_mbia_ceremony_may_30_09.pdf (accessed May 24, 2014).

Will, W. M. 1991. "From Authoritarianism to Political Democracy in Grenada: Questions for U.S. Policy." *Studies in Comparative International Development* 26 (3): 29–57.

Williams, G. 2007. *U.S.-Grenada Relations: Revolution and Intervention in the Backyard*. New York: Palgrave Macmillan.

Williams, M. 2003. "Economic History of Grenada, 1960–1990." Unpublished paper, Eastern Caribbean Central Bank.

World Bank. 1990. "Grenada: Updating Economic Note." Report No. 8270-GRD. Washington, DC: World Bank.

12. The Spirit and Ideas of Maurice Bishop Are Alive in Our Caribbean Civilization

Ralph E. Gonsalves

The spirit and ideas of Comrade Maurice Bishop, revolutionary icon and indomitable fighter for justice, popular democracy, and self-determination, are alive and flourishing among the people of Grenada and the Caribbean.[1] This extraordinary gathering at Point Salines embraces this anti-imperialist and anticolonialist titan whom Grenada has selflessly given to the Caribbean and the world. This belated honor of naming this international airport in his memory, and as testimonial acceptance of his heroic contribution to its construction, is just and long overdue. The vanities of parochial, vengeful, and backward politics have at long last been exorcised from the citadels of the state apparatus. What we are doing today formalizes a condition which has been indelibly etched in the people's collective memory for quarter of a century. The outpouring of joy is palpable on this day which the Lord has made. Let us thus be thankful and rejoice in it.

From ancient times, our people have been enjoined to honor and celebrate the lives of our fallen sons and daughters who have distinguished themselves in the service of the people. Thucydides' *History of the Peloponnesian War* and more particularly the funeral oration of Pericles, in extolling the glory of Greece and the majesty of its heroes, resonate with aptness for Comrade Maurice:

> For the whole earth is the sepulcher of illustrious men, nor is it the inscription on the columns in their native land alone that shows their merit, but the memorial of them, better than all inscriptions in every foreign nation, reposited more durably in universal remembrance than on their tombs. For to be lavish of life is not so noble in those whom misfortunes have reduced to misery and despair, as in men who hazard the loss of a comfortable subsistence and the enjoyment of all the blessings this world affords by an unsuccessful enterprise. Adversity, after

a series of ease and affluences, sinks deeper into the heart of a man of spirit than the stroke of death insensibly received in the vigor of life and public hope.

Maurice Bishop was one such illustrious man who lived as a beacon of hope for the poor, the marginalized, and the dispossessed, bearing his pain and struggles with a calming equanimity. Beaten on the anvil of experience and forged in the cauldron of struggle, Maurice has emerged as the embodiment of the political virtue of our peoples' quest for self-mastery. The stone which some builders had refused has become the head cornerstone. Now that the historical dust is settling, even Maurice's severest critics and political opponents must now recognize that he was one of the most outstanding sons produced by our Caribbean civilization. Pericles had astutely commented in times of yore: "Envy will exert itself against a competitor while life remains, but when death stops the competition, affection will applaud without restraint." The honor being bestowed today on Maurice Bishop constitutes, too, an historical reckoning; it represents the closure of a chapter of denial. At the same time it is symbolic of a catharsis, a cleansing, which purifies and unifies with an amazing grace. Those who are blind can now see; those who were lost have been found.

On March 13, 1979, at 10:30 a.m., on Radio Free Grenada, Maurice Bishop, a young man barely into his thirties, leader of the New Jewel Movement (NJM), delivered his first address to his nation as leader of the Grenada Revolution. His opening lines were memorable, calm, sparing, and simplicity itself:

Brothers and Sisters,

This is Maurice Bishop speaking. At 4:15 a.m. this morning the People's Revolutionary Army seized control of the army barracks at True Blue. The barracks were burned to the ground. After half-an-hour struggle, the forces of Gairy's army were completely defeated, and surrendered. Every single soldier surrendered, and not a single member of the revolutionary forces was injured.

After detailing the efforts of the People's Revolutionary Army in seizing state power, Maurice did something remarkable. He put the revolution in the hands of the people. Thus he intoned:

I am appealing to all the people, gather at all central places all over the country and prepare to welcome and assist the people's armed forces when they come into your area. The revolution is expected to consolidate the position of power within the next few hours.

Without popular support, the revolution would have collapsed. Fidel was later to comment that Maurice had led "a big revolution in a small country." Make no mistake about it, the revolution and its popular acceptance provided the political foundation for the construction of the international airport at Point Salines.

Maurice addressed precisely this issue in a national broadcast on March 29, 1981, titled "Together We Shall Build Our Airport," in the following terms:

> To begin with, sisters and brothers, we must all be clear that this project rep-
> resents the biggest and single most important project for our future economic
> development. In fact, as you all know, this represents the single biggest project
> ever undertaken in the history of our country. More than this, we must under-
> stand that the idea for the project has been with various Grenadian governments
> for twenty-five years or so, a reality that can be proved from the existence of
> numerous airport study projects dating back several years. However, with our
> popular revolution of March 13, 1979, the People's Revolutionary Government set
> out with seriousness and determination to transform the dream of our interna-
> tional airport into a concrete reality.

Without substantial external grant assistance, in cash or kind, it was virtually impossible for the Grenada Revolution to build this international airport.
From which source or sources was the grant assistance to come? The so-
called traditional allies, including the United States of America, were unhelp-
ful. Indeed, the USA, to use Maurice Bishop's own words, was in 1981 "engaged
in an all-out massive and vulgar attempt to dissuade various countries from
attending a co-financing conference to be hosted by the European Economic
Community aimed at raising vital financing" for the international airport
project.

At first, Maurice and his government received so little positive feedback
from potential donors that he mused that the dream of its realization would
remain unfulfilled. However, solemn assurances of practical support and
uplifting inspiration were to come from Fidel Castro, the leader of the Cuban
Revolution, at the Non-Aligned Conference in Havana in August 1979 and
again at the United Nations General Assembly gathering in October 1979.
Cuba pledged immediate assistance in kind in four areas: technical expertise,
skilled manpower, heavy-duty equipment, and some construction materials
such as steel and cement. In November 1979, Cuba started to make good on its
commitment. The International Airport was thus on its way, but much, much
more was left to be done. Maurice's confidence in the Grenadian people, their
revolution, and their friends overseas, combined with determined, astute

leadership, were the central pillars of turning the airport dream into reality. Maurice saw this venture as a great cause; and great causes have never been won by doubtful men and women. He and his revolution were not doubtful!

In time, Maurice built a coalition to construct the airport. Grenada and Cuba were foundation members of that coalition. Along the way they were joined by Venezuela, Canada, Libya, and some European and Middle-Eastern countries. I was in Tripoli in July 2001, when the Libyan government forgave the residue of the indebtedness of Grenada on the airport loan in the sum of US$6 million.

Mr. Chairman, the commitment of the people of Grenada to this marvel of regional and international solidarity will be told ages and ages hence. Ordinary Grenadians of all walks of life volunteered their labor, free of any remuneration, on weekends, to assist in the construction of their airport. These volunteer brigades of free labor were more than matched by the absolute determination of the Cuban workers to give life and meaning to Fidel's generosity and selflessness for which the heroic people of Cuba are known internationally. The Cuban workers toiled in comradeship with their Grenadian counterparts six days per week, twelve hours per day. Most of them volunteered to work on their rest days. One such Cuban comrade was Ramon Quintana, who sadly met a sudden and unnatural death on this very site when he was crushed, accidentally, by a piece of heavy-duty equipment. We remember, especially, Ramon Quintana, today. We send special thanks to his family and to all the Cuban people. We salute Fidel; we wrap his name in glory. Fidel lives forever in the hearts and minds of Grenadians, with a love that looks on tempests and is never shaken.

We ought never to forget that those in our hemisphere who were seeking to destabilize the Grenada Revolution and to sabotage the construction of this airport were among the same persons who had, a short while before, allied themselves militarily with the racist regime of apartheid South Africa against Nelson Mandela's African National Congress (ANC) and Augustino Neto's Movement for the Liberation of Angola (MPLA).

In that momentous struggle in southern Africa, the Cubans, in selfless solidarity with the freedom fighters of the ANC and MPLA, took on the mighty army of racist South Africa, which was supplied by weapons from countries which sought subsequently to strangle revolutionary Grenada and its right to self-determination. The defeat of the hitherto impregnable army of apartheid South Africa by the Angolan and Cuban combatants at the Battle of Cuito Cuanavale was instrumental in opening the prison cell of Nelson Mandela and paved the way for the founding of a free and democratic South Africa. What the Cubans did with arms in defense of the freedom of the people of

Angola and South Africa, they did with construction equipment, building tools, expertise, and labor at Point Salines in Grenada. We will never forget Cuba's sacrifice, selflessness, and generosity of spirit.

Let us put this phenomenal achievement of the construction of the international airport in perspective.

During the Second World War, the British and the American governments entered certain agreements concerning the leasing of large tracts of land in the British colonial possessions in the Caribbean. In several of these countries, the Americans built international-size runways and rudimentary landside facilities to accommodate their warplanes. These airports were constructed in countries with a sufficiency of flat lands to make the ventures feasible, in engineering and financial terms, in a short time. Three islands were too mountainous to benefit from this wartime American effort, namely, Dominica, Grenada, and Saint Vincent.

After the Second World War, the Americans left the British Caribbean to the devices of the British. And the British were, as always, uninterested in enhancing the region's physical infrastructure for sustainable development. After all, the British were the colonial masters in Saint Vincent and the Grenadines for some two hundred years, unbroken from 1773, and they built only two small secondary schools, one for boys and one for girls, one for each century of damning colonialism. Thus it was never contemplated that they would build or contribute to building international airports in Dominica, Grenada, and Saint Vincent, where the terrain and topography were challenging for airport construction.

Grenada had to await the revolution's arrival to lay the basis for the practical elaboration of the international airport project and its implementation. Dominica and Saint Vincent and the Grenadines were insufficiently revolutionary to launch such a project. Nearly twenty-five years after the completion of the international airport at Point Salines did an anti-imperialist, nationalist, and patriotic people-centered government in Saint Vincent and the Grenadines, which I have the honor to head, in the evocative spirit of Maurice, commenced the construction of the Argyle International Airport. It is scheduled for completion in the first quarter of 2013. As in Grenada, Cuba and Fidel have been instrumental in turning our similar dream in Saint Vincent and the Grenadines into a reality. In the process, we are moving one mountain and two hills, filling three valleys, and spanning a river to build our international airport. My government has fashioned a "Compact of the Willing" for this purpose, comprising the governments of Cuba, Venezuela, Trinidad and Tobago, Mexico, the Republic of China (Taiwan), Austria, Turkey, and now Iran and Libya. The government of Dominica, led by my dear friend Roosevelt Skerrit, is on a similar path. We are following, in this regard, the road traveled by Maurice, a road less traveled by, and that has made all the difference!

Between 1979 and 1983, imperialism told enormous lies about this airport at Point Salines and was determined to sabotage its construction. Laughable tales that the airport was for military purposes only, to facilitate fighter jets and other warplanes from Cuba and the Soviet Union, were actually believed by supposedly serious people. Ideological blinkers and imperialist indoctrination made such people not see, or see doubles, as we say in the Caribbean. Ignorance, the mother of all suspicion, enjoyed a full flowering. A kind of "Midsummer's Night Madness" gripped the imperial ideologues; and those of a lesser light, invariably paid hacks of imperialism, voiced corresponding follies and fables about this awesome project. They must today hang their heads in shame! Do not expect apologies, only more sophistry and vaunted vanities.

One month after the triumph of the revolution, Maurice Bishop put down his marker with crystal clarity in a national broadcast titled "In Nobody's Backyard." It is well with our soul to quote it at some length:

> We are a small country, we are a poor country, with a population of largely African descent, we are a part of the exploited Third World, and we definitely have a stake in seeking the creation of a New International Economic Order which would assist in ensuring economic justice for the oppressed and exploited peoples of the world, and in ensuring that the resources of the land and sea are used for the benefit of all the people of the world and not for a tiny minority of profiteers. Our aim, therefore, is to join all organizations and work with all countries that will help us become more independent and more in control of our own resources. In this regard, nobody who understands present-day realities can seriously challenge our right to develop working relations with a variety of countries.
>
> Grenada is a sovereign and independent country, although a tiny speck on the world map, and we expect all countries to strictly respect our independence just as we will respect theirs. No country has the right to tell us what to do or how to run our country, or who to be friendly with. We certainly would not attempt to tell any other country what to do. We are not in anybody's backyard, and we are definitely not for sale.

This fighting spirit, these noble ideas, are what fueled the drive to build this international airport; they, too, sustain us in our legitimate, ongoing quest to further ennoble our Caribbean civilization.

I cannot recall when I first met Maurice Bishop. It was some years prior to the revolution, but we had known each other in revolutionary spirit long before that. So we knew each other long before we met each other. In the decade prior to the revolution, I had come to the attention of the security forces of the region and hemisphere in the Cold War era, not for the commission of any crime, but on account of my anti-imperialist, revolutionary democratic, and socialist-oriented political activities. On October 16, 1968, at the age of twenty-two years, as leader of the Students' Union at the University of the West Indies, Jamaica, I led arguably the largest protest in that country since the momentous and popular anticolonial uprising of 1938. The symbol of our defense and affirmation of solidarity was the Guyanese scholar and revolutionary activist Walter Rodney, who was banned by the Jamaican government from returning to his post as a university lecturer consequent upon his attendance of a black writers' conference in Montreal, Canada. We were beaten and teargassed by the Jamaican security forces; and the leadership of the popular mass movement was vilified, harassed, and persecuted by imperialism and neoimperial surrogates. Between October 1968 and 1979, for example, at one time or another, I was denied entry into several Caribbean countries, including Grenada, Saint Lucia, and Antigua. In December 1979 my work permit as a university lecturer at Cave Hill was revoked by the Barbadian government, and my residency in that country canceled. I was, in the language of the day, "persona non grata" in the eyes of the established authorities. At one stroke I was denied an opportunity to work in my chosen profession in my region. I had a wife and child to feed. This is, alas, but a glimpse of those terrible days when the faces of ordinary men and women across the Caribbean were strained and anxious. Still, as my Rastafarian brethren and sistren would say: "I and I survived and thrived; there is no malice, just the love of Jah from I and I."

In Grenada, Maurice Bishop and his comrades fared worst of all. They were threatened with imminent physical liquidation, a matter on which no chances could be taken, given the history of barbarism against them and the working people by the regime of the day.

I shall never forget the morning of March 13, 1979. I was living at Paradise Heights near to the university in Barbados, where I was employed as a lecturer. My friend, a young Saint Lucian student named Didacus Jules, who subsequently worked in the field of education under the People's Revolutionary Government and is now the chief executive officer of the Caribbean Examination Council, telephoned me around 7:00 or so that morning and reported that the Gairy regime had been overthrown in Grenada, but he was unsure as to what had in fact transpired. Swiftly thereafter I ascertained the truth. I was ecstatic: weeping had endured for a long night, but joy had come that morning. God is a good God; yes, He lives! A redemption song was being sung on the streets of Grenada, in the undulating valleys, on the hillsides, the plains, and beaches.

Within a week of the revolution, Maurice invited me to visit Grenada. I did so on the second Saturday of the revolution and immediately immersed myself in political work, under his direction, at his home, where I was to be accommodated for a few days. There was so much to be done; sleep barely encroached. In any event, when I was shown my room of abode, in which was located the telecommunications equipment, I knew immediately that the nights would be long and sleepless. Frequently there were noisy radio calls for "Papa Mike," the code name for Maurice.

The next day, the second Sunday of the Revo, there was a massive rally at Sea Moon in Grenville. I rode in Maurice's vehicle with him and his wife, Angela. Along the way, people lined the streets and waved in celebration with their revered leader. At the Rally, Maurice delivered a most substantive speech, on both domestic and foreign policy matters. A significant part of his speech was in my handwriting; the other part was in his own hand. I do not know if a record of it exists anywhere.

At the onset of the French Revolution in the late eighteenth century, the English poet William Wordsworth approvingly declaimed: "Bliss was it in that dawn to be alive, but to be young was very heaven." The revolution's enormous strength and energy flowed immensely from the work of the young people who constituted one of its important bases and from which was drawn the leadership of the principal organs of the state and party. In retrospect, this youthfulness was also a weakness in that at critical points, a more mature, reflective, and experienced judgment would have been most helpful. Certain errors, even tragedies, could have been avoided.

Like me, most of the supporters of, and activists in, the revolution have now lived more years than we have remaining to live. If Maurice were physically with us today, he would be sixty-five years old. He has his name on his airport before his seventieth birthday, the proverbial three score and ten years. That is a cause for rejoicing.

I last saw Maurice alive in February 1983. I was passing through Grenada to get a ride on a plane going to Cuba for a celebration of the life and work of José Martí, the Cuban patriot and national hero. I spent the entire night in Maurice's company. I attended some functions with him that evening, including one at Point Salines, where the Cuban engineers and construction workers were engaged in building this airport. Afterward we went back to the prime minister's residence and talked through the night, mainly about politics in the Caribbean and Grenada. I spoke to him frankly about my unease concerning certain developments in Grenada and thought that the mass support for the revolution was becoming indifferent, in important respects. He shared my concerns, and we addressed possible solutions, strategically. As comrades we were honest with each other. One day I will write about all this, God's willing.

We agreed that on my return from Cuba we would continue the conversation face-to-face. This was not to happen. The Cuban aircraft took me to Barbados; LIAT was unable to get me to Grenada that day. So I went home to Saint Vincent and the Grenadines. We kept in touch over the next few months, but I never saw my dearest comrade and friend again. When he was murdered, I cried uncontrollably like a baby. He still lives in me.

Thereafter, in the eastern Caribbean, Rosie Douglas of Dominica, Tim Hector of Antigua, George Odlum of Saint Lucia, and I, among others, kept fanning the flame for justice and freedom, for the further ennoblement of our Caribbean civilization, and for the central struggle against imperialism. I eulogized Rosie, Tim, and George at their funerals. I am the remaining survivor. I have to do their work and mine. I was never able to say of, and for, Maurice, as I did for the others, the heartrending poetic lines of the celebrated Guyanese poet Martin Carter, in his epic "Death of a Comrade": "Too soon, too soon . . . now from the mourning vanguard moving on dear Comrade I salute you and I say death will not find us thinking that we die."

Maurice Bishop was a builder in the tradition of the prophet Nehemiah. In his quest to fashion a better society for his people, he was traduced by his enemies, day and night. He was a towering success; no one really remembers in glory, or at all, his puny adversaries. In communion with his people and friends overseas, he set about building this international airport in a focused manner, as Nehemiah did in respect of the wall around Jerusalem, which was broken and in a dilapidated condition for 112 years. Nehemiah was mocked by his enemies; they were indignant; they were moved to anger and conspiracy; they tried every ruse, including violence, to prevent the wall's reconstruction; and when all that failed, they sought to draw him out onto the plains of Ono to ambush him. It is all reported in the book of Nehemiah. Similar things were done to, and against, Maurice. But like Nehemiah, he and his people prevailed. A committed people, properly led for noble purposes, will always triumph. Maurice's life and work taught us this splendid lesson.

Ladies and gentlemen, this ceremony would not have been possible had the people of Grenada not elected a government which pledged to do exactly what is now being done. The Grenadian people have given their overwhelming permission and approval for what is now being done in their name. In the process, an historic wrong has been righted. Today Grenada stands tall in this region and the world for this profound act of historical reclamation in which you the people view your collective achievements of the past through the prism of your own eyes and not by way of an externally imposed imperial perspective, amidst local vanities and grudges.

Let us face it squarely: this ceremony would not have been possible without the advocacy and approval, the imprimatur, of a most humble but remarkable patriot known as Tillman Thomas, the distinguished prime minister of Grenada. My friend and brother, Tillman, is courageous and devoid of malice or bitterness. This easygoing but battle-hardened warrior and visionary was imprisoned by the People's Revolutionary Government headed by Comrade Maurice. I have spoken to Tillman, more than once, about his experiences in this regard. He bears no hatred for, or ill will to, those who caused him and his family much pain and suffering. He looks forward with hope and optimism, not backward with hurt and anguish. His Christian fortitude and love for people have touched me most deeply. His calming presence induces you to love him dearly. Grenada is blessed to have such a leader at this time. His joyous hopefulness will always endure beyond a debilitating learned hopelessness and helplessness.

The people of Grenada, in a spirit of reconciliation, have shone a light of the most illuminating clarity in the interest of their humanization. In their actions they have accepted the poetic summation of the Caribbean poet Daniel Williams: "We are all time; yet only the future is ours to desecrate. The present is the past, and the past our fathers' mischief."

This naming of the Maurice Bishop International Airport is an act of the Grenadian people coming home to themselves out of their agony and compromises, their pain and joys, and their triumphs and defeats of the past. It has been an uplifting and redemptive journey. One of my favorite poets, the great Vincentian "Shake" Keane, puts it all well in his poem "Private Prayer," written in 1973 on the occasion of the publication of Walter Rodney's pathbreaking volume *How Europe Under-developed Africa*: "To understand how the whole thing run I have to ask my parents and even my daughter and son. To understand the form of compromise I am I must in my own voice ask how the whole thing run. . . . To understand history I have to come home."

We have come home. Grenada and Maurice have come home symbolically and in reality. I thank you and Almighty God for being present here. I feel infused by the spirit of Comrade Maurice; I believe that each of us feels it. It is a noise in our blood, an echo in our bones.

Thank you! Forward Ever! Backward Never!

Notes

1. This chapter reprints the feature address delivered at the formal ceremony of the naming of the Maurice Bishop International Airport, at Point Salines, Grenada, on May 30, 2009. Reproduced with permission of Dr. the Honourable Ralph E. Gonsalves, Prime Minister of Saint Vincent and the Grenadines.

CONTRIBUTORS

Horace G. Campbell is a professor of African American studies and political science at Syracuse University in Syracuse, New York. At Syracuse University, Campbell is a member of the International Relations Faculty in the Maxwell School and director of the Africa Initiative in the university. Professor Campbell has published widely. His most important book, *Rasta and Resistance: From Marcus Garvey to Walter Rodney*, is going through its eighth edition. His recent book *Barack Obama and Twenty-first Century Politics* was published by Pluto Press in 2010.

Ralph E. Gonsalves is the prime minister of Saint Vincent and the Grenadines (2001 to the present). In 1974 and 1981 he obtained a Ph.D. in government and a degree of utter barrister at University of Manchester, England, and Gray's Inn, London, respectively. Concurrently while pursuing his political career and before his becoming the prime minister of Saint Vincent and the Grenadines, Dr. Gonsalves practiced law extensively and successfully before the Eastern Caribbean Supreme Court in a wide range of matters. Dr. Gonsalves has researched, written, and published extensively on a range of matters touching on the Caribbean, African, trade unionism, comparative political economy, and developmental issues generally. Among his latest publications are *History and the Future: A Caribbean Perspective* (Saint Vincent: Quik Print, 1994) and *The Politics of Our Caribbean Civilization: Essays and Speeches* (Saint Vincent: Great Works Depot, 2001).

Kari H. I. Grenade is a Grenadian born and an economist currently employed with the Caribbean Development Bank (CDB) in Barbados. Before joining the CDB, she was employed with the Eastern Caribbean Central Bank in Saint Kitts and Nevis for five years. She holds a Ph.D. in public policy and administration from Walden University, a master's degree in financial economics from the University of Toronto, and an undergraduate degree in economics (first class honors) from the University of the West Indies. Dr. Grenade has published in international and regional journals, mainly in the areas of economic development, economic growth, and general macroeconomics. Some of her publications include "On Growth Diagnostics and Grenada," *Journal of*

Eastern Caribbean Studies (2012); and, with Sukrishnalall Pasha, "Accelerating Guyana's Growth Momentum," *Developing Country Studies* (2012).

Wendy C. Grenade is a Grenadian born who is a lecturer in political science in the Department of Government, Sociology, and Social Work at the University of the West Indies, Cave Hill Campus, Barbados. She holds a Ph.D. and M.A. in international studies from the University of Miami, with concentrations in international relations and comparative politics. She has published several articles on politics in Grenada, Caribbean integration, governance, and security. Her publications include "Party Politics and Governance in Grenada: An Analysis of the New National Party (1984–2012)," *The Round Table: The Commonwealth Journal of International Affairs*; "Engendering Security: HIV/AIDS and Human (In)Security in the Caribbean," in *Love and Power: Caribbean Discourses on Gender*, edited by Eudine Barriteau (University of the West Indies Press, 2012); and "Small States and Risky Global Intercourse: The Grenada-Taiwan Dispute," *Social and Economic Studies* (special issue) (2013).

David Hinds is an associate professor in the Caribbean and African Diaspora Studies Department at Arizona State University. His areas of teaching and research include race, ethnicity, and politics; African diasporan political thought; and popular culture as political expression. His publications include "Problems of Democratic Transition in Guyana: Mistakes and Miscalculations in 1992," *Social and Economic Studies* (2005); and *Beyond Formal Democracy: The Discourse on Democracy and Governance in the Anglophone Caribbean in Commonwealth and Comparative Politics* (2008). His book *Ethno-politics and Power Sharing in Guyana: History and Discourse* was published by New Academia Press in 2011.

Curtis Jacobs is a historian. He holds a Ph.D. in history from the University of the West Indies. His research focuses on Caribbean history with special emphasis on Grenada and the eastern Caribbean. He has published widely, and his publications include *Joy Comes in the Morning: Elton George Griffith and the Shouter Baptists* (1996) and "A Review of the Political Languages of Emancipation in the British Caribbean and the U.S. South," published by University of North Carolina Press (2002) and in *Journal of Caribbean History* (2004).

Tennyson S. D. Joseph is head of department and lecturer in political science, Department of Government, Sociology, and Social Work, at the University of the West Indies, Cave Hill Campus, Barbados. He attained his Ph.D. from the University of Cambridge in 2001. His teaching and research interests revolve around Caribbean political thought (with a special focus on C. L. R. James), globalization and anticolonialism, sovereignty and decolonization, and the post-1945 political history of Saint Lucia. His publications include *Decolonization in St. Lucia: Politics and Global Neoliberalism, 1945–2010* (University Press of Mississippi, 2011); *At the Rainbow's Edge: Collected Speeches of Kenny D. Anthony*, coedited with Didacus Jules (Ian Randle, 2004); and *General Elections and Voting in the English-Speaking Caribbean, 1992–2005*, coauthored with Cynthia Barrow-Giles (Ian Randle, 2006).

Patsy Lewis is a professor at the Sir Arthur Lewis Institute for Social and Economic Studies (SALISES), University of the West Indies, Mona. Her areas of research include the developmental challenges of small states, regional integration movements, and trade agreements. Her publications include *Surviving Small Size: Regional Integration in Caribbean Ministates* (University of the West Indies Press, 2002).

Brian Meeks is a professor of social and political change, director of the Sir Arthur Lewis Institute of Social and Economic Studies, and director of the Centre for Caribbean Thought in the Department of Government at the University of the West Indies, Mona Campus. He has also taught at Michigan State University, Florida International University, and Anton de Kom University of Suriname and served as a visiting scholar at Cambridge University, Stanford University, and Brown University. Professor Meeks has published seven books and edited collections, including *Envisioning Caribbean Futures: Jamaican Perspectives* (2007) and *The Thought of New World: The Quest for Decolonisation*, edited with Norman Girvan (2010). His first novel, *Paint the Town Red*, was published in 2003. Professor Meeks has doctor of philosophy, master of science, and bachelor of science degrees from the UWI.

Hilbourne A. Watson is Professor Emeritus, Department of International Relations, at Bucknell University. He taught at Bucknell from 1994 until his recent retirement. Professor Watson specializes in areas within international political economy, international relations, and political theory. Professor Watson has published widely. Among his recent publications are "W. Arthur Lewis and the New World Group: Variations within the Analytic Framework of Neoclassical Economics," *Nordic Journal of Latin American and Caribbean Studies* (2008); "Alienation and Fetishization: A Critical Analysis of 'Radicalism and Innovation' in the New World Group's Approach to and Rejection of

Metropolitan Intellectual and Political Hegemony," *Nordic Journal of Latin American and Caribbean Studies* 38, nos. 1–2 (2008); and "Raciology, Garveyism, and the Limits of Black Nationalism in the Caribbean Diaspora," *Shibboleths* 2, no. 2 (2008): 85–95.

CREDITS

Chapter 4, "A Retrospective View from Richmond Hill: An Interview with Bernard Coard," by Wendy C. Grenade

An earlier version of the work was part of a special issue of the *Journal of Eastern Caribbean Studies* 35, nos. 3–4 (September–December 2010), which was edited by Wendy C. Grenade. The *Journal of Eastern Caribbean Studies* has granted permission for this essay to be reproduced in *The Grenada Revolution: Reflections and Lessons*, published by the University Press of Mississippi.

Chapter 5, "Grenada Once Again: Revisiting the 1983 Crisis and Collapse of the Grenada Revolution," by Brian Meeks

An earlier version of this work was published in the 2012 collection *Caribbean Political Activism: Essays in Honour of Richard Hart*, edited by Rupert Lewis. Permission was granted from the Centre for Caribbean Thought, University of the West Indies, Mona Campus, for this essay to be reproduced in *The Grenada Revolution: Reflections and Lessons*, published by the University Press of Mississippi.

Chapter 6, "Remembering October 19: Reconstructing a Conversation with a Young Female NJM Candidate Member about Her Recollections of October 19, 1983," by Patsy Lewis

An earlier version of the work was part of a special issue of the *Journal of Eastern Caribbean Studies* 35, nos. 3–4 (September–December 2010), which was edited by Wendy C. Grenade. The *Journal of Eastern Caribbean Studies* has granted permission for this essay to be reproduced in *The Grenada Revolution: Reflections and Lessons*, published by the University Press of Mississippi.

Chapter 8, "C. L. R. James and the Grenada Revolution: Lessons Learned and Future Possibilities," by Tennyson S. D. Joseph

An earlier version of the work was part of a special issue of the *Journal of Eastern Caribbean Studies* 35, nos. 3–4 (September–December 2010), which was edited by Wendy C. Grenade. The *Journal of Eastern Caribbean Studies* has granted permission for this essay to be reproduced in *The Grenada Revolution: Reflections and Lessons*, published by the University Press of Mississippi.

Chapter 9, "The Challenges for Revolutionary Change in the Caribbean," by Horace G. Campbell

> An earlier version of the work was part of a special issue of the *Journal of Eastern Caribbean Studies* 35, nos. 3–4 (September–December 2010), which was edited by Wendy C. Grenade. The *Journal of Eastern Caribbean Studies* has granted permission for this essay to be reproduced in *The Grenada Revolution: Reflections and Lessons*, published by the University Press of Mississippi.

Chapter 10, "The Grenada Revolution and the Caribbean Left: The Case of the Guyana Working People's Alliance," by David Hinds

> An earlier version of the work was part of a special issue of the *Journal of Eastern Caribbean Studies* 35, nos. 3–4 (September–December 2010), which was edited by Wendy C. Grenade. The *Journal of Eastern Caribbean Studies* has granted permission for this essay to be reproduced in *The Grenada Revolution: Reflections and Lessons*, published by the University Press of Mississippi.

Chapter 11, "Exploring Transitions in Party Politics in Grenada, 1984–2013," by Wendy C. Grenade

> An earlier version of the work was part of a special issue of the *Journal of Eastern Caribbean Studies* 35, nos. 3–4 (September–December 2010), which was edited by Wendy C. Grenade. The *Journal of Eastern Caribbean Studies* has granted permission for this essay to be reproduced in *The Grenada Revolution: Reflections and Lessons*, published by the University Press of Mississippi.

Chapter 12, "The Spirit and Ideas of Maurice Bishop Are Alive in Our Caribbean Civilization," by Ralph E. Gonsalves

> An earlier version of the work was part of a special issue of the *Journal of Eastern Caribbean Studies* 35, nos. 3–4 (September–December 2010), which was edited by Wendy C. Grenade. The *Journal of Eastern Caribbean Studies* has granted permission for this essay to be reproduced in *The Grenada Revolution: Reflections and Lessons*, published by the University Press of Mississippi.

INDEX

ACLM (Antigua Caribbean Liberation Movement): close ties with the NJM, 219; as part of preparatory committee for sixth Pan-African conference in Tanzania, 224; speaking out against the excesses of the Grenada revolution, 238; and WPA, 219

Advisory Council (AC): established by, 242; establishment of, 258; major objectives of, 242; Nicholas Brathwaite as chair of, 259

African National Congress (ANC), 267

Agriculture, and PRG, 40, 41

Alexis, Francis: as leader of Grenada Democratic Movement, 242; resignation from NNP and co-founding of NDC, 259

ASCRIA (African Society for Cultural Relations with Independent Africa), 220–22; and close relationship with NJM, 224; as a founding group of WPA, 219

Authoritarianism: as deeply-rooted ruling-class norm, 122; indigenous regional traditions of, 94; and revolutionaries from Gairy and colonial regime, 97

Bishop, Maurice: death of, 96; on decision to overthrow Gairy, 33; as leader of NJM, 219; as leader of the Opposition, 30; and MAP-forged relationship with JEWEL, 24; on spirit and ideas in Caribbean civilization, 265; strengths compared to Bernard Coard, 90; on Walter Rodney's assassination, 227

Black Power, Gairy's response to, 24

Black Power Movement, and roots of Grenada revolution, 214

Black Power Revolution, in Trinidad and Tobago in 1970, 23

Blaize, H. A.: as first premier of Grenada, 21; as leader of the NNP, 243; and 1989 parliament in and launching of National Party, 245; and proposed Unitary Statehood with Trinidad and Tobago, 20

Bloody Sunday, 26

Bolivarian Revolution, 8, 182, 184, 201–2

Bourgeoisie, 129, 131, 138, 140, 153, 162

Britain, and PRG strategic partnership with, 66

Brizan, George, 35, 259; as co-founder of NDC, 245; as educator, historian, and prime minister of Grenada, 259; on Grenada's 1990 SAP, 246; as leader of National Democratic Party, 242

Burnham, Forbes: assistance to NJM, 224; opposition to invasion of Grenada, 234

Capitalism: crisis of, 170, 174; structural reversals in viability of, 171

Caribbean Basin Initiative (CBI), 125, 141

Caribbean Civilization, 264–65, 267, 269, 271–73, 275, 280

Caribbean Development Bank (CDB), 51, 53–55, 275

Caribbean Left: rise of, 214; after reversal in Grenada, 152

Castro, Fidel: assistance to Grenada's airport project, 266; as maximum-leader model, 79; on RMC, 164

CC (Central Committee): identified as Bishop's and Coard's areas of strength, 77; meeting on September 14–16, 1983, 76; minutes of October 1983, 126

CDLP (Christian Democratic Labor Party), 259

Che Guevara and Contemporary Revolutionary Movements, 205, 208

Coard, Bernard: influence in party and state, 89; release from prison, 6; resignation from PB, CC, and OC, 100; and Workers Liberation League, 94

Cold War, 3–5, 13, 22, 42, 74, 82, 202, 215, 243, 270

Colonialism, 33, 123, 167, 181, 188, 190, 192, 215, 217, 223

Constitution: 1959 suspension of, 20; 1966 restoration of, 21; 1967 "associated state," 21

Contras, 194–95, 198, 206, 209

Cuba: disapproval of NJM party's joint leadership decision, 78; influence on PRG's leadership, 79; ties with, 74; training of Grenadian professionals, 60

Cuban Revolution, 18, 62, 79, 180, 184, 190–93, 205–7, 215, 266

Democracy: beyond the vote, 200; contradictions of, 254; enlargement of, 160; parliamentary, 29, 242, 249, 257; participatory, 167, 258; and socialism linked to, 166

Democratic Centralism, 100

Demonstrations: against Gairy, 114; following expulsion of Walter Rodney from Jamaica, 216

Dictatorship: overthrow of, 34; of proletariat, 146

Duffus Commission, 26–27, 64

Economic growth, 41, 43, 46–48, 52, 132, 275

Emmanuel, Patrick, 241–42, 244, 261

Eusi Kwayana, 219

FARC (Revolutionary Armed Forces of Colombia), 180

Fort Rupert, 6, 107, 114, 117, 137, 140–41

Gairy, Eric, regime of, 28, 53, 65, 81, 161–62, 256–57, 270

Gairy's GULP, 245, 247

General elections: in 1976, 29; in 1984, 243; in 1990, 245; in 1995, 247; in 1999 and NNP gain of all seats, 249; in 2003, 250; in 2008 NDC defeat of NNP, 253; distortions of FPTP, 249; incumbents' defeat in Caribbean elections, 260; PRG's views on, 70

General strike, 25–27, 64, 66, 107, 235

GMMWU (Grenada Manual and Mental Workers' Union), 17, 30

GNP (Grenada National Party): alliance with NJM, 224; formation of, 17

Governance: alienation of people from, 257; NDC's technocratic approach to, 246; and NNP, 251

Grenada Democratic Movement (GDM), 242, 259

Grenada Documents, 9, 95, 110, 113, 176

"Grenada 14," 254, 259

"Grenada 17," 206, 250, 259

Grenadian economy, 38, 48, 50, 54, 179, 231, 254

Grenadian Left, 250, 252, 257

Haitian Revolution, 62, 173, 180–81, 184, 188–90, 204, 237

Hurricane Ivan, 50, 53, 55, 262

Imperialism, 72, 82–83, 126, 215, 238, 269–70, 272

Indian People's Revolutionary Associates (IPRA), 220–21

Invasion of Grenada, 3, 5, 48, 87, 198, 234, 241

James, Liam "Owusu," 92, 103
Jamesian perspective, 155, 164–65, 168, 174
James's mass party, 153, 167
JEWEL (Joint Endeavors for Welfare, Education, and Liberation), 24–25, 130, 159–60
JLP (Jamaica Labor Party), 95
Joint leadership, 75–78, 83, 89–90, 92–93, 96, 99, 102–6, 115, 136–39, 143, 232

Leninism, 102, 135, 145, 157, 162–63, 166, 219
Louison, George: against joint leadership, 78; and deciding vote to overthrow Gairy, 33

MAP (Movement for Assemblies of the People), 23–25, 85, 105, 130, 159–60
Marryshow, T. A., 14–16, 21, 29, 34, 194
Marxism-Leninism, 64, 66–67, 94, 121–23, 145, 197, 230, 236
Mass organizations, 40, 76, 81, 98, 132, 134–35, 148, 191
Maurice Bishop International Airport (MBIA), 8, 253, 273–74
MBPM (Maurice Bishop Patriotic Movement), 245, 247, 249–50, 259
Mexican Revolution, 184, 186, 190, 206, 208
Mitchell, James, 242–43
Mitchell, Keith, 245, 247, 256
Mixed-economy approach, 40–41, 48, 53–54
MNIB (Marketing and National Importing Board), 60–61, 83, 133–34
MPLA (Movement for the Liberation of Angola), 267

National Democratic Party (NDP), 242, 259
National Liberation Army. See NLA
National Party, 242, 245, 255
National Women's Organization (NWO): formation of, 66; massive growth of, 135
NDC (National Democratic Congress), 8, 242, 245–57, 259, 262

Neo-liberalism, 122–25, 147–49, 170–71, 198–99, 202, 204, 262
New Jewel Movement. See NJM
Nicaraguan Revolution, 184, 194–95
NJM (New Jewel Movement): as Leninist vanguard, 162; call for Leninist path, 135; formation of, 25; ideological tactic of populism, 131; on independence, 25; as mass party, 68; 1974 independence manifesto, 159; and overthrow of Gairy, vii; on social reforms, 179
NJM-PRG, 125–26, 132, 134, 140, 148
NLA (National Liberation Army), 26, 28, 205
NNP (New National Party): as coalition of three parties, 242; electoral dominance, 8; formation of, 242; and gain of all seats in 1999 general elections, 249; and gain of all seats in 2013 general elections, 256; main strengths of, 256; splintering of, 245
Non-capitalist path, limits to, 127–29

OREL (Organization for Revolutionary Education and Liberation), 63–64, 92, 97, 130, 219–20
Organization of Eastern Caribbean States (OECS), 43, 45, 53, 55, 252, 262

Patriarchy, 122–23, 141, 191, 203
People's Alliance, 28–29, 31, 259
People's Convention on Independence, 25, 65
PPP (People's Progressive Party): as led by Cheddi Jagan, 142; and WPA opposition to US invasion of Grenada, 233
PRA (People's Revolutionary Army): and control of Gairy's army barracks, 265; as successor to NLA, 26
PRG (People's Revolutionary Government): approach to planning economy, 40; composition of, 66; foreign policy, 73

Radix, Kenrick, 26, 29, 32, 139–40, 160
Revolutionary Military Council (RMC), 142, 164, 232–34

Rodney, Walter: and critique of vanguardism, 195; expulsion from Jamaica,
  216; as foremost leader of WPA in a
  collective leadership approach, 219; as
  renowned scholar-revolutionary, 220
Russian Revolution, 195, 206, 208

SAPs (Structural Adjustment Programs),
  125, 243, 246
Scoon, Paul, 31, 33, 35
Seamen and Waterfront Workers' Trade
  Union (SWWTU), 30
Singham, Archie, 15–20, 35, 126, 151
Social Democracy, 148
Socialism: and conditions necessary to
  build, 140; critique of state as facilitator
  of, 154; difference between Stalinism
  and Jamesian view of, 154; influence on
  NJM leadership, 62; link to movement
  for democracy, 165; NJM and conflict-
  ing definitions of, 160
Soviet Union, 13, 46, 63, 73–74, 82, 99, 139,
  197, 223, 252, 269
Strachan, Selwyn, 33, 91, 93

TNP (The National Party), 245, 247, 255,
  259
Tourism, 38–40, 50–51, 128, 134, 179, 254,
  260
TRC (Truth and Reconciliation Commission), 249–50

Ubuntu, 187, 197
United States: and Cold War rivalry with
  Soviet Union, 13; PRG's blind spot with,
  67
United Workers Party (UWP), 226

Vanguard party: comparison to mass party,
  77; as critical element for success of
  March 13 overthrow, 98; reasons for,
  67

Wallerstein, Immanuel, 154, 169–70, 178
Whiteman, Unison: execution of, 259; as
  founder of JEWEL, 130; as key supporter of Bishop, 126
WLL (Workers Liberation League), 94, 110
Women: and Cuban revolution, 191; and
  equal pay, 41, 134; on Fort Rupert, 117;
  role in society after revolution, 60
World Bank, 42–44, 55, 61, 125, 170, 231, 244,
  263
WPA (Working People's Alliance), 8, 144,
  214, 216, 218–40
WPJ (Workers Party of Jamaica), 62, 93–94,
  96, 110, 144, 197, 219–20, 227–30

Youth movements, 63, 66

Zapatistas, 8, 191, 201–2